OUT OF THE ASHES?

THE SOCIAL IMPACT OF INDUSTRIAL CONTRACTION AND REGENERATION ON BRITAIN'S MINING COMMUNITIES

David Waddington
Chas Critcher
Bella Dicks and
David Parry

Regions, Cities and Public Policy

London: The Stationery Office   *London:* Regional Studies Association

First published in the United Kingdom by The Stationery Office in 2001 *with* the Regional Studies Association (registered charity 252269).

A CIP catalogue record for this book is available from the British Library
A Library of Congress CIP catalog has been applied for

ISBN 0 11 702729 4

'Last Shift', written by Richard Thompson © 1997

Printed in the United Kingdom by The Stationery Office
TJ4243 C8 06/01 619965 19585

CONTENTS

LIST OF FIGURES

LIST OF TABLES

ACKNOWLEDGEMENTS

We are grateful to a wide range of individuals and organisations who have helped to make this publication possible. We extend our deepest appreciation to the residents of the mining communities of Askern, Dunscroft/Stainforth, Rossington and Woodlands (all near Doncaster), Thurcroft (Rotherham) and Warsop Vale (near Mansfield) for patiently answering our questions in surveys and interviews. We also thank many whose intimate knowledge and experience of the mining industry proved invaluable: full-time officials of the National Association of Colliery Overmen, Deputies and Shotfirers (NACODS), the National Union of Mineworkers (NUM) and Union of Democratic Mineworkers (UDM); and workers and managers at RJB Mining's Kellingley, Maltby and Rossington collieries (all Yorkshire), its Harworth colliery (Nottinghamshire), and at the independently run pits at Tower and Betws (Wales) and Longannet and Monktonhall (Scotland).

The research on which this book is based would have been impossible without the financial assistance, encouragement and advice of the following institutions: the Economic and Social Research Council (ESRC), to whom we are indebted for grant number X206252004 and an extension to this initial award (L20652004); the Anglo-German Foundation for the Study of Industrial Society; Rotherham Metropolitan Borough Council and the Rotherham Training and Enterprise Council; and the Communications, Media and Communities Research Centre at Sheffield Hallam University.

Many academic colleagues, past and present, at Sheffield Hallam University have contributed to our work. We particularly wish to thank Maggie Wykes for being instrumental in securing our ESRC award and helping to design and implement a questionnaire survey of four Doncaster communities. Similar thanks are due to: Sheffield Hallam University's Survey Unit for assisting us with our surveys of communities in Doncaster and Rotherham; Lesley Marchant for carrying out in-depth interviews with our Thurcroft respondents; Joanna Motamedi for her endless hours of interview transcription; Simon Masterson for helping with the literature review; and Vanessa Pittard for carrying out statistical tests on stress measures. We are also indebted to our secretarial and administrative colleagues, for helping us to prepare our manuscript: Beverley Chapman, Vicky Marriott and, especially, Pam Hibberd, whose patience and diligence appear inexhaustible.

Academic colleagues outside our own institution have also lent their support. Of these, we would especially like to thank the editor, Ron Martin, for agreeing to include our work in the Regional Policy and Development Series. Our understanding of the coal industry and communities in Germany and Spain was enhanced by reviews commissioned from Gerda Speller (of Speller Consultants) and Juan Vázquez and Ignacio del Rosal (of the University of Oviedo). We are indebted to these colleagues for their contribution to our study. We are also grateful for the encouragement and advice received from Rick Ball, Adam Edwards, Ray Hudson and Eric Swyngedouw.

Earlier versions of some of the chapters were previously published elsewhere: chapter 6 in the *British Journal of Industrial Relations* (Parry et al. 1997); chapter 7 in *Work, Employment and Society* (Waddington et al. 1998b); chapters 8 and 9 in a collection edited by Paul Edwards and Tony Elger (Critcher et al. 1999).

The evocative lyrics from Richard Thompson's 'Last Shift' are taken from the album *Industry* by Richard and Danny Thompson. We are greatly indebted to Bug Music for granting us permission to use these lyrics.

While collective responsibility for the contents of this book is accepted by all the authors, three of them would like to make it clear that it exists only because of the foresight, enthusiasm and energy of Dave Waddington.

Last but not least, we wish to thank our families, particularly our partners in life, Joanna, Val, Ken and Caroline. We very much hope that the publication of this work repays them for the patience, encouragement and support they so selflessly devoted while we were 'at the coal face'.

David Waddington,
Chas Critcher,
Bella Dicks and
David Parry

Sheffield, December 2000

LIST OF ABBREVIATIONS

ACAS	Advisory, Conciliation, and Arbitration Service
BCC	British Coal Corporation (British Coal)
BCE	British Coal Enterprise
BS(I)	British Steel (Industry)
C of E	Church of England
CCC	Coalfield Communities Campaign
CCGTs	combined-cycle gas turbines
COSA	Colliery Overmen and Staff Association
CTRU	Civic Trust Regeneration Unit
CVP	Christian-Democrat Party
DETR	Department for the Environment, Transport and the Regions
DIDA	Derwentside Industrial Development Agency
DM	Deutschmark
DTI	Department of Trade and Industry
DVP	Dearne Valley Partnership
EC	European Commission
ECSC	European Coal and Steel Community
ENISA	Empresario Nacional di Innovación (Spanish innovation company)
EP	English Partnerships
ERC	European Recreation Centre
ERDF	European Regional Development Fund
ESF	European Social Fund
ESI	Electricity Supply Industry
ESOP	Employee Share Ownership Plan
ESRC	Economic and Social Research Council
EU	European Union
EURACOM	European Action for Coal Communities
GDP	Gross Domestic Product
GHQ	General Health Questionnaire
HUNOSA	Hulleras del Norte Sociedad Anónimia
IEEC	International Economic and Energy Consultants
IFR	Institute for Regional Development
IGBE	IG Bergbau-Energie
JACCS	Job and Career Change Scheme
KS	Kempische Steenkoolmijnen N.V.

MW	megawatt
NACODS	National Association of Colliery Overmen, Deputies and Shotfirers
NCB	National Coal Board
NUM	National Union of Mineworkers
NVQ	National Vocational Qualification
PSOE	Partido Socialista Obero Español
PWL	Permanente Werkgroep Limburg
quangos	quasi non-governmental organisations
RAG	Ruhrkohle AG (German mining company)
RDAs	Regional Development Agencies
RDC	Rural Development Commission
RECHAR	Reconversion Charbonnage
RECs	Regional Electricity Companies
SAYPE	El Servicio de Asesoramiento y Promoción Empresarial (Spanish business assessment and promotional service)
SCEBTA	Scottish Colliery Enginemen, Boiler-firemen and Tradesmen's Association
SME	small and medium-sized enterprises
SODECO	Society for the Development of Comarcas Mineras
SRB	Single Regeneration Budget
TEBO	Tower Employee Buy-Out
TECs	Training and Enterprise Councils
TUC	Trades Union Congress
TUPE	Transfer of Undertakings (Protection of Employment) Regulations 1981
UDCs	Urban Development Corporations
UDM	Union of Democratic Mineworkers
VIAE	Valleys Initiative for Adult Education
WDA	Welsh Development Agency
WTOs	worker take-overs
ZAK	Zukunftsaktion Kohlegebiete (Campaign for the Future of Coal-Mining Areas)

Last Shift

Stow your gear and charge your lamp
Say goodbye to dark and damp
DSS will pay your stamp
Last Shift, close her down

Leave your manhood, leave your pride
Back there on the mucky side
Take the cage for one last ride
Last Shift, close her down

Put the business in the black
And they stabbed us in the back
With old school ties and little white lies
They left our town for scrap

Golden handshake, sling our hooks
Now we're nursemaids, now we're cooks
Now our kids steal pension books
Last Shift, close her down

Now the scrapper boys infest
And the wrecking balls caress
Like vermin round a burial ground
They catch the smell of death

Old Grimey's lost its soul
Fifty million tons of coal
And we're beggars on the dole
Last Shift, close her down
Last Shift, close her down

Introduction: Coal *Was* Our Life

This is a book about the decline of the coal industry and its communities, the ways in which it was experienced by those affected and the fitful efforts to regenerate the villages which progress had left behind. Though this process has accelerated in the last fifteen years, its history has much deeper roots. The title of this introduction is a counterpoint to the classic *Coal Is Our Life: An Analysis of a Yorkshire Mining Community* (Dennis et al. 1956), which analysed social, political and industrial relations in the pseudonymous village of 'Ashton' (actually, Featherstone in Yorkshire) not long after the nationalisation of the mines in 1947. At the time of nationalisation, there were nearly one thousand collieries in the UK. However, in just twenty years two-thirds of them disappeared, leaving only 317 in 1968.

As a result, thousands of miners and their families relocated throughout the United Kingdom. The local economies they had deserted were often left, unmanaged, to survive as best they could. The 1969 introduction to the second issue of *Coal Is Our Life*, was prescient:

> *The mining industry, or certainly a large part of it, has been condemned to death. Yorkshire is not one of those coalfields which has already been virtually closed, but more and more of its pits face extinction. We do not mourn the death of a dangerous and health-destroying industry as such, any more than do the miners themselves. Insofar as this decline is part of the abolition of arduous manual labour then it is a step along the path to human freedom. But in the social relations actually existing it is not yet any such thing. Social relations do not adapt to the cultural basis of progress automatically or according to the course of reason. As a worker, the miner has only one basic right: to sell his labour-power. As a member of the working class, he exercises that right under conditions established through a century and a half of organization and struggle. For miners today, the death of their industry means that the heart is torn from their communities. There is no overall planning of new industries or of education for leisure; there is no more than marginal provision for economic security. We did not paint the mining community in any* couleur de rose, *but this community without the mine and mineworkers is in danger of becoming merely an aggregate of socially isolated and culturally condemned human beings. (Dennis et al. 1969, pp.9–10)*

During this era of apparently irreversible decline, academic scrutiny of the impact of pit closures was virtually non-existent, despite evidence of their repercussions:

Throughout mining history closures and depression have hit particular localities, perhaps relieved here and there by the migration of those out-of-work to new sinkings and growing prosperity elsewhere. There has long been a tradition of settlements which have lost their original mining function and have declined or decayed. The landscape has often been scarred and the miner's family has been accustomed to all this as part of the way of life in the coalfields. The hardships have in earlier history been great but have largely gone unchronicled. (House and Knight 1967, p.1)

As we shall explain in chapter 1, mining underwent an economic revival in the 1970s. The National Union of Mineworkers exerted considerable political clout, inducing the election defeat of the Conservatives in 1974. However, the election of a Conservative government in 1979, determined to vanquish the miners once and for all, led inexorably to the miners' strike of 1984–5 and eventually to their defeat.

Our research into the aftermath of the strike (Waddington et al. 1991) emphasised the social fragmentation, economic insecurity and political disempowerment evident even in mining communities as yet untouched by pit closure. While popular and journalistic accounts stressed the apocalyptic nature of closure, the process of disintegration often began well before and lasted long after the pit shut:

The reality, as ever, was less dramatic, if arguably more depressing: a pit closure announcement, far from catapulting a community into a sudden spiral of decline, merely sets the seal on nearly a decade of quiet disintegration. Rather than focusing on the final moment of closure, which simply represents the culmination of years of relentless job loss, we need to look instead at the decline of the mining industry over a number of years – particularly those since the 1984/85 strike – in order to chart the actual process of social and community disintegration. (Dicks et al. 1993, p.175)

The perspective required was longitudinal, encompassing the incremental nature of decline. This is the main objective of this volume. For the past fifteen years, two of the present authors (Waddington and Critcher) have been engaged in a programme of research which has documented and analysed the accelerating, late 20th-century demise of the British coal industry and its dependent mining communities. There have been four phases to this research.

The first phase began in 1984 with a study of public disorder in South Yorkshire during the miners' strike, published as a book (Waddington et al. 1989). This constructed a model of the factors involved in determining the likelihood of disorder occurring in specified situations: picketing, demonstrations and inner-city disturbances.

The second phase consisted of a follow-up study, in 1987–8, of social relations in mining communities in the aftermath of the strike. We selected three communities in South Yorkshire, Nottinghamshire and Derbyshire to see if differences in their degree of support for the strike had implications for the ways they experienced its aftermath. The three empirical foci were on the nature of the communities, everyday life (work, gender relations and family networks) and relationships with authoritative institutions (the law, mass media and politics). The theoretical focus was on the applicability of Bulmer's (1975) model of change in mining communities to the new situation of the late 1980s. The results were published as a second book (Waddington et al. 1991).

The third phase began in late 1991 when we were successful in obtaining funding under an ESRC Programme on the Management of Personal Welfare to look at how four communities were coping with the reality or prospect of widespread local unemployment following pit closure. While fragments of that research have been published previously (cf. Waddington et al. 1994; 1998a), it appears here in full for the first time. We also draw on a separately published study commissioned by Rotherham Council, investigating the impact of pit closure on a village on the outskirts of the town (Critcher, Parry and Waddington 1995).

The fourth phase broadened the focus to consider the impact of economic regeneration initiatives in ex-coalfield areas, and to analyse the changing nature and constitution of the coal industry. Between 1992 and 1996, an internally funded research assistant (David Parry) undertook a study of such initiatives in three locations: South Yorkshire, North Nottinghamshire and South Wales. In 1994, we hosted an international conference, funded by the Anglo-German Foundation for the Study of Industrial Society, to compare experiences of restructuring and regeneration in Britain and Germany. Its proceedings were published the following year (Critcher, Schubert and Waddington 1995). As an extension to the original project on unemployment, the ESRC funded us to commission two reports on the current state of the industries in Germany and Spain, produced in 1995 and subsequently published (Critcher et al. 1999).

In 1996 we embarked on a two-year, internally funded project which explored the possible changes in working conditions, industrial relations, health and safety at work, and employee attitudes consequent on the recent privatisation of the coal industry. Aspects of this research, which focused on collieries in Yorkshire, Nottinghamshire, Scotland and South Wales, were published as a pair of journal articles – on industrial relations in mining (Parry et al. 1997) and worker take-overs in the industry (Waddington et al. 1998b). Finally, in 1998, we carried out a commissioned study of a small Nottinghamshire community on behalf of the present government's Coalfields Task Force.

Our work overall thus focused on local communities, national industries in Europe and the globalised energy market. At each level, we were concerned simultaneously with the economics of the industry and the political strategies adopted by national – and in the case of the EU supra-national – government.

The cultures of local mining communities gave a particular shape to the economic, political and cultural impacts of industrial contraction and also posed specific challenges to any attempts at economic regeneration.

The Structure of the Book

These concerns are reflected in the contents and structure of this book, which offers a longitudinal analysis of the decline of the most socially and politically important industry of the 20th century (Hall 1981). The following chapters contain some statistical data but our primary emphasis is on the spoken contributions of the men and women living or working in current or former mining communities. In part, this is an oral history of the decline of mining.

The book's contents are organised as follows:

Part I: 'The Overview' contextualises the decline of the UK coal industry in terms of domestic, and increasingly, global economic and political developments. Thus, in chapter 1, we chart the patterns of industrial and political conflict that are inseparable from the de-industrialisation of Britain's former coal regions.

Part II: 'The Impact of Industrial Contraction' presents data from studies of ex-mining communities in the Doncaster, Rotherham and Nottinghamshire areas, which reveal how pit closure or its prospect is experienced by ex-miners, their wives, families and the community as a whole. The bulk of this part (chapters 2–4) is devoted to a comparative case study, based on survey methods and in-depth interviews, of four Doncaster mining communities, two recently experiencing pit closure, with the other two still benefiting from working mines. The remaining chapter (chapter 5) assesses the generalisability of the Doncaster findings by studying the impact of pit closure on the villages of Thurcroft (Rotherham) and Warsop Vale (Nottinghamshire).

Part III: 'The Restructured Industry' examines what is left of the coal industry since its major upheavals of the 1990s. It looks at the implication of privatisation for working practices and industrial relations (chapter 6), the viability of worker-ownership of the mines and the prospects for what is left of the industry (chapter 7).

Part IV: 'The Economic Regeneration of Mining Communities' has separate chapters on such efforts in the UK (chapter 8) and other major coal-producing countries in Europe (Belgium, Spain and Germany) (chapter 9). Programmes of land reclamation, inward investment, skills training and community-based initiatives are evaluated for their effectiveness in replacing lost jobs and for empowering mining communities.

The Conclusion: 'Coal and Communities in the 21st Century' (Part V) returns to some of the themes of the introduction: how the local is linked to the global by economic shifts and political decisions, and how macroeconomic forces are experienced by individuals, families and communities. If de-industrialisation is inevitable and lost jobs cannot be replaced, the most constructive measures may be those which at least attempt to restore some sense of dignity and control to those whose original economic activity is no longer regarded as useful in a post-industrial society within a global economy. It suggests a different way of reorienting the future lives for people of whom it is now more accurate to say not coal *is*, but coal *was* their life.

PART I:
THE OVERVIEW

1   The Background to the Crisis

It is perceived by the community as a story of political revenge: for 1974, even for 1945. Who knows what dark atavisms stir in Tory breasts at the mere mention of miners, those heroes of Labour, those barely human creatures of the early industrial era, who toiled in their true element, the earth, whose villages were sooty blots on the landscape, and whose ways were alien and terrifying to the cultivated society that resented its dependency upon them. (Seabrook and Blackwell 1993, p.18)

INTRODUCTION

On Monday 14 August 2000 a previously unthinkable newspaper headline – 'British mining could fall to a US group' (*The Guardian* 14 August 2000) – appeared to portend the latest, and perhaps most ignominious, chapter in the recent history of the UK coal industry. The news that RJB Mining, owners of thirteen of the seventeen remaining British deep mines, had spent the previous three months negotiating a possible take-over by the American Renco coal and steel company was symptomatic of an inexorable demise which had seen the coal industry's total workforce shrink from 700,000 to a mere 13,000 in fifty years. In 1947, the nationalised industry was so staple to the nation's industrial and political affairs as to warrant the proud epithet 'King Coal' (Hall 1981). By August 2000 the re-privatised industry had long relinquished its reign. Now, it seemed, the crown jewels were about to be pawned abroad.

The story of coal's demise is not merely one of industrial disintegration; it is also one of political and economic conflict. It is impossible to grasp the socio-political, economic and psychological impact of the ongoing coal crisis without first appreciating the main stages in the rise and fall of the deep-mined coal industry over the past two hundred years and the conflict that generated its decline. We therefore begin by tracing coal's development from the industrial revolution of the 19th century, through its heyday of the 1920s, to its current rapidly shrinking state. Second, we focus on the process of industrial and political conflict from 1947 to 1994, which catapulted the industry and its workers to the centre of the British class struggle and made mining communities its grim casualties. Finally, we examine the uncertain progress of the coal industry since its privatisation in January 1995 and the attitude of recent governments, in whose hands the future of what little remains of the British coal industry now lies.

Coal's Disappearing Kingdom

The industrial revolution was pivotal to coal's rapid development as Britain's primary source of energy from the mid-19th to late 20th centuries. The use of coal quadrupled in the period from 1770 to 1830, due to increasing industrial consumption and its growing domestic use by an expanding urban population (Hall 1981, pp.19–20). Thereafter, coal gradually supplanted hydro energy. Between 1830 and 1880, its annual production grew by over 600 per cent, from 23 million to 147 million tonnes (one tonne: 1,000 kilos). Thus, 'Within the space of half a century, coal was truly king and the men who were winning it had become politically and socially one of the most important and catalytic elements of the British working class' (Hall 1981, p.20).

Coal's expansion was further stimulated by the introduction of steam power throughout British industry. At its all-time peak of 1913, the coal industry comprised 3,024 pits employing 1,127,900 miners, with an annual production of 287,430 million tonnes (Allen 1981, p.13). However, internecine competition among the industry's multitude of small owners during inter-war trade depressions resulted in successive rounds of pit closures. By 1940, the number of collieries had reduced by one half, and its workforce by one third, compared with 1913.

The post-war General Election of 1945 produced a Labour government committed to nationalisation. The Coal Industry Nationalisation Act 1946 paved the way for the conversion of the mines to public ownership on 1 January 1947. Mineworkers anticipated a new era in which the National Coal Board (NCB) would deliver a coherent energy policy, guaranteeing a secure and prosperous future for Britain's 980 collieries and their 718,400-strong workforce. They were to be sorely disillusioned.

In 1950 the NCB published its 'Plan For Coal', which embodied the expansionist aim of producing 240 million tonnes of coal per annum by the early 1960s, 40 million tonnes more than in 1947 (Hall 1981, p.28). However, immediately following nationalisation, the Coal Board set about the systematic closure of scores of the smaller, less efficient mines. Paradoxically, the industry also had problems attracting suitably qualified workers. This meant that production targets were not achieved and the shortfall had to be met by importing foreign coal.

Perceptions that the industry could not satisfy its markets encouraged larger consumers to seek alternative sources of fuel. The railways began to phase out steam engines in favour of diesel trains. Many power stations were converted to oil-burning instead of coal. In 1955 the Government commissioned the building of the country's first ever nuclear power installations (ibid., p.29). The combined effect of these developments was a rationalisation of the industry: 158 mines were closed between 1947 and 1957. In the following decade coal was displaced by oil as Britain's premier fuel. As Hall (ibid., pp.30–1) explains:

By 1960, the respective costs of oil and coal for electricity generation were almost the same. And as soon as coal lost its overwhelming price advantage, its many drawbacks became a very real handicap. Oil, for example, was cleaner than coal, easier to handle and had no ash to get rid of. Railways and industry shunned coal; householders put hardboard over their fireplaces, and warmed themselves in front of Magicoal fires. Only power stations increased their usage of coal. Successive governments tried to soften the blow, but nonetheless, by the early seventies, oil had become the dominant fuel in the British economy.

In the words of Allen (1981, p.44), 'Miners in the 1960s were caught in a pincer movement between pit closures and mechanisation'. Both reduced the labour force. Between 1957 and 1969, 505 collieries were closed, costing 378,000 jobs, mostly in the 'peripheral' coalfields of Scotland, Durham, Northumberland and South Wales.

The first oil crisis provided a temporary respite. Between 1970 and 1973 the price of Saudi Arabian light crude oil steepled from $1.80 to $11.65 per barrel. Western governments consequently placed a higher strategic value on their own coal industries. With the election in 1970 of a Labour government, the NCB disclosed plans to increase its coal output by 42 million tonnes a year, largely by reprieving 'condemned' collieries, developing existing pits and sinking new shafts.

In the early 1980s coal looked to have a viable future:

There are proved, workable reserves which are sufficient for 300 years, even at faster rates of production. At the same time, new technologies are being developed which will increase the potential use of coal. The fluidised bed combustion of coal, for example, will result in the burning of coal in a vastly more efficient manner in power stations and factories. The rise in the price of oil has also brought about a renewed interest in the synthetic production of fuels made from coal. As oil becomes more scarce and even more expensive, coal will also become more important in the production of chemicals. Few would doubt, in the midst of all this, that the future for coal in Britain is secure. (Hall 1981, p.32)

Such optimism was subsequently confounded by global developments. World coal production multiplied as major multinational oil companies diversified into coal – mainly opencast – in developed countries (such as the USA, Australia and South Africa), and in newly industrialising countries (e.g. Colombia, Indonesia and Venezuela) (Rutledge and Wright 1985). Supply quickly outstripped demand. The world price of steam coal fell by over 50 per cent, from $60 per tonne in 1982 to $26 per tonne between 1982 and 1987 (Sadler 1992). Such prices became volatile since 'the discrepancy between volumes of world production and trade meant that the price rested on a delicate balance' (ibid., p.44).

The emergence of new energy sources further reduced the demand for European coal. In Britain, the use of gas increased, supplied indigenously and from Russia. Britain and France produced nuclear power for electricity generation, threatening what had become the staple market for coal. The privatisation of the electricity industry, both generation and supply, exacerbated coal's difficulties, since the new private companies had freedom to purchase their energy sources. The nuclear power industry had a guaranteed market share through a government subsidy, based on an 11 per cent levy on all fuels. The rapid increase in gas turbine power-generation in the early 1990s dealt a further blow to coal (Parker and Surrey 1992).

This diversity of energy supplies made governments feel less vulnerable to sudden shortages in one sector. The net effect of all these factors has been that major European coal-producing countries like Britain, Germany and Spain have been forced to decrease production and subsidise remaining capacity. Figure 1.1 shows the gradual diminution of the coal industry from the early 1980s to the year 2000. Between 1985 and 1992, 119 pits were closed, the number of miners falling from 171,000 to 44,000. Following the sudden acceleration of the Conservative Government's pit closure programme in October 1992 a further 30,000 jobs were lost.

FIGURE 1.1 REDUCTION IN UK MINING CAPACITY 1984–2000

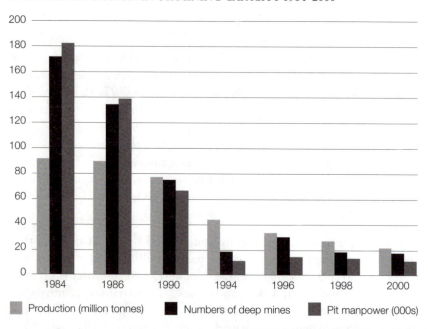

Production (million tonnes)   Numbers of deep mines   Pit manpower (000s)

SOURCE: COALFIELD COMMUNITIES CAMPAIGN

The restructuring of the coal industry was precipitated by shifts in the global energy market but the events and the process of change involved cannot be fully explained by economic arguments alone. The endemic economic problems of the UK coal industry have been compounded by policies in which long-term planning was replaced by short-term political expediency. Ideological confrontation has had an undue influence on economic factors. A relatively sound industry would not have been subjected to such draconian rationalisation were it not for a political strategy based on historical antagonisms (Turner 1997; Winterton and Winterton 1993). The following examination of both the roots and the course of this conflict will cast doubt on the apparent inevitability of pit closure programmes.

Coal and Confrontation

In the generally positive climate immediately following nationalisation, pit closures were accepted with little protest. Even the massive pit-closure programmes of the late 1950s and early 1960s provoked little resistance, even though 'It appeared scandalous to lose pits today that would be economically and financially sound, because oil enjoyed a temporary price advantage' (Hall 1981, p.113). Pit closures were accepted because miners and their trade union leaders had been conditioned to see them as economically necessary: 'It was all happening through the cold, rational, impersonal, uncontrollable operation of the price mechanism. Oil was cheaper than coal; the demand for coal, therefore, must fall' (Allen 1981, p.60).

Additionally, alternative employment was abundant. As Wilsher et al. (1985) point out:

> There were plenty of alternative jobs – 346,000 miners left voluntarily in the eight years prior to 1968 – and there was plenty of work, too, for those who chose to stay. The rich central coalfields in Yorkshire, Nottingham and the Midlands saw an influx of displaced Scots, Welshmen, Lancastrians and North-Easterners on a scale unequalled since the late Victorian growth years, and the character (and accent) of whole villages and districts were transformed by the newcomers. But gradually, as economic horizons darkened and men who had often uprooted their families two or three times already became reluctant to face further change, a new spirit of resistance stirred. (p.8)

This 'new spirit' was harnessed within the National Union of Mineworkers (NUM). From around 1967 onwards left-wing NUM officials and rank-and-file activists, particularly in Yorkshire and South Wales, started to promulgate a more oppositional ideology (cf. Francis and Smith 1981, pp.425–85; Taylor 1984, pp.163–211). A greater sense of unity among NUM members was promoted by the introduction of a centralised bargaining structure. This new militancy was manifested in two national strikes against the Conservative Government of Edward Heath in 1972 and 1974 (Winterton and Winterton 1993).

The earlier dispute is remembered for the enforced closure of the strategically important Saltley cokeworks in Birmingham by a mass picket, led by the future NUM president Arthur Scargill. Intent on avoiding a similar debacle during the re-run confrontation of two years later, Ted Heath called an emergency general election, based on the slogan 'Who runs the country?' This was a gross miscalculation, for Labour were returned to government where they remained until 1979.

During their five years spent in opposition the Conservatives reacted to the humiliation of their successive strike defeats by preparing a blueprint for defeating the miners. The so-called Ridley Report recommended that any future Tory administration should steel itself for such a confrontation by: stockpiling coal at the power stations; having a contingency plan for importing coal; introducing dual oil-and-coal fired burning in power stations; curtailing social security relief for those on strike; establishing mobile police units to deal with flying pickets; and enlisting non-union drivers prepared to cross picket lines (*Economist* 27 May 1978).

Following their return to power under Margaret Thatcher in May 1979 the Tories soon set about delivering their pre-election pledge to pacify British trade unionism. Early in 1980 the Government took on and defeated a national strike by the steel unions. As Hall (1981, p.32) reports, by the summer of 1980 there was a growing feeling in the coalfields that the miners would be next: 'The belief was gaining ground that the consensus of support for the industry was coming to an end. By the end of 1980 many in the coalfields were predicting that the possibility of closures could lead to conflict.'

It was predictable that coal should become the focal point of the industrial conflict of the 1980s:

> For the industry was seen by the Conservative Government as epitomising
> the post-war settlement – the series of compromises between capital,
> Government and trades unions that the Thatcherite project both (rightly or
> wrongly) identified as a prime cause of the UK's economic decline, and also
> set out to break, irrevocably if possible. The coal mining regions were seen as
> amongst the last remaining bastions of support for labourism and the
> collectivist values of social democracy. In this sense, restructuring the coal
> industry was vital to the Thatcherite political project, undertaken as much
> for its ideological effects as for its economic benefits. (Hudson and Sadler
> 1990, pp.435–6)

Confrontation between the miners and Mrs Thatcher's government almost occurred in February 1981. Faced with coal flooding the world market, the NCB submitted proposals to the coal unions for the 'accelerated closure' of twenty-three collieries. When an NUM threat immediately to ballot its members on strike action was accompanied by a spate of unofficial action at collieries nationwide, the Government backed down. As Mrs Thatcher subsequently explained in her memoirs, the Department of Energy had committed no forward planning to the possibility of a strike. Since stocks of coal at the power stations were not sufficient to withstand sustained strike action, 'It became very clear that all we could do was to cut our losses and live to fight another day, when – with adequate preparation – we might be in a position to win' (Thatcher 1993, p.139).

That this 'climbdown' was merely a stalling device to enable the Thatcher administration to prepare for later confrontation was confirmed on 1 September 1983 with the provocative appointment of Ian MacGregor as NCB chair. MacGregor had recently presided over successful confrontations with the car and steel unions at British Leyland and the British Steel Corporation, respectively. Similar confrontation with the miners was expected – though this time on the Government's own terms (Winterton and Winterton 1993).

In March 1984 the NCB's stated intention of closing down twenty mines, starting with the Cortonwood colliery near Sheffield, became the trigger for arguably the most momentous dispute in British industrial relations history. Initially, the NUM's National Executive sanctioned strike action by its militant Scottish and Yorkshire areas, based on the supposition that other areas would fall into line, obviating the need for a national ballot. However, the determination of key sections of the union, especially in Nottinghamshire, to continue working throughout the dispute, allied to the strike-breaking activities of the police, enabled the Tories to gain full revenge for their humiliating setbacks of 1972, 1974 and 1981 (cf. Wilsher et al. 1985 for an overview of the main events).

Mrs Thatcher has since disclosed that she had been afraid during the strike that Ian MacGregor 'would unwittingly give away basic principles for which the strike was being fought' – specifically, by replacing the insistence on closing 'uneconomic' pits with an emphasis on closing those pits which could not be 'beneficially developed'. She felt it was 'crucial for the future of the industry and for the future of the country itself that the NUM's claim that uneconomic pits should never be closed should be defeated, and be seen to be defeated, and the use of strikes for political purposes discredited once and for all' (Thatcher 1993, p.364).

The post-strike formation of the recalcitrant Nottinghamshire area into the breakaway Union of Democratic Mineworkers (UDM) left the main coal unions fatally divided. Over the next seven years, British Coal (as the NCB was renamed in March 1987) ruthlessly pared down its operations. With national industrial action now futile, miners also rejected the industry's Modified Colliery Review Procedure, ostensibly designed to assess the viability of a threatened pit. No colliery ever remained open as a result of the review procedure – due, in large part, to British Coal's refusal to accept any outcome as 'binding' (Beynon et al. 1991).

With a now profitable industry Cecil Parkinson could tell the Tory Party conference of October 1988 that a re-elected Conservative government would administer the 'ultimate privatisation' of the coal industry, which 'would mark the end of the political power of the National Union of Mineworkers and would make the coal industry what it should always have been, another important industry, no more and no less important than many others' (Parkinson 1992, p.280).

Parkinson acknowledged his party's indebtedness to the nation's nuclear power industry, maintaining 'if nuclear had not been available here, Scargill would have won' (*The Guardian* 13 October 1988). Parker and Surrey (1992) argue that favouring nuclear power was crucial to defeating the miners and privatising the industry. Leaked cabinet documents and the memoirs of ministers demonstrate how Conservative energy policy was driven by a desire to 'break the power of the NUM and the perceived stranglehold of coal on the Electricity Supply Industry [and] demonstrate the failure of public ownership' (ibid., p.58).

Arguments shifted to suit this political agenda. As the economic and social arguments in favour of coal (in terms of relative cost and safety) became virtually irrefutable, government rhetoric turned to environmental considerations:

> *Coal-fired power stations were often portrayed as the main danger to the planet even though they were responsible for less than one tenth of the total emissions of greenhouse gases world-wide. This mood was reflected in the Government's White Paper on the Environment, 'Our Common Inheritance'. The only references to coal were as a source of pollution: there were no suggestions as to how this could be mitigated. There was no reference to clean coal technology, particularly of the potential of such technology to reduce emissions and BCC's internationally acknowledged expertise in this field. Coal was seen as a liability, not an asset. (ibid., p.23)*

The agenda also structured the privatisation of the Electricity Supply Industry (ESI). The monopolistic Central Electricity Generating Board was divided into two central private generating companies (PowerGen and National Power) and the state-owned Nuclear Electric. They would compete to supply twelve privately owned Regional Electricity Companies (RECs). Before 1991 the coal industry could depend on the guaranteed custom of the publicly owned ESI for some three-quarters of its sales. Granted government permission to seek out new sources of supply, the RECs immediately began to construct twenty gas-fired power stations. Compared with coal-fired stations, gas stations are relatively cheap to build and produce cleaner energy than coal-fired stations, though the latter's production costs are lower (Coalfield Communities Campaign (CCC) 1993). The two main generators entered the 'dash for gas', preferring imported coal and Venezuelan Orimulsion [a bitumen-in-water fuel, so called because its base is extracted from the Orinoco river basin], the latter approved by government regardless of its reputation as an unrivalled air pollutant (*The Guardian* 14 August 1993).

Other disparities were apparent in the Government's treatment of the coal and nuclear power industries. Written into the electricity privatisation settlement was a clause guaranteeing a market share to nuclear power under the 'non-fossil fuel order' created by the Electricity Act 1989, even though this is easily the most expensive method of generating electricity (CCC 1993).

Acting under an EC rule limiting the provision of state support to only one power-generating industry, ministers chose to subsidise nuclear power, unlike the Germans whose preference was for coal (McAvan 1993).

Paving the way for privatisation, in May 1991 the Department of Energy commissioned merchant bankers NM Rothschild to identify those collieries whose long-term profitability was most secure. Their report was leaked in October 1991. Just fourteen collieries were identified: seven in Yorkshire (Frickley, Kellingley, Maltby, Riccall, Rossington, Stillingfleet and Wistow), five in the Midlands (Daw Mill, Harworth, Ollerton, Thoresby and Welbeck), and one each from the North-East (Wearmouth) and Scotland (Longannet) (Fothergill and Witt 1992).

In the autumn of 1992 the Government agreed a renewed five-year contract for the supply of coal with the main power generators. The contract anticipated coal sales of 40 million tonnes in 1993–4, falling to 30 million tonnes in the remaining four years, well down on the 65 million tonnes for 1992–3. Another round of pit closures was implied. With its goal of privatisation apparently in sight, the Government committed the tactical error, on 13 October 1992, of disclosing plans for the immediate closure of twenty-seven collieries and the 'mothballing' of four others (cf. Turner 1995, pp.26–7).

The memoirs of the then Secretary for Trade and Industry Michael Heseltine reiterate his justification for pit closures:

> *The generators' case was unanswerable. They could purchase coal on the world market considerably more cheaply than from British Coal. They could produce electricity more cheaply and more cleanly from gas than from coal. They had coal stocks in their balance sheets of a value indefensibly against their competitors' interests. They had a fiduciary responsibility to run the companies on behalf of the shareholders effectively and efficiently. They were offering to buy coal to the maximum extent that prudence permitted. Any costs we imposed on them would adversely affect the competitiveness of British industry, which would have to pay. (Heseltine 2000, p.435)*

Unwilling to consider any form of subsidy, Heseltine authorised the escalation of the closure programme. This disconcerted the European Commission who were 'unhappy with a situation where the lowest-cost Community coal producer faced rapid contraction while high-cost German and Spanish production continued at a high level' (Parker and Surrey 1992, p.28). In Britain itself there was a major national outcry:

> *The bungled announcement of the closure of 31 pits and 30,000 sacked miners triggered a spontaneous outburst of popular revulsion against the Government unprecedented in the Tories' 14 years in office. Hertfordshire housewives wept into their washing-up, up to a quarter of a million people demonstrated in London twice in one week, Tory MPs were besieged by angry constituents and the Government was forced to retreat in the face of a*

backbench rebellion. Even Cheltenham marched for the demoralised miners, who emerged blinking into the light of unaccustomed media acclaim. For a fortnight, the miners' case was trumpeted around the land, the 'irrational' rigging of the energy market in favour of gas and nuclear power minutely explained and stoutly denounced. Arthur Scargill was transmogrified from most hated man in Britain into vindicated folk hero. (The Guardian 7 June 1993)

Patently unsettled, the Government hastily authorised a pair of Select Committee Inquiries (on employment, and energy policy and the market for coal). A subsequent White Paper of 25 March 1993 granted a temporary reprieve for twelve of the thirty-one named pits, which were to be kept open for a period of 'market testing'. The White Paper also contained a £75 million financial package to support training, counselling and job-search programmes in mining areas and an equivalent sum for the provision of sites and premises (Department of Trade and Industry (DTI) 1993).

The White Paper was regarded by experts as a cynical device to silence government detractors. Few, if any, of the mothballed or market-tested collieries could survive when government policies were shrinking the market for coal (Fothergill 1993). By December 1993 all but four of the thirty-one mines had gone. Whole areas, such as Derbyshire and Wales, now had no pits.

Miners' apparent readiness to accept closure at the twenty-seven affected pits had a simple logic. British Coal used threats and bribery to induce mineworkers to accept redundancy rather than opt for the review procedure. For example, at Calverton colliery in Nottinghamshire in November 1993, where miners initially voted for review, British Coal raised redundancy payments to £7,000 per employee – on condition that the mine shut down forthwith. Three days later, on 10 November, management's offer was reluctantly accepted (CCC 1993).

Heseltine has recently conceded that the Government misjudged the public mood in announcing the thirty-one pit closures, especially that of the middle classes who 'appeared to feel more strongly than the miners themselves' (Heseltine 2000, p.439). However, he clearly considers himself vindicated:

The outcome was in all practical senses what I had originally announced. A large number of working miners had taken the redundancy terms on offer and left the industry. My colleagues on the back benches had come to terms with what was happening. Time had served to replace the initial shocked reaction with a degree of acceptance of harsh reality. Given the circumstances, there was simply no alternative. From that day to this nobody has come forward with a credible rival set of options that I could have pursued. Overall closures have taken place on the scale we anticipated. The long-overdue rationalisation of the industry had to happen. But, as I write today, seventeen major deep mines are still operating in this country, and coal still accounts for 29 per cent of national electricity generation. The false

*prophecies of the Opposition spokesman Robin Cook that we would see
wholesale closure of the industry have proven to be no more than the
overblown rhetoric he should have known them to be at the time. (ibid.,
pp.442–3)*

With some difficulty the way had been cleared for privatisation. A small
number of the market-tested or mothballed collieries were put up for sale in
advance of the main privatisation process: five of these were purchased by Coal
Investments and four others by RJB Mining. Betws colliery and Hatfield Main,
near Doncaster, were leased to management buy-out teams. In the autumn of
1994 bids were submitted by a variety of companies for the remainder of the
mining industry. A new – and perhaps final – chapter in the history of the
British mining industry was starting to unfold.

Coal's Dying Light?

The privatisation of British Coal's deep mines and opencast sites, their core
mining assets, was finalised on 30 December 1994. Unexpectedly, a large part
of the available assets was purchased by a single bidder, RJB Mining, who paid
£815 million for a total of seventeen pits, fourteen operating opencast sites and
nineteen disposal sites. The company could now boast 600 million tonnes of
coal reserves, with guaranteed contracts of 29 million tonnes of coal to the
power stations until March 1998. The remainder of the assets were shared out
among a small number of independent applicants: the Tower Employee Buy-
out Team, who were to reopen and manage their former mine in South Wales;
Celtic Energy, who took on the majority of most of the Welsh opencast mines;
and Mining (Scotland), a consortium of private companies backed by the
Scottish NUM and TUC, who acquired the Longannet pit and Scotland's
opencast mines. On New Year's Day 1995 the British coal industry was
returned to the private sector after almost half a century of state ownership.

The early months of coal's new era were fraught with controversy and
recrimination as one of the unsuccessful bidders for the English coal regions,
Coal Investments, objected to government bias in the form of an unsecured
three-year loan of £16 million to RJB Mining (*The Independent* 6 April 1995).
In February 1996 Coal Investments called in administrators, having failed to
resolve a cash-flow crisis stemming from the costs of reopening and developing
closed mines (*Financial Times* 7 February 1996). A month later RJB Mining
disclosed pre-tax profits of £173 million, compared with the last British Coal
surplus of £118 million. Each employee was rewarded with £500-worth of
shares. Together, they owned 6 per cent of the company (*Financial Times*
29 March 1996).

RJB's financial success was obscuring other problems, especially its inability
to reduce unit costs. An attempt in May 1995 to freeze wages for three years
almost provoked an all-out strike. In early 1996 the Brunner Mond chemicals
company shelved plans to build the first coal-fired power station for twenty

years because gas prices had fallen substantially (*Financial Times* 29 January 1996). The fall also had implications for future contracts with power generators. Some hoped the election of a Labour government in May 1997 would secure a stable long-term future for the coal industry. However, political developments since have questioned this assumption.

Accusations that the new administration was politically indifferent toward the mining industry arose three months into the new Parliament. The closure of RJB Mining's Asfordby 'superpit' in Leicestershire due to 'adverse geological conditions' came just as the Government authorised the construction of a new gas-fired power station. Three hundred million pounds had been invested in Asfordby before privatisation and £40 million has been invested since. Its closure reawakened fears of trade union and coal industry representatives that the coal industry would lose out to gas. NUM president Arthur Scargill called upon the Government to honour previous pledges to reinvigorate the industry, while the director general of the Confederation of UK Coal Producers complained in writing to the Prime Minister that 'We have had 100 days of New Labour and no indications of support for the British coal industry' (*The Guardian* 19 August 1997).

RJB Mining's marketing development director Colin Godfrey lamented the bias of the energy market towards gas-fired power stations. On BBC Radio Four's *World At One* (17 November 1997) he said RJB would not produce coal it could not sell. Difficulties in renewing contracts with the main power companies were jeopardising the future of ten of RJB's seventeen mines. Government should recognise the centrality of domestically produced coal in the energy market (*The Guardian* 18 November 1997).

Further embarrassment was caused to New Labour on 23 November 1997 when *The Independent on Sunday* revealed the contents of a leaked DTI document. This document underlined the Government's unwillingness to intervene in negotiations between RJB and the power generators, and its determination to deflect the blame for any consequent pit closures. It advised ministers that 'Once closures are announced, we need to be able to deploy a strategy to be able to mitigate the impact.' The document also recommended ministers to shift the blame to RJB for failing to negotiate new contracts while other 'major producers' had successfully concluded theirs; or failing that, hold the previous government's strategy – 'or lack of it' – responsible for the current crisis. Alternative strategies were a 'high profile' intensive broadcast campaign which closed 'once and for all any possibility of public funds to rescue the Budge mines [a reference to Richard Budge, RJB's chief executive]', or a 'low profile' option based on briefings to selective journalists, a ministerial interview with a specialist magazine, or a pre-prepared article supposedly written by a minister.

The political fallout was immediate. In a Commons debate, Elizabeth Peacock, the former Tory MP for Batley and Spen who had famously opposed the Conservative pit closure programme of 1992, accused the Government of allowing the coal industry to die: 'planning its funeral and who to blame for its death' (*The Guardian* 27 November 1997).

Early the following month the Government announced a moratorium on the building of gas-fired power stations. Energy Minister John Battle informed members of the trade and industry committee: 'Views have been put to me recently from various quarters that the increasing dependence on gas in power generation raises issues concerning the security of supply of our electricity system – put simply, the ability to keep the lights on, reliably' (*The Guardian* 4 December 1997). Two weeks later the Government brokered a deal between RJB Mining and the power generators to extend the coal contracts for a further three months (until the end of June 1998), supposedly to give ministers time to re-examine energy policy (*The Guardian* 16 December 1997).

During the ensuing debate industry representatives reiterated the need for long-term measures to ensure the security of the nation's future energy supplies. The Coalfield Communities Campaign advocated a minimum guaranteed market share of 30 per cent for coal and a 'framework of long-term stability (15–20 years) that would justify investment in opening up new coal reserves to replace those being exhausted' (CCC 1998, p.7). The CCC argued that, whilst it would be legally improper under European rules to operate a ring-fenced market exclusively for British coal, it was none the less permissible to create a market defined in terms of 'EU-produced coal'. This would block the 6–8 million tonnes currently being imported from places like Columbia, South Africa, Australia and the USA. The high cost of alternative EU-produced coal supplies would ensure that only British coal was used for power generation. The implications of this policy were that:

> *With the UK electricity sector's total fuel demand running at around 140 million tonnes a year (coal equivalent) a 30 per cent market share implies a minimum coal-burn of 42 million tonnes a year. This compares to a 1997 figure of 48 million tonnes, though falling quickly. Allowing for other markets for UK coal and for opencast production, this minimum market would be sufficient to maintain colliery production at around the present level of 30–35 million tonnes a year. Most if not all of the threatened colliery closures could therefore be avoided. (ibid., p.9)*

The Government's White Paper on energy sources for power generation, published in October 1998 (DTI 1998), offered some optimism for the industry. It concluded that, based on current trends, the UK would have to import 90 per cent of its gas by 2020, creating an unhealthy dependence on a single source of fuel exposed to political disruption and price volatility. The Government had decided to apply a stricter consents policy to the building of gas-fired power stations and to reform the electricity wholesale market (the 'Pool'), which discriminated against the use of coal. In addition, the two main generators were encouraged to divest power stations in the hope of increasing competition. By 2000 generating capacity was shared by nine major companies with multinational portfolios as well as a plethora of independent producers (DTI 2000).

Intent on promoting a free market principle, the Government refused to ring-fence a specific market share for coal. Industry Secretary Peter Mandelson declined to give 'a God-given right to Mr Budge to produce coal that others will buy' (*The Guardian* 9 October 1998). Conspicuously absent from the White Paper was any governmental commitment to investing in clean-coal technology.

The energy review did galvanise negotiations between RJB Mining and the generators. In late 1998 RJB reached agreements with PowerGen to supply 35 million tonnes until March 2003 and with Eastern to supply 37 million tonnes of coal until April of the same year. RJB's chief executive acknowledged that 'Although we have been successful in agreeing additional sales contracts, they are for significantly reduced volumes and at a lower price than we previously received. The contracts do, however, provide a basis for stability in our mining operations and a future income stream for the business' (RJB Mining 1998, p.4).

On 1 December 1998 the Government launched the publication of its response to a report by the Coalfields Task Force, a specially commissioned team of experts and practitioners set up in October 1997 by the Deputy Prime Minister John Prescott to 'develop a specific and comprehensive programme of action to assist communities which had been affected by pit closures and job losses' (Coalfields Task Force 1998, p.5). The Government response emphasised that, in addition to the more than £1 billion per annum it was already spending towards the regeneration of 'local authority areas with coalfield areas', it also planned an additional £354 million of investment over the next three years. Deputy Prime Minister Prescott described the package as recompense for the abrupt run-down of the industry and its knock-on effect on local communities. The Coalfield Communities Campaign pointed out that an element of previously committed funding was also included in the total, but 'the most important thing is that the Government has pledged a long-term commitment. This is a ray of hope after years of decline' (*The Guardian* 2 December 1998).

In the spring of 1999 further disquiet emerged when RJB Mining announced pre-tax profits of £40.1 million, well down on the previous year's £171 million. The company blamed this reduction on the proliferation of gas-fired power generation which had reduced coal's share of the electricity production market to 36 per cent, compared with 53 per cent when privatised (*Financial Times* 3 March 1999).

On 7 April 1999 the Secretary of State for Trade and Industry formally approved the construction of a 500 MW gas-fired power plant project at Baglan Bay in South Wales. This initiative was to be based on the most up-to-date and efficient gas turbine currently available. As one independent energy consultant explained, emissions from this type of turbine are almost devoid of dust, sulphur and nitrogen oxide, whilst its carbon dioxide emissions are one-third the extent of those of coal-fired stations. In addition:

> *The turbine promises an efficiency improvement of a full 5 percentage points over the best of the UK's current gas-fired plants (i.e. around 60% efficiency versus a typical figure of 54–55% today). The efficiency is nearly double the efficiency of the older coal-fired power plants that some wish to retain.*
> *(White 1999, p.21)*

Such arguments serve to amplify the problems of the coal sector hemmed in by environmental policies. Despite being able to produce the cheapest electricity (a fact conceded in the 1998 White Paper), coal use was increasingly constrained by imposed emission limits. Coal's long-term commercial viability remained questionable.

Two days after the Baglan Bay disclosure, on 9 April, RJB announced the closure of its Calverton colliery near Nottingham, citing 'deteriorating geological conditions' to have made it unviable (RJB Mining press release 9 April 1999). Yorkshire's principal regional newspaper identified 'an ill omen for the future of coal'. Arguing that the Government's readiness to endorse gas-fired stations despite its moratorium was jeopardising the coal industry, the paper maintained that the previous year's energy White Paper amounted to 'little more than a politically expedient fudge. The effect of the Government's policy is not to save the coal industry, but to extend its demise over a number of years, thus minimising any potentially damaging political impact' (*Yorkshire Post* 10 April 1999).

Paradoxically, the Government had been secretly involved in bailing out Mining Scotland's deep mine at Longannet where geological difficulties had produced a cash-flow crisis. The jobs of 750 workers were saved by the provision of 'bridging finance' enabling the development of new reserves. Though Mining Scotland would not comment on the precise details of the deal, the Scottish Office revealed how 'the government and Scottish Enterprise worked with Mining Scotland and Scottish and Southern Energy to produce a package of bridging finance which is intended to allow the development of the new reserves to proceed' (*McCloskey's Coal UK* April 1999, p.8). Speculation was rife that the Government was matching the private finance used to prop up the mine (ibid.).

On 13 April 1999 RJB Mining celebrated a four-year agreement with National Power for the delivery of up to 46 million tonnes of coal up to and including 2003. This contract represented an extension of an existing three-year agreement for RJB to supply 18 million tonnes, starting in April 1998. However, the deal involved an undisclosed level of options, estimated by one analyst at two-thirds of the whole (*McCloskey's Coal UK* April 1999). These options introduced a similar degree of uncertainty to that inherent in RJB's deals with other generators: Eastern's contract with RJB for 37 million tonnes was said to carry 'an intricate web of options', while at least 20 per cent of the

PowerGen deal for 35 million tonnes was reputedly optional (ibid.). In speaking of the PowerGen agreement, the coal analysts Merrill Lynch explained, 'The deal gives RJB security and breathing room for a couple of years, but longer term it still faces the challenges of tighter environmental legislation and competition from gas and imported coal which will drive demand for UK coal lower' (*Financial Times* 14 April 1999).

The precise nature of these problems is specified by Parker (1999, p.33). The prices agreed in the replacement contracts with the power companies are 15 per cent higher than the market price for imported coal but 20 per cent lower than the prices in previous British Coal contracts. 'In 1998, operating profits of deep mines were only £26m (compared with £137m in 1997) and even that much-diminished profit was earned mainly in the first quarter of the year, when the old "British Coal" contract prices still applied' (ibid.). The negligible margin between RJB's operating costs and the contract prices agreed for power station coal leaves little scope for profit or investment in mine development. With additional pressures resulting from the tightening of environmental regulations and governmental approval for the commissioning of thirty-six combined-cycle gas turbines (CCGTs), further reductions in coal-producing capacity seemed inevitable.

In a May 1999 interview, Richard Budge welcomed the new power contracts as giving the company breathing space to become more internationally competitive. Despite the dedication of the 'vast majority' of the workforce, there were still 'a number of people who do not seem to be committed to the survival of their colliery' who should not be allowed to 'undermine the good progress' so far made and the 'continued progress' necessary for 'longer term security' (*NewScene* May 1999).

In the same month, the chief executive told the 3,000 miners at RJB's Selby complex that they must raise productivity and recover profitability within the next three months or face possible redundancies and closures (*The Guardian* 5 May 1999). The company was committed to a £20 million reduction in its annual operating costs. Voluntary redundancies would account for 400 jobs – 7 per cent of the workforce – in the Midlands and Yorkshire coalfields. Problems at Selby, where output was down by half a million tonnes at a cost of £15 million to the company, would mean a hundred jobs would go:

> *The job reductions are part of the measures being implemented to reduce the most significant yardstick of our efficiency – the cost of each unit of energy, measured in gigajoules, that we produce. By a combination of constant downward pressure on costs and rises in productivity, we can further narrow the gap between the price of British-mined coal and the price of that on the world market. By achieving that goal, we will maximise sales and jobs and enhance future security.* (NewScene *June 1999*)

In mid-June RJB's chief executive met a deputation of MPs at Westminster to argue that, in order to invest, he required a guarantee of future markets for indigenous deep-mined coal (*Yorkshire Post* 22 June 1999). In the context of the Government's recent £152 million subsidy to Rover's Longbridge factory, the chair of the Coalfield Communities Group of MPs maintained the coal industry could not be left to the mercy of the market. The provision of guaranteed markets for home-produced coal, investment in clean-coal technology and the relaxation of tough curbs on emissions were necessary since, 'Unless we get some understanding that priority will be given to British deep-mined coal then we may not have a viable industry by 2005' (*Yorkshire Post* 22 June 1999).

On 17 April 2000 the Secretary for Trade and Industry Stephen Byers announced a subsidy for the coal industry. This was ratified by the EU Commission in November 2000 and was worth £110 million over two years. This aid was justified as helping the industry through a 'period of transition' during which the energy market would be reorganised. The German coal industry was receiving £23.3 billion per annum of government subsidy (*The Guardian* 18 April 2000). Beyond the two-year subsidy period when the European Coal and Steel Treaty ended, the coal industry would have to cut costs further to survive. Nevertheless, the Government had overturned an important principle: the payment of operating aid to the coal industry had been dismissed out of hand just two years before.

The subsidy announcement was accompanied by controversy. One week earlier two senior civil servants, held to be part of an anti-coal faction within Whitehall, had been removed from key energy posts for objecting to the scheme. Journalists speculated that government ministers were abandoning economic realism, fearing an 'armchair revolt' by traditional Labour voters alarmed by the continuing decline of the mining industry (*The Guardian* 17 April 2000). The subsidy was interpreted by Conservative politicians as a ploy to shore up the Labour's vote in local elections immediately and the general election in the long term (*Daily Telegraph* 18 April 2000).

Within the coal industry itself, reaction was divided. The majority mine owner Richard Budge was understandably euphoric. Earlier in the year, he had informed ministers that a six-year deal to provide almost 5 million tonnes of coal to the Drax power station near Selby was dependent on assurances to the station's American owners, AES, that the agreed price would include a government subsidy (*Yorkshire Post* 23 March 2000). Byers' announcement now guaranteed that deal and ensured the survival of threatened collieries at Ellington and Clipstone. On a BBC regional news magazine programme, Budge remarked:

> *It's very good news. The Government have seen the major distortion that's created by European subsidies where our European competitors get £3.3 billion a year to produce 70 million tonnes of coal and the UK produces 45 million tonnes of coal a year without subsidy. So I'm delighted it levels that playing field up ... The subsidy will be there for two years but it will help us to secure the additional sales that we need to keep places like Selby sold out until 2006. (*Look North, BBC1 17 April 2000*)*

Asked by the interviewer whether this now guaranteed the safety of RJB's other mines outside the Selby complex, he replied:

Safe is a relative term. Certainly, we'll be looking at sufficient sales for our business until 2004 across the piece and that will include the Ellington mine in the North-East and the Clipstone mine in Nottingham, which I'm particularly pleased to say we will not now be closing. (ibid.)

An NUM representative from Selby, interviewed on the same programme, was unimpressed by a short-term subsidy. Miners were looking for a twenty- or thirty-year plan 'and that takes more commitment than just saying, "Here's some money, you've got two years"' (*Look North*, BBC1 17 April 2000). Andrew Cox, editor of the *UK Coal Review*, insisted that ministers' failure to invest in clean-coal technology made the majority of UK collieries vulnerable to closure within a decade (*The Guardian* 18 April 2000).

Broadsheet editorial writers condemned the coal subsidy as driven by sentimentality rather than economic rationality. A *Financial Times* editorial cautioned the British Prime Minister 'not to slide into a new role as curator of a museum for dark satanic mills'. *The Independent* leader-writer thought the £100 million 'would have been better spent on helping miners adjust to change than an ultimately futile attempt to underwrite markets that no longer exist. When gas is cheaper and more environmentally friendly, in the end sentiment can count for nothing' (*The Independent* 18 April 2000). Finally, *The Times*'s editorial took the view that:

It would be a minor miracle if the essentials of coal economics had altered in the intervening period. The limited protection for subsidies that EU arrangements might afford today will have disappeared. Mr Byers, or his successor, will need to make the decision then that he is willing to spend £100 million to avoid taking now. (18 April 2000)

In August 2000 Renco's bid for RJB Mining's collieries was made public, only for the American company to withdraw its interest later in the autumn. These negotiations, allied to ministerial ambivalence since the 1997 general election, suggested that neither the largest UK coal owner nor the current Labour Government were wholeheartedly committed to the future of the British mining industry.

By the turn of the new millennium the size of coal's industrial workforce had shrunk to approximately 9,000 employees (see figure 1.1). A mere nineteen deep mines now littered the UK industrial landscape (figure 1.2). Change was occurring at a disconcerting rate. After decades of industrial decimation and accompanying political conflict, coal-mining communities were once again waiting with bated breath. The attitudes within such localities, the mental health of local residents during the recent concentration of industrial decline and the way that such people have been assisted or impeded in their attempts to reposition themselves in times of social and economic adversity can only be properly understood against the historical backdrop just recounted in this chapter.

FIGURE 1.2 MAP OF UK COLLIERIES 2000

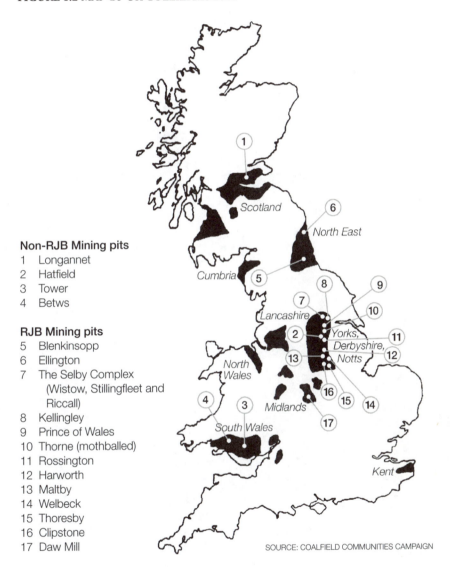

Non-RJB Mining pits
1 Longannet
2 Hatfield
3 Tower
4 Betws

RJB Mining pits
5 Blenkinsopp
6 Ellington
7 The Selby Complex
   (Wistow, Stillingfleet and
   Riccall)
8 Kellingley
9 Prince of Wales
10 Thorne (mothballed)
11 Rossington
12 Harworth
13 Maltby
14 Welbeck
15 Thoresby
16 Clipstone
17 Daw Mill

SOURCE: COALFIELD COMMUNITIES CAMPAIGN

PART II:
THE IMPACT OF INDUSTRIAL
CONTRACTION

2 Men's Experience of Industrial Contraction

BACKGROUND TO THE STUDY

The following three chapters comprise a comparative study of four neighbouring Doncaster mining communities affected to varying degrees by industrial contraction in the early 1990s. In two of these communities, Askern and Brodsworth,[1] the local colliery had been closed, for periods of six and eighteen months, respectively. At a third community, Hatfield,[2] the future of the mine was widely regarded as being in serious jeopardy; while at the fourth, Rossington, the pit's future was generally considered secure. The project was funded by the Economic and Social Research Council and carried out between the summer of 1992 and the spring of 1993. Our principal objective was to examine the possible impact of the loss of mining jobs through redundancies and pit closure. We concentrated on three types of impact: on the miners themselves; on their partners and families; and on the communities as a whole. To this end, we obtained a wide range of quantitative and qualitative data on employment prospects, individual, family and community stress, and sources of coping. The three main methods of data collection were:

1. A questionnaire survey of 420 respondents. This comprised:

- a 'main sample' (n = 320) of 40 miners/ex-miners and their female partners from each of the four communities;

- a sub-sample of 40 *voluntary* redundant ex-miners (20 each from Hatfield and Askern) and their female partners; and

- a further sub-sample of 80 Rossington residents (equal numbers of men and women) not employed in mining.

What distinguished the voluntary redundants from other ex-miners in this sample was that they had successfully applied to leave the industry before the scheduled closure of their mines.

2. In-depth interviews with 30 current or former miners and their female partners. These 60 respondents were drawn from all four of our chosen communities, having previously taken part in our survey.

3. Similar in-depth interviews with 60 key informants (e.g. educationalists, social or community workers, police officers and health workers).

More precise details of our methodology, including sampling methods, are provided in the appendix.

A key research objective was to develop a multi-method and interdisciplinary perspective for analysing the human impact of industrial contraction. We combined quantitative and qualitative methods and would claim some triangulation, given the range and sources of data. The claim to interdisciplinarity arises from our utilisation of the full range of disciplinary perspectives offering relevant concepts and methods: psychological instruments for measuring stress, social psychological profiles of support networks, sociological perspectives on community and, more recently, economic analysis of the local labour market.

Since the start of the 1984–5 miners' strike 150 pits have closed with the loss of 170,000 mining jobs. Our 1992 study provides a snapshot of one moment in this process as two communities coped with pit closure, another with the constant threat of closure and a fourth apparently remained secure. In subsequent chapters, we examine the impact of actual or threatened pit closure on miners' wives and families (chapter 3) and on community life as a whole (chapter 4). This present chapter reviews how former and current miners coped with these prospects. Initially, we review male employment status in the two communities where the pit had closed, Brodsworth in September 1990 and Askern in December 1991. From these two communities a total of 80 miners and 80 miners' wives participated in the survey. Roughly a quarter were subsequently interviewed in depth. In subsequent chapters, we then look at three groups of men: those remaining unemployed after pit closure, those staying in the industry and those re-employed outside it. In each case we present our quantitative survey evidence and qualitative interview material. These findings are then related to previous studies.

Male Employment Status After Pit Closure (Askern and Brodsworth)

It can be seen from table 2.1 that the effect of pit closure was to make around half the male workforce unemployed, slightly fewer (48 per cent) at the pit shut for six months, rather more (58 per cent) at the pit shut for eighteen months.[3] The largest single area of re-employment was in mining, largely in the form of transfers to other pits or working for mining contractors. In Askern nearly half (45 per cent) manage this in the first instance. However, Brodsworth shows a much lower percentage of men (15 per cent) who continued to find work in mining. The second largest area of re-employment is in the categories of labouring, manual and factory work. Eighteen months after closure 20 per cent of miners had been re-employed in those sectors, though six months after closure this had dropped to only 3 per cent. Thus, in the long run, the redundant miner was likely to experience at least one of three options. In order of frequency these were: (1) unemployment; (2) continued employment in some form in the mining industry; and (3) general labouring. There was no evidence that, given time, the rate of unemployment would gradually decrease.

There was evidence that re-employment in mining is slowly replaced by other forms of employment. However, this does not have the effect of increasing the overall rate of employment: eighteen months after closure, around half of all ex-miners remained unemployed.

TABLE 2.1 EMPLOYMENT DESTINATIONS OF REDUNDANT MINERS: BY GENERAL CATEGORY

Employment destination	Brodsworth (18 months shut)		Askern (6 months shut)		Total	
	N	%	*N*	%	*N*	%
Non-mining	11	27.5	3	7.5	14	17.5
Mining	6	15.0	18	45.0	24	30.0
Unemployed	23	57.5	19	47.5	42	52.5
Total	*40*	*100*	*40*	*100*	*80*	*100*

Note: percentage totals in all tables may not add up to 100% because of rounding.

The Unemployed

Survey Data

We asked survey respondents (both male and female) about their previous experience of unemployment and whether they had found this stressful when compared with other life events. It is evident from table 2.2 that three out of ten respondents had previously experienced the unemployment of their partner and marginally fewer their own. Yet the dominant view was that these were not stressful events. Of the 96 respondents whose partner had been unemployed, only 20 per cent experienced this as highly stressful, 32 per cent as fairly stressful, but 48 per cent – nearly half – as not stressful at all. Of the 93 who had themselves experienced unemployment, the figures – highly stressful (29 per cent), fairly stressful (26 per cent) and not at all stressful (45 per cent) – were not much different.

TABLE 2.2 UNEMPLOYMENT AND PERCEIVED STRESS: MAIN SAMPLE

	Men (%)	Women (%)	All (%)
Own unemployment			
Experienced	35	23	29
Of whom finding it:			
Very stressful	30	27	29
Fairly stressful	29	22	26
Not stressful	41	51	45
Unemployment of partner			
Experienced	25	35	30
Of whom finding it:			
Very stressful	17	22	20
Fairly stressful	22	40	32
Not stressful	61	38	48

(*N* = 320)

There were some telling gender differences here. Men were slightly more likely than women to report that they found their own unemployment highly or fairly stressful (59 per cent compared with 49 per cent). Conversely, women were more likely than men to say that they found the unemployment of their partner fairly or highly stressful (62 per cent compared with 39 per cent). The unemployment of a man is regarded by all as a more stressful experience than that of a woman. Nevertheless, in virtually every case, the dominant category of response (minimum 38 per cent, maximum 61 per cent) was that unemployment was not a stressful experience.

However, we provoked different responses in another section of the questionnaire which asked about the type of issue that caused 'worry' to respondents. Here, the insecurity of work was rated as a major source of worry. The rank order for the seven most salient issues was:

1.   children's upbringing;

2.   work insecurity/redundancy;

3.   bereavement;

4.   the aftermath of the strike;

5.   unemployment;

6.   health; and

7.   separation/divorce.

If we aggregate some of these topics together (see table 2.3), then we find that work-related 'worries' are as prominent as family-related ones. Clearly, in the minds of survey respondents, 'stress' was defined in terms of permanent changes in life circumstances, such as bereavement or illness, whereas 'worry' was about disruptions to the normal patterns of life, whether in the family or at work. Perhaps our respondents were operating a more sophisticated series of categories than social scientists concentrating on stress.

TABLE 2.3 MOST WORRYING THING (EXCLUDING NOTHING): MAIN SAMPLE

	%	Sub-total %
Work security	19	
Strike aftermath	12	
Unemployment	11	
All work-related		42
Child welfare	23	
Bereavement	17	
All family-related		40
Health	8	
Separation/divorce	4	
All personal		12
Other	7	7
Total	*100*	*100*

(N = 259)

The voluntarily redundant and their wives (table 2.4) differed significantly from the main sample (table 2.2) in terms of their experience of, and attitudes towards, unemployment. They experienced unemployment more frequently: 55 per cent, compared with 29 per cent in the main sample, had experienced their own unemployment. Voluntary redundant men and their wives were also more likely to experience unemployment as stressful: 43 per cent classed their own unemployment as highly stressful, compared with 29 per cent of the main sample. Since the proportion defining it as not stressful is roughly the same (43–45 per cent), the difference appears to be that, amongst the voluntarily unemployed, those who found it stressful were more likely to define it as highly, rather than fairly, stressful. This also extends to the unemployment of their partner. Amongst the voluntarily redundant and their wives, 51 per cent had experienced the unemployment of their partner, of whom 42 per cent classed it as very stressful. The comparable figures for the main sample were 30 per cent and 20 per cent. Even within the same community, such as Askern, the voluntarily redundant and their wives were more likely to have experienced unemployment and more likely to have found it stressful than those men and their wives currently in the mining industry or made compulsorily redundant from it.

TABLE 2.4 UNEMPLOYMENT AND PERCEIVED STRESS: VOLUNTARY REDUNDANCY SAMPLE

	All (%)
Own unemployment	
Experienced	55
Of whom finding it:	
Very stressful	43
Fairly stressful	14
Not stressful	43
Unemployment of partner	
Experienced	51
Of whom finding it:	
Very stressful	42
Fairly stressful	14
Not stressful	44

(N = 80)

As part of our survey we administered a short stress-rating scale to all respondents (see appendix). This scale, which checks for each individual's experience of psychological, behavioural and physical 'symptoms' associated in the literature with high stress, provides an illuminating index of the apparent stressfulness of unemployment compared with relevant sections of the working population. It is evident from table 2.5 that the currently unemployed men in our sample show consistently higher mean levels of stress than comparative groups of redeployed ex-miners (those in 'new work'), working miners and men employed outside the coal industry (working non-miners). These mean differences are significant at the 6 per cent, 0.01 per cent and 0.02 per cent levels, respectively. While the first of these scores offers relatively inconclusive statistical verification of the higher stress levels experienced by the unemployed, the remaining two outcomes comprise powerful evidence of the greater stress endured by unemployed people relative to their employed counterparts (see explanation of significance levels accompanying table 2.5).

TABLE 2.5 STRESS SCORES – CURRENT EMPLOYMENT COMPARISONS (MEN)

Current employment comparison	N	Mean	Median	Mann-Whitney (W) test of differences[†]		
New work	29	7.2	7	W	=	1765
Unemployed	59	9.4	9	p	=	0.06
New work	29	7.2	7	W	=	2028
Working miner	104	7.3	6	p	=	0.64
New work	29	7.2	7	W	=	968
Working non-miner	31	6.1	5	p	=	0.22
Unemployed	59	9.4	9	W	=	14704
Working miner	104	7.3	6	p	=	0.001***
Unemployed	59	9.4	9	W	=	9510
Working non-miner	31	6.1	5	p	=	0.002***
Working miner	104	7.3	6	W	=	7291
Working non-miner	31	6.1	5	p	=	0.25

Note: maximum individual stress = 42 (see appendix for details of calculation).

Key for significance tests:
The following explanation of symbols also applies to tables 3.4, 4.6, 4.7, 4.8 and 4.9, appearing elsewhere in this book.

*** = significant at least at a 0.5% level. There is only a 0.5% probability that the difference(s) between these samples occurred purely by chance. Therefore there are proven strong differences in stress levels between these groups.

** = significant at least at a 1% level. There is only a 1% probability that the difference(s) between these samples occurred purely by chance. Again, proof of a significant difference in stress levels between the groups.

* = significant at least at a 5% level. There is a 5% probability that the difference(s) between these samples occurred purely by chance. This is commonly used as the significance 'threshold', above which results are not normally seen as significant. Significance at this level, again, can be treated as strong proof of difference between the groups.

Obviously, the lower the probability that the results occurred by chance, the more significant the findings – the more asterisks, the stronger the difference. Where *p* is above the significance 'threshold' but still fairly low (between 0.05 and 0.1, i.e. a 5–10% probability of chance differences), researchers can take this as suggestive of a difference between the samples. However this is not conclusive and usually merits some further investigation (e.g. there could be differences, but there may be 'confounding' variables).

[†]The Mann-Whitney test is a non-parametric test based on a calculation of the sum of ranks in two independent samples (cf. Daniel 1978 for a fuller explanation).

What is equally striking about these results is that there are no statistically significant differences between the mean stress scores for the three categories of employed respondents. Clearly, the most crucial variable here is whether the individual is in work or not, regardless of the relevant employment sector. It is worth pointing out, however, that the mean stress score for working non-miners (6.1) is lower than the comparable scores for working miners and redeployed ex-miners (7.3 and 7.2 respectively), even though the difference is non-significant.

Interview Material

We asked Askern and Brodsworth miners about their decision to vote for pit closure. Most ex-employees of these mines emphasised that they were given little time in which to speculate about their possible unemployment:

> *Obviously, the decision was hard – which way to go, for transfer or redundancy. Deep down, you think, 'It's been my livelihood for over 15 years and what am I going to do now?' But it happened that quick, I don't think anyone had that much time to become stressed over it. (Mr P, Brodsworth)*

Askern and Brodsworth miners agreed that negative feelings about closure were counterbalanced by relief that the waiting was over: 'It was like a black cloud hanging over you all of the time when you were working at Brodsworth. So that black cloud's gone, now' (Mr W, Brodsworth).

Nevertheless, in our visit to Askern colliery, days before pit closure in December 1991, we met many traumatised miners:

> *They're like in a state of shock. They don't actually know ... you know what's happening but I don't think your mind wants to accept it. You know, it's something that comes gradually. I don't think it will show through until after Christmas when they've actually got their Christmas holidays over and realised they're not getting up to go to work, they haven't got a job. (NUM official, Askern)*

Interviews with men from Askern pit, whose experience of unemployment had been short-term, suggested that the buffer of redundancy payments absolved them from immediate pressure to find a job. Some had confidence in their potential employability while others seized the opportunity to pursue interests and hobbies. A pit carpenter, for example, never saw himself remaining unemployed for long:

> *I think you asked us this before, when we were winding down the pit, and a group of us said we weren't bothered: it didn't stress us, it was like water off a duck's back, probably because we'd got a trade and we'd be lucky enough to get another job. If I didn't get a job I was prepared to go on the dole and I've got my tools so I could go and do spare time work. (Mr W, Askern)*

This man had worked outside mining before and had his own survival strategies: 'I would manage. Perhaps if I didn't have the money behind me it would be a different matter.'

Others found things to do with their time. One man went on every course available. Another decorated the house from top to bottom and played golf extensively. In such cases, a positive marital relationship and a willingness to engage in housework undoubtedly helped. Others were not so fortunate; for some, the novelty of having time to burn soon wore off:

> I think it was more because I was bored than anything else. It was getting repetitive, day after day. Getting up in a morning and thinking, 'What am I going to do with myself today for the rest of the day?' and trying to find something to do. I was getting snappy with everybody else because I wasn't settled in myself. When I was working, my life was sort of arranged. Whereas, when I finished, all that arrangement in my life had gone and there was a bit of a hole to fill that was normally filled at the pit. I sort of hit the bottle. (Mr C, Askern)

This particular individual refused to help much with housework, even though his wife worked full time. Regular drinking bouts led to growing marital tension until, finally, he went to his doctor and was diagnosed as having high blood pressure. After an unsuccessful stint as the driver of an ice-cream van, he eventually found more satisfying and stabilising work as a taxi-driver.

Ill health of various kinds was common amongst unemployed miners. This was often compounded by other problems, such as advancing age or social isolation. One man in this situation conveyed his anxiety in the following terms:

> I've been on the sick, now, for three months with my nerves, and I think what it is, they're expecting you to look for jobs and you don't know where to start, because I've worked for 27, 28 years at one place and everything's totally different now. I think I'm nervous of interviews and how to apply – things like that. I'm comfortable at the moment because my wife's working, but I'm nervous and worried that I'll never get another job. I'm thinking too much, putting pressure on myself. Everything seems to go through my head: I worry about money, although I've got plenty. I think it's going to disappear if I don't do something. (Mr M, Askern)

Entire weekdays were spent brooding in total isolation while his wife and two teenage children were out at work. On their return, he would pick arguments on the slightest pretext. While many such interviewees were remarkably frank about their behaviour, others clearly needed to put a brave face on things in public. As a working miner explained:

> I've got a mate [in Askern] who's the same age as me. He can't get a job. His wife's just had a kid and, since he packed in at the pit, he's been going out nearly every afternoon and night and he must be going through his money

summat rotten, and everybody knows it, but he's trying to make out he's not
and he's having a whale of a time. It's just trying to save face, I think. A lot
of them are trying to show that they're doing better than they actually are.
(Mr S, Askern)

Longer-term unemployment for those who had worked at Brodsworth pit was patently even more difficult to cope with. A lot depended upon both the man's perspective on his unemployment and the support he received from those around him. Some stood up to it remarkably well. Having spent over thirty years in the mines, 47-year-old Mr Wa bemoaned the loss of a regular routine, the company of 'smashing workmates' and the feeling of being useful to society; but his new life had ample compensations. A prize-winning gardener with well-stocked flower-beds and a pair of bulging greenhouses, he could always find plenty to keep himself occupied. When not active in the garden, he was busy doing repairs and carrying out improvements on the house. Meanwhile, the full-time jobs of his wife and two adult daughters gave him a sense of financial security.

A second man, Mr T, thought he was 'coping pretty well'. A member of the local Job Club, a keen ornithologist and useful snooker player, he had recently completed a college computer course. As with Mr Wa, the fact that his wife had a full-time job and they had savings to fall back on relieved the financial pressure. Nevertheless, it was apparent that his inability to obtain a job in the face of repeated rejections by employers was slowly sapping his morale.

For some, like Mr We (Brodsworth), the day-to-day experience of unemployment involved unremitting anxiety:

Well, you're out of work and you're looking for work and you've got pressure
on you to get work from such as the unemployment people. And you see
young lads there who can't get work and you're in your fifties and you think:
'What chance have I got?' I applied for plenty, but they didn't even answer
your letters, the majority. They'd no need. I even put stamped addressed
envelopes in, but no answers. I couldn't see the light at the end of the tunnel,
so I got over-anxious: I started having palpitations and tightness in the
stomach. I went to the doctor's and he put me on beta-blockers. He said,
'Most of the people I treat for anxiety are people who have lost their job and
people moving house.' So he put on my notes 'anxiety' and I was on the sick
for six months. I found it very hard to sleep.

Subsequently this respondent became resigned to his new status:

I think I just got used to being unemployed. I just got it into my head that
I wouldn't get a job, it's as simple as that, so I may as well accept it. It didn't
mean I didn't try to get jobs but I didn't get as over-anxious if I got a job
or not.

Lack of money was a recurrent theme in other interviews. The idea of the unemployed man being a breadwinner failing to provide for his family frequently resurfaced, as in the following comments by Mr C, a Brodsworth man in his late thirties:

> *It's constant agitation because all the time you're thinking – it's at the back of your mind when the kids want an ice-cream and things like that – can we afford it? You're copper counting all the time and it's something that I've never had to do in my life. We're sort of living hand to mouth. When the giro cheque comes in, we know it's not going to be ours in a way because we've got things to pay straight out: the mortgage has to go, the electric. That's something I thought I'd never have to do: pay the electric weekly. And shopping. We've never been people that ever went round supermarkets looking for cheaper brands, but that's what we're doing now.*

In this case, Mr C resented his wife working, since it meant that she was 'keeping' him when it should have been the other way round. His response, which we found recounted time and again, was to become habitually bad-tempered towards the family:

> *I stopped smoking for five years and I've started again. Worrying, whittling, you're copper counting all the time. I get so uptight about being unemployed. Everybody says, 'My dad's grumpy.' If I'm that way inclined, I just go barmy with them all – if they don't move a cup, or knife, or anything like that, I go absolutely crazy. When I finished at the pit, the wife wanted a dishwasher, so I bought her one but they still put the pots in the sink and that's when I start losing my temper. Very, very irrational in my behaviour, temper-wise. I'm hoping that there is going to be a future but it's really making me whittle about what sort of future there is. I just can't cope at times with the stress I'm under now of being unemployed.*

Some hope had appeared in the form of a place on a welding course. Yet even in such an extreme case there were alleviating factors. The eldest of three daughters had married and left home, leaving one less teenager to support. He also had a best mate on whom he could depend:

> *I've got a good friend, Stewart. We'll probably have a few drinks in the house – which we can just about afford. He's in the same position as me: he was a long-distance lorry driver. He was made redundant so we're more or less in the same boat.*

Moreover, his wife was clearly willing to stand by him through thick and thin:

> *We both enjoy each other's company. We have terrible rows, which is stress to me. We've got a good relationship where we can talk things out. It does get a bit stressful at times when we're going through a phase where we've both got the monk on with each other, but it does boil down to we've got each other to talk to. She goes through hell with the finances, trying to balance the books. She talks to me about it but it's like talking to a brick wall. I'd sooner her do*

it because if she didn't do it it wouldn't get paid because I'd take all the money and go to Asda and just blow out.

Such domestic support was not always in evidence. Another man from Brodsworth, Mr G, had been divorced two years earlier. His ex-wife's new husband had become increasingly violent towards her and the children. A new relationship with another woman expecting his child had collapsed amidst arguments over money. To resolve the situation he had become active in the local informal economy:

I do gardening work. I've got a couple of jobs I do each week; that makes me a few quid but even that goes on bills. I might go out tonight and get a job for tomorrow, even if it's just a day's work. Everybody who goes into the Broad Highway wants to know if there's anything going. Like, I know a welder who's unemployed and I get him bits of work while I'm out gardening because people want garden gates, railings and things like that. Same with plasterers, joiners – mates of all kinds – and they'll keep a lookout for owt that might suit you.

Unable to depend, like Mr C, on a close, supportive relationship, Mr G was also discovering that such a risky and unreliable career was, in itself, a considerable source of stress. Lacking the security of either a legitimate job or reliable social support, and concerned about the welfare of his children and pregnant partner, he increasingly resorted to a coping device which was becoming commonplace in the area:

Everybody I know smokes grass or cannabis. That started during the strike because people never had the money to go out and have a drink, and so they used to stop at home and have a smoke. That's how I got introduced to it. When the strike came, it started coming out round here in the pubs and that. It's increased; it's available, it's cheaper than going to the ale house. When I was about eighteen, it was just isolated in town, there was none round here, but now it's a lot of young 'uns – seventeen- and eighteen-year-olds.

It is apparent that experiences of and reactions to unemployment are complex. A range of factors are involved: financial circumstances; a sense of self-identity; the availability of other activities to replace the rhythms of work; the extent of support from family and friends. Unemployment is rarely a positive experience but the extent of its negative repercussions is mediated by variations in individual circumstances. The patterns we have identified are largely consonant with those in the psychological literature.

The Psychology of Unemployment

Factors linking unemployment to impaired psychological well-being have been well researched. Warr (1985) identifies these as reductions in: income; activity outside the home; scope for autonomous decision-making; the use and development of skills; the quality of social interaction; prestige and social acceptability; and engagement in goal-related tasks and activities which tie in with those of other people. Unemployment increases a range of psychologically threatening activities (e.g. borrowing money or unsuccessfully applying for jobs), and insecurity and uncertainty about the future. We found evidence of all these tendencies amongst unemployed ex-miners, notably financial problems, reductions in social activity outside the home and increased tensions within it, and lowered self-esteem.

Strandh (2000) has recently re-emphasised the significance of 'economic strain' and a reduction in the individual's capacity to control their lives as factors liable to impair the mental health of the unemployed: 'Economic problems diminish short-term control of the life situation: it becomes difficult to uphold the desired standard of living. This, in turn, reduces long-term control of the life course, as financial problems make planning impossible' (ibid., p.463). This loss of control was much evident in our interviews, over the routine of the day, the disposition of the family budget and in interactions with neighbours and friends.

Some of those we interviewed or surveyed exhibited the symptoms which Warr (1985, pp.304) suggests affect between 20 and 30 per cent of unemployed men: poor concentration and application to activities; a lack of confidence; apathy; nervousness and anxiety; irritability; and depression. We also encountered men suffering from 'psychophysical' conditions, such as skin problems, headaches, high blood pressure and stomach complaints. After consulting a doctor, such men either became classed as too ill to work or finally accepted the existence of stress and resolved to take positive action about it.

The differences found between short-term unemployment at Askern and longer-term unemployed at Brodsworth confirm Gallie and Marsh's (1994 p.15) summary of 1970s research:

> If the very first days of unemployment were experienced as a relief from the constraints of the rat race, this soon gave way to a sharp decline in morale. Anxiety about finding a new job and coping with financial worries made it difficult to concentrate upon, let alone enjoy, alternative activities. The unemployed were beset by difficulties in sleeping, by tiredness during the day, and by loss of appetite. As the length of unemployment increased, they lost a sense of meaning in their lives and even their sense of identity.

In line with Brenner and Starrin's (1988) study of Swedish blue-collar workers, we also found that stress, though highest amongst the long-term unemployed, was also high amongst those still at work but anticipating redundancy.

Overall, our findings validate Ezzy's (1993, p.41) comment that 'It is now clear that the relationship between employment status and mental health is complex and subtle.' As Ezzy suggests, unemployment, like bereavement, sickness and divorce, constitutes a form of 'divestment passage' capable of causing a crises of 'identity legitimation', involving self-doubt, anxiety, depression and lowered self-esteem. Although our survey respondents declined to define unemployment as stressful outright, our interview material graphically illustrates such processes in operation.

It also showed the importance of variations in the capacity of individuals to cope with, or adapt to, unemployment. Warr and Jackson (1987) refer to the possible significance of such factors as: age and basic health; extent of social contact outside the family; and one's level of 'employment commitment' (i.e. motivation to become re-employed). These authors also distinguish between two forms of adaptation: 'resigned adaptation' involves a process of psychological adjustment where expectations of life are reduced to a level compatible with unemployment; whereas 'constructive adaptation' involves active attempts by the individual to cope with or offset the effects of unemployment. We found evidence of both these forms of adaptation, with contrasts between those finding ways to cope with unemployment and those becoming its resigned victims.

Nordenmark and Strandh have suggested that the mental health of individuals 'who mainly fulfil their need for a social identity in ways other than employment' is relatively unaffected by being out of work (1999, p.583); and that it is those individuals 'who manage to satisfy their need for a social identity through activities other than employment' who maintain positive psychological well-being during the period spent out of work (ibid., p.588). This was the case with our respondents who could construct a meaningful lifestyle around hobbies, interests and family responsibilities, including housework. By contrast, people unable to find a substitute role are likely to become resigned to their negative situation, or seek consolation or distraction in less constructive activities, such as an increased use of alcohol or substance abuse (Hammer 1992; Iversen and Klausen 1986). Many unemployed men had no interests and refused to participate in housework or childcare. Some interviewees frankly admitted to resorting to drugs and alcohol to obliterate the stress of unemployment.

Such responses are characteristic of men in occupational communities where the experience of unemployment has a particular meaning. As Harding and Sewel (1992, p.269) point out, 'The majority of recent research on unemployment and psychological well-being has decontextualized unemployment from its community context'. The individual responds in context where the identity of whole communities and all of the local economy is jeopardised.

A Swedish study of former shipyard workers and their families (Joelson and Wahlquist 1987) identified the stress associated with prolonged uncertainty over closure and the removal of structure and identity when the shipyard closed:

Now when they had all the time in the world, they found it difficult to meet their old friends, because one of the main things they had in common was lost. Besides a shipyard worker tends to look upon himself as a man of men. To be unemployed and to live all day at home does not fit that role and is nothing to share with others. (ibid., p.181)

These were almost exactly the effects in a different occupational community in another country just a few years later. These are not unexpected. In a pioneering study of redundant mineworkers in the north-east of England over thirty years ago, House and Knight (1967) contrasted the adjustment of those who interpreted unemployment as premature unemployment with the dislocation of those still seeking work. They also found the long-term unemployed to be divided between resignation to their fate and bitterness at its injustice. In this study, wives showed remarkable resilience in their willingness to make material and financial sacrifices.

More recently, Wass (1989; 1994), studied miners made redundant at Markham colliery in South Wales. Out of 505 employees working at the time of closure in 1985, 179 men were transferred. Wass conducted a postal survey of the 326 made redundant. Of those remaining 'economically active', a third had not worked in the twenty-two months since closure. Eighty per cent had been unemployed for at least two months.

In interviews, she found a marked contrast between the positive psychological health of those who viewed redundancy as a form of early retirement, saw closure as an inevitable fact of life, used their redundancy money to pay off mortgages, and remained active, and the inferior mental well-being of those already suffering ill health, who were unable or unwilling to find a surrogate work activity, and who were depressed by continual rejection by employers.

That the responses of unemployed ex-miners were along the lines predicted by the psychological literature on unemployment in general and on miners specifically validates both social science and those who warned of the consequences of pit closure. The rates of unemployment and sickness amongst men in ex-mining communities, as updated in chapter 5, remain disturbingly high. What we found in 1992 will, in many cases, have changed only little in the intervening nine years. Unemployment, whenever, wherever and whoever it affects, damages identity and health, dislocating men from their roles within the family, community and local economy.

Working Miners

Survey Data

Miners and ex-miners were asked whether nine aspects of the mining industry had improved, worsened or stayed the same since 1985. The answers (represented in table 2.6) were fairly clear-cut. The features seen most clearly to have worsened were job security and the attitudes of British Coal, with industrial relations and pit management style not far behind. There were not quite majority views for the worsening of discipline and safety standards. Little change was perceived in hours of work or relationships with workmates. The one aspect seen to have improved was pay.

There was considerable agreement about these changes across the communities, even where the pit had shut. The most idiosyncratic group was working Hatfield miners. They agreed with the others that British Coal attitudes and job security as well as safety had worsened and that pay had improved. They were, however, less likely to see a worsening of pit discipline, pit management style or industrial relations. Clearly, working at the local pit was an exceptional experience. This contrast was confirmed by our interviews.

TABLE 2.6 PERCEIVED CHANGES IN THE MINING INDUSTRY SINCE 1985

	Main sample Men only (%)	Voluntarily redundant Men only (%)
Saying had worsened		
Job security	96	90
British Coal attitude	86	90
Industrial relations	74	72
Pit management style	72	75
Discipline	49	52
Safety	48	52
Saying had stayed the same		
Hours of work	56	83
Workmate relations	66	67
Saying had improved		
Pay	46	50
N	*160*	*40*

Interview Material

In interviews, we explored the implications of new technology, management styles and attitudes to unions, safety issues and job insecurity. We also sought the experiences of those transferred to other pits or in contract mining.

Many of those interviewed emphasised the positive aspects of technological innovation which had made the job simpler and less arduous. Craft personnel responsible for the fitting and maintenance of machinery were swift to endorse such changes. As one Hatfield Main electrician informed us: 'It actually makes it a lot easier. A lot of the time now I can be rung up and asked to do a belt or a bunker and they can tell me the problem before I get there' (Mr L, Hatfield).

However, automation was also seen as reducing autonomy. The men were now being 'dictated to by their machines':

It's more stressful actually. It was hard work with a shovel but that's all you were doing, more or less, looking after your head and shovelling. Now it's speed all the time. You have to keep going all the time, plodding on. (Mr R, Rossington)

The traditionally strong solidarity existing between mineworkers had not completely survived the post-strike transformation of the industry. One man moving from Brodsworth to Hatfield had found more repartee and camaraderie at the new pit. This was attributed to a commitment to old management styles despite the new pressures from above. Union officials confirmed that variations in management attitudes were discernible even between neighbouring mines:

> *I don't know how much this is determined by the manager – how much rope they get – but we get one style of management at Hatfield and they get the opposite style of management at Markham Main within the same period of time. (Hatfield Main NUM official)*

At Rossington, the second of our working mines, the situation was less satisfactory:

> *The atmosphere is dowdy, it's not very good. It's gone down hill since the strike. The comradeship that used to exist between workers has gone. I think management's tighter discipline has affected ... I think pride – that's the word – there's less pride. I don't think anybody's bothered. They don't know whether they're coming or going; whether it's going to close, stay open or what. (Mr S, Rossington)*

Here, central directives were converted into orders to dispense with tried and tested working practices:

> *Many a time a deputy will say, 'I've had my orders from above, you've got to do this.' We'll say, 'Why? That's not right. Why don't we do what we normally do?' But they say, 'No, you've got to do this.' They're working it from the offices and it doesn't work like that. It gets you mad at times if they're trying to cause aggro, which sometimes they do. That stresses you up. They seem to want you to rag up and go on strike. They seem to want you to do that. It's a pressure on you not to do it at times. (Mr M, Rossington)*

Both the pressure to work harder and a decline in the number of deputies were seen to jeopardise safety standards. A NACODS official (from the National Association of Colliery Overmen, Deputies and Shotfirers) admitted that they were sailing close to the wind:

> *Sometimes, unfortunately, we get caught up in the trap where we have more of a production head on than we do safety and we end up going out on a limb; and it's getting that balance that is the difficulty. We've had a lot of new officials who have learned quickly because they've had to. But when they've gone training, they're trained with a production head. They've still got a high regard for safety but the production head is highlighted. It's, 'What is the delay going to cost us in terms of getting coal off?' (Rossington NACODS official)*

At Hatfield Main workers were more split in their opinions on safety. Nevertheless, here too NACODS officials suggested that the declining number of deputies, allied to the growing obsession with maintaining production, was impairing safety standards.

Above all, however, it was insecurity and uncertainty about the future that seemed to be the primary source of stress among working miners. Media stories and rumours were experienced as constantly unsettling:

I might have no job in a month's time or might still be working in five years' time. That's how they treat you now: they don't tell you anything. I don't lie awake thinking about it; I don't fall out with people or become moody, but it gives me cause for anxiety. (Mr L, Hatfield)

As with unemployment, the capacity to cope with the pressures often depended on life outside work. A working miner, Rossington's Mr M, told us how his son had returned home following the break-up of a relationship, bringing with him a baby whose mother was refusing to look after it. This had upset Mrs M so much that she had gone sick from her job as a machinist. Since both father and son worked at the pit, and each was fatigued by the arduousness and insecurity of the job, Mrs M had taken on responsibility for the baby but found it all too much to take:

Before, we could go out as often as we wanted or just stop in, and that's what we did. We'd just get in the car, drive off and go anywhere we wanted. Now she feels hemmed in, she can't get out. I don't go out so much any more because I stop in to keep her company. She can't go out if he is on nights because she has to look after the baby. She [Mrs M] sleeps well; she whittles in the day. With time on her hands, now, especially, she's worrying about the baby and the pit closing all the time. She gets very depressed at times. She's under one of these psychoanalysts. She's been going for a while now. She broke down there a few weeks ago. (Mr M, Rossington)

With little social support, the family struggled along. With problems at work and at home, Mr M's refuge was the local working-men's club where the pressure would be temporarily lifted. He still had a job but, on the whole, he and his wife found life every bit as stressful as did many of those who were unemployed.

Some had found a solution to the unwelcome prospect of unemployment by opting for transfer or contract work. Respondents in the former category had mixed stories to tell. On the whole, transferees appreciated their greater sense of job security, especially at the apparently invincible Selby complex, and often found the work less demanding. On the debit side, however, there were problems with commuting, the stress of taking on new roles and responsibilities (often without adequate training) and forging new relationships with workmates who were sometimes resentful of newcomers. One reaction was psychological detachment, as in this account from a man in his late forties who had transferred from Askern to Selby:

*Looking at it from my side, what I think myself at 47 is I'm not ready to
finish work yet. I've got no love for the coal industry. I've no love for Riccall
colliery at all: I'm not bothered about the place, I haven't any loyalty towards
it. It's a matter of a job now. I do my job and I come home. I don't volunteer
for anything; I just do what's necessary. I'm like, in my own way, thinking,
'I'll screw them for the next five or six years as much as I can, just like they've
done to us over the last twenty-odd years since I've been in.' (Mr B, Askern)*

There were other kinds of adjustment. A 30-year-old former Brodsworth
miner was now working long hours at Rossington to maintain his family's
comfortable lifestyle. The psychological tensions this caused were handled by
resort to drugs and alcohol:

*I've been smoking it for quite a few years but not as a stress-related thing –
just purely for enjoyment. Alcohol made me more of a violent type person
whereas I found if I had a smoke of marijuana, it had more of a calming
influence. What I've found now is, since I've had this job, it works wonders.
I can come home really stressed up and in a terrible mood and Elaine will
see it straight away and say, 'Get yourself one rolled up,' and I'll sit there,
roll a joint and … I'm not saying that I'm smoking them all night; just one
joint and I'm okay. You talk to some of the lads and there's a few of them
that smoke. Obviously, it's kept well away from work. I wouldn't even dream
of smoking before I went to work. I don't drink heavily but, if I've got a
weekend off, I'll go for it. If I know I've got to get up for work in the
morning I'll go out and have a couple of pints, a game of pool, and I'm
alright. But if I'm not going to work the next morning, I don't know why,
I've got to go for it and I get arseholed. (Mr S, Brodsworth)*

Some miners made redundant from British Coal found new jobs difficult
to find and chose to work for mining contractors. It provided a job but at a
price. Contracts were issued according to demand, for short periods and in any
part of the country. Mr M of Rossington conceded that his typical day was
more arduous and uncomfortable than that of corresponding British Coal
employees:

*The main difference is that you're doing more than your own job. You're
helping with everything else on the running of whatever part of the
development you're doing. Twelve months out of the hard, strenuous work
and then going back into it took its toll. It took me about three or four
months to get used to it again.*

Trends in Mining Management

Such experiences reflected the strategies of British Coal between the end of the
strike in 1985 and privatisation in 1995, which have been well documented
(Edwards and Heery 1989; Gibbon and Bromley 1990; Prowse and Turner
1996; Taylor 1988; Winterton and Winterton 1989; 1993).

These involved greater reliance on retreat mining methods of coal extraction, new technologies for extraction and transportation and microelectronic data systems. All were clearly more efficient but could also be interpreted as increasing management control and de-skilling the workforce (Gibbon and Bromley 1990). Trade unions were progressively marginalised by the dismantling of previous agreements over conciliation, unfair dismissal and disciplinary codes. Wages were increasingly determined at local rather than national levels, increasing differentials between pits (Winterton and Winterton 1993). Short-term contracts and weekend working became commonplace. Trade union activists were isolated or transferred to surface work:

> Colliery managers now rarely consult the union branch ('unless they want something') whereas before the big strike it was customary for any change to be negotiated. Management now issue unilateral instructions or bypass the union altogether, dealing with individuals on a 'take it or leave it' basis. Some colliery managers are more approachable and, in units which are of strategic importance, local concessions have been won ... However, pit-level bargaining is characterised by informality giving management the power to withdraw concessions. (Winterton and Winterton 1993, p.91)

The use of contract labour and the erosion of demarcation further weakened the unions. Communication was targeted via bulletins and videos to reach workers 'over the heads' of union officials (Leman and Winterton 1991). Safety training emphasised the need to minimise costs in lost production (Tucker and Clark 1991).

As we shall see in chapter 6, these trends would be continued in the privatised industry after 1995. By that time, Hatfield and Rossington, though both still working, would have shed their workforces still further, causing even more miners to join the ranks of the unemployed – or else enter the final category of our respondents: those who had found work outside the mining industry.

Men Re-employed in Non-mining Jobs

Survey Data

As was clear from table 2.1, almost half the miners redundant from Askern found employment elsewhere in the industry (table 2.7); but in Brodsworth, where the pit had been shut longer, only one in six remained in the industry. With over a half unemployed there, just over a quarter (28 per cent) had found new jobs outside mining. These were all unskilled, mainly manual and labouring. There was little evidence of retraining into skilled or semiskilled employment. Nor did there seem much likelihood of self-employment, with just one man out of eighty exercising this option.

TABLE 2.7 EMPLOYMENT DESTINATIONS OF REDUNDANT MINERS:
NON-MINING JOBS

Employment destination	Brodsworth	Askern	Total	
	N	N	N	%
Caring	1		1	7.1
Domestic	1	1	2	14.3
Labouring/manual	6	1	7	50.0
Factory work	2		2	14.3
Self-employed	1		1	7.1
Craftsmen		1	1	7.1
Student				
All new employment	11	3	14	100

Interview Material

Miners re-employed outside the mining industry had to adjust to new types
of work, conditions and pay. It should be remembered that mining was, and
still is, a dirty, dangerous and debilitating occupation, so new jobs were
occasionally an improvement.

Self-employment was one option. One ex-craftsman, Mr K of Askern, had
previously worked for himself as a commercial fisherman in Cornwall. He had
the technical skills, experience and confidence to start a business fitting and
decorating kitchens, bedrooms and bathrooms. It compared favourably with
mining:

> *It doesn't compare at all. It's up in the fresh air every day and it's great. I
> enjoy it. We've just painted a chap's house, just round the corner. Out in the
> fresh air, sunshine on your neck – lovely! You don't get that at the pit.*

Self-employment was rare. Casual or seasonal employment driving ice-
cream vans or taxis was more typical. Those who had found secure employment
earned less but there were compensations. One man working as a joiner for
the local council found his working life had been greatly enhanced:

> *I'm enjoying my work better. I'm not having to get up at 5 o'clock in the
> morning. Now, I've got the lump sum behind me I don't have to work
> overtime. I can work my five days, eight while half past four. We go round
> repairing houses. We do some decent work, it's varied. I'm doing a job I enjoy
> and my peace of mind is great. I'm a different person. (Mr W, Askern)*

He missed pit humour and wages were lower but otherwise his life had
improved. Even a part-time, unskilled job was better than nothing, as another
respondent explained:

> *It's only cleaning but I enjoy it more than the pit. You're not working as
> many hours, that's one thing. You're not getting mucky. There's no pressure on
> you, as long as you do your job of course. I'm a lot happier. There's a bit of
> money coming in. It's only a part-time job but, as things are with the wife*

working especially, we're quite happy. But there must be people who haven't even got a part-time job in the same boat as me. I don't know how they carry on. It must be really upsetting for them. We've been really lucky. (Mr We, Brodsworth)

This sense of having been lucky compared with others often appeared in interviews. The reference point was no longer previous work down the pit but others who had remained unemployed. Attitudes to new jobs were always tempered by this sense of relief.

This is not to pretend that that the transition from mining to non-mining was always so smooth and unproblematical. We heard numerous accounts of jobs taken on that proved either too insecure or financially or socially unrewarding to last for long. For example, Mr C of Brodsworth had spent a brief spell as a coal-delivery man (which he abandoned because 'the effort almost killed me'), followed by a two-week period labouring on a building site, at which point the business he was working for folded, another casualty of the recession. Such patterns of 'chequeredness' and instability were common characteristics of the employment available to former Askern and Brodsworth miners. They reflected changes in the labour market and working conditions evident in the economy as a whole over the last fifteen years.

New Working Conditions

In the 1980s psychologists quite understandably turned their attention to the problems of the unemployed but, in doing so, they may have underestimated the increased pressures on those remaining in work in terms of work intensification, job insecurity and consequent stress (Burchell 1992).

Cartwright and Cooper (1997) have catalogued the nature of work intensification occurring since the 1980s. This incorporates: onerous working conditions; long working hours; increased shiftwork; and commuting further afield. All of these developments were confirmed by Burchell et al. (1999) in their study of twenty organisations in both the private and public sectors. The relationship between poor psychological health and job insecurity has also been demonstrated in numerous studies (cf. Burchell 1994; Hartley et al. 1991; Iversen and Sabroe 1988). Work intensification and job insecurity produce stress, with raised levels of depression, negative moods, sleep problems, anxiety, fear and anger (Nolan et al. 2000). Stress at work correlates with psychosomatic complaints (e.g. chest pains and raised blood pressure), anxiety, irritability, exhaustion and depression (Cartwright and Cooper 1997). Individuals may choose to react to, or cope with, the stress they encounter at work in a variety of different ways: they may become apathetic or indifferent to their job; they may turn to alcohol or substance misuse; absent themselves more often; or leave the company altogether (Iversen and Klausen 1986; Leigh 1991; Seeman et al. 1988; Watson 1997).

Re-employment following redundancy does seem to have an immediate and positive effect on mental health. Using survey sub-samples of unemployed, re-employed and continuously employed workers, Kessler et al. (1989, p.655) discovered that: 'Respondents who found new jobs showed dramatic decline in distress compared to those who remained unemployed and were, in fact, functioning as well as the stably employed at the follow-up interview'. However, this and other studies emphasise that a period of unemployment may leave the re-employed vulnerable to enduring feelings of self-doubt and insecurity (Fineman 1987).

The ramifications for miners were explored by Witt's (1990) postal survey of 302 redundant miners from the Woolley and South Kirkby collieries, near Wakefield. New jobs were sought within a narrow range of occupations, notably manufacturing and warehousing, and to a slightly lesser extent in building, driving or back into mining. Often, as with our Doncaster respondents, employment was 'chequered' and unstable:

> It is important to note the instability of much of this employment. In the Yorkshire survey, 101 of the 222 men who had been employed at some point (45 per cent) had had two or more jobs. Almost a fifth of the entire group had had two or more spells of unemployment. And even eighteen months after closure 17 per cent were in jobs of a temporary or contract nature. Given that many of these would have taken some months to find their first job, the picture which emerges is one of considerable uncertainty and insecurity for a significant proportion of former miners. (ibid., p.26)

Wass (1989; 1994) found the same for miners made redundant at Markham colliery in South Wales: 'For those who did work their new jobs were often insecure and miners soon found themselves out of work again' (1989, p.17).

We shall return to these questions, of the quality and insecurity of replacement jobs in chapter 5, since they emerged in our own later (1995) survey in Thurcroft. In the meantime, it is reasonable to conclude that, for ex-miners from Brodsworth and Askern, finding any job at all was an achievement in itself, one that only a minority managed. For the lucky ones, this involved a positive and refreshing change from the mines. For the majority, however, it entailed a continuation of the insecurity they had been exposed to at the pit, the disruption of moving from job to job and a marked reduction in pay.

Conclusion

We have examined the employment experiences as they existed in 1992 of men in four mining communities. In two where the pit was still open, Hatfield and Rossington, we found men confronting a bewildering variety of changes in working practices and management attitudes. The intensification of work and job insecurity had produced its own kind of stress. For those made redundant six months earlier at Askern, continued employment in the mining industry was still the preferred option; but at Brodsworth, where the pit had been shut for eighteen months, re-employment in mining was less evident. The majority here were unemployed. Case histories demonstrated great variety in the capacity to cope with long-term unemployment but overall it had a range of negative economic and psychological effects of the kind well established in the literature. The minority of men successful in finding new employment did so in low-grade occupations though working conditions were often an improvement. In chapter 5 we shall update this picture, though in many of its essentials it has changed very little. Pit closure causes a crisis in the local economy, which has demonstrable effects on the psychological health of those affected. In this chapter we have concentrated exclusively on men but their wives and families are intimately involved as well. The next chapter therefore examines the position and experiences of women in the mining communities we studied.

NOTES

1. The village surrounding Brodsworth colliery is actually called Woodlands. However, to avoid unnecessary confusion, we shall continue to refer to it as Brodsworth.

2. Likewise, Hatfield Main colliery is encompassed by three small, but interrelated localities: Dunscroft, Hatfield and Stainforth. For ease of reference, we shall refer to the larger amalgamation as Hatfield.

3. It should be noted that these figures are inclusive of those respondents registered as unemployed (and therefore claiming unemployment benefit) and any individuals not currently in paid work due to long-term sickness.

3   The Impact on Women and Families

INTRODUCTION

In the last chapter we focused on men's experience of industrial contraction. In this chapter we look at the experiences of women. We look initially at their own experience of work and unemployment. Then we examine how women perceived the work of men remaining in mining and those redeployed elsewhere. Since unemployment was such a common outcome of pit closure, we discuss at some length how women handled the unemployment of their partners, the sources of conflict which arose and the kinds of resolutions achieved. Our objective here is to draw conclusions about the impact of unemployment on family and marital relations by analysing 'the different meanings men and women attach to the experience of unemployment and to their marriages and family lives ... [one which] incorporates a review of the man's work status but gives equivalent rating to his family membership, especially his relationship with his wife and children' (McKee and Bell 1985, p.387). This wider impact on families is situated within women's greater responsibility for the emotional maintenance of family life. Two case studies are used to illustrate what we identified as the variables compounding or moderating the stress caused by unemployment. Finally, we suggest that, in these communities, women's experiences were framed by the responses of their partners so that the male agenda predominated. In most of the sections, we discuss, in turn, survey data and interview material which is then related to previous studies.

Women and Work

We begin by examining what our survey revealed about local patterns of female employment. To see if there are variations in women's employment by area or the employment status of their husband it is first useful to look at the figures for all the women who were partners of present or past miners. In this group as a whole, 45 per cent were housewives and almost exactly 50 per cent in paid work (see table 3.1). There were two main clusters of female employment. The first cluster, caring/catering/retail sales, provided employment for 29 per cent of all women, well over half those in paid work. The second cluster, domestic/factory/labouring, amounts to 11 per cent of all women or one fifth of those in paid work. More skilled work, managerial/office was undertaken by 6 per cent of all women, about 12 per cent of all employment.

If over thirty-one hours is taken to be full-time employment, then just over a quarter (29 per cent) of working women were in this category (table 3.2). Thus, the vast majority, 71 per cent, worked part-time. One in three working women worked 11–20 hours, one in five 21–30 hours and one in seven less than 10 hours. So the norm for female employment was a half/two-thirds time job. Women not currently working had worked in the past. A third of them used to work in manual/factory employment, more than did at present. The majority of women (51 per cent) said they had stopped work to look after young children but sizeable minorities did so because of illness (26 per cent) or redundancy (15 per cent). If the first is a choice, the second two are not.

TABLE 3.1 EMPLOYMENT STATUS OF WIVES OF WORKING, COMPULSORILY AND VOLUNTARILY REDUNDANT MINERS

Employment status/sector	All women				Employed only	
	N	*%*	*N*	*%*	*N*	*%*
Caring	18	9.2				
Catering	20	10.2				
Retail sales	19	9.7				
			57	29.1	57	58.8
Domestic	7	3.6				
Factory work	7	3.6				
Labouring/manual	7	3.6				
			21	10.8	21	21.7
Managerial	8	4.1				
Office work	4	2.0				
Self-employed	3	1.5				
Other	4	2.0				
			19	9.6	19	19.5
All employed	*97*	*49.5*	*97*	*49.5*	*97*	*100*
Housewife	87	44.4				
Unemployed	8	4.1				
Student	3	1.5				
Retired	1	0.5				
Total	*196*	*100*				

Note: employment status of 10 wives unknown.

TABLE 3.2 WORKING HOURS OF WIVES OF WORKING, COMPULSORILY AND VOLUNTARILY REDUNDANT MINERS

Hours per week	*N*	*%*	Sub-total %
less than 10	14	14.4	
11–20	33	34.0	48.5
21–30	22	22.7	
31–40	24	24.7	
over 40	4	4.1	51.5
Total	*97*	*100*	*100*

Working miners' wives were slightly more likely to be housewives than the group as a whole (50 per cent compared with 45 per cent) but this is wholly attributable to the generally lower rate of economic activity in one of the communities, Hatfield. The most frequent employment status in pit closure communities was that of housewife. This was higher in Brodsworth (42 per cent) than in Askern (33 per cent), part of a general pattern of differences in female economic activity between areas, possibly attributable to contrasting opportunities in the local jobs market. The variations were within an overall pattern. In both areas, two-thirds of all female employment was in caring/catering/retail sales or domestic/factory/labouring. Pit closure does not have the same impact on female employment as it does on that of men. The most important influence on female economic activity seems to be the area in which they live and whether the local economy generates the kinds of jobs miners' wives are likely to take up.

The impact of male unemployment on family income and relationships might be expected to vary according to the employment status of female partners. Table 3.3 shows the profile of female employment status in relation to male employment status for the whole of the main sample. The tendencies are slight but consistent. Wives of unemployed ex-miners are less likely to be working full-time and more likely to be working part-time than the wives of continuing miners, though there is less difference in the proportion who are housewives. In the absence of longitudinal data, we cannot say that male unemployment is a cause of women forsaking full-time for part-time employment.

All this seems to confirm that the paucity of employment prospects for women in mining communities means that families have traditionally depended wholly or mainly on the male wage. Generally, the data does not suggest that redundant miners' wives were in a position to compensate for the loss or reduction of their husbands' wages by going out to work. The restrictions of the local jobs market, in addition to other contributory factors such as the stage in the life cycle, mean that women's employment opportunities in mining communities remain restricted and cannot be expanded to compensate for the loss of male jobs.

We asked working women interviewees about their jobs. Nearly all responded positively, regardless of the pay or skills involved. One woman explained the satisfaction of being a school canteen supervisor in the following terms:

> *I enjoy the work. I especially like the cooking part. You get a lot of satisfaction when things come out well, especially if they look nice. At the moment I've been moving round and doing cook-in-charge jobs at different schools and meeting the girls there. I was a bit apprehensive at first and I couldn't sleep at first for the thought of going but after the first day it was alright and I've enjoyed it since. (Mrs E, Hatfield)*

TABLE 3.3 EMPLOYMENT STATUS OF COUPLES: MAIN SAMPLE

Male employment status	Female employment status					
	Full-time work	Part-time work	House-wife	Not known	No partner[†]	Total
Mining work (N)	29	62	103	10	2	206
Mining work (%)	14	30	50	5	1	100
Other employment (N)	4	14	17	–	1	36
Other employment (%)	11	39	47	–	3	100
Unemployed (N)	4	31	34	3	3	75
Unemployed (%)	5	41	45	4	4	100
Not known (N)	–	1	2	–	–	3
Total (N)	37	108	156	13	6	320
Total (%)	12	33	49	4	2	100

[†] Six men had no partner at the time of interview.

Another woman worked as a care assistant and was taking an NVQ qualification. Since her relationship with her unemployed husband was problematic, the job provided compensation:

I feel as though I'm doing some good. I don't feel trapped. I'll be honest, I think if I hadn't had a job I'd have had a breakdown. That was my outlet. You're getting out of the house, getting away from it all. I could get out that door and shut it and just forget for seven hours. It doesn't go away – you've got it to come back to – but it doesn't seem half as bad when you've been out of the house for so many hours and then come back. (Mrs M, Brodsworth)

Only one interviewee, to be encountered later, disliked her job, feeling resentful that she was being made to work hard for low pay at a Hatfield supermarket.

While the kinds of job available to women in these communities were restricted, they clearly enjoyed them. Interview material confirmed the conventional wisdom that it is psychologically more beneficial for women to have an arduous and demanding job than for them to have no job at all (Brown and Harris 1978; Nathanson 1975). We did not explore the issue of childcare sufficiently to comment on its strategic importance in enabling women to work (Ross and Mirowsky 1988) but we did find great emphasis placed by working women on the autonomy it offered them. For some, it clearly was the case that employment compensated for problems at home so 'that positive conditions in one sphere of life may compensate for negative conditions in another' (Lennon and Rosenfield 1992, p.324). The mere fact of having to cope with paid and domestic work does not necessarily cause women stress. As Baruch et al. (1987) suggest, it is the quality, not quantity, of their dual responsibilities, which is crucial. Where both work and life at home were unsatisfactory, then stress would be compounded. This complicated interaction of variables may account for the lack of statistical difference between the mean stress scores of working and non-working women, revealed in table 3.4.

TABLE 3.4 STRESS SCORES OF WORKING/NON-WORKING WOMEN

Whether working	N	Mean	Median	Standard deviation
In work	128	9.5	9.0	4.8
Not in work	112	7.8	7.0	4.2
	Mann-Whitney test: W = 14302; p = 0.06			

Note: maximum individual stress = 42 (see appendix for details of calculation).

Women's Own Unemployment

In our survey sample only a few women – between 4 and 8 per cent – were classified as unemployed but the few who experienced it took it hard. We interviewed one. When Askern colliery closed 45-year-old Mrs R was made redundant from her full-time job at the pit canteen. Her electrician husband, who had suffered a heart attack the previous year, returned to the pit only just before it closed. He was now depressed and withdrawn, convinced that, since he was approaching 50 and plagued by a heart problem, he stood little chance of finding another job. Mrs R felt constantly aware of his vulnerable health as well as his depressed state of mind:

> *I think he just feels useless. It worries you; and with him being at home all day, you're living on your nerves because you tend to watch all the time – 'Does he look well today?'*

Mrs R had three school-age children to look after but this scarcely substituted for the loss of her job which she had thoroughly enjoyed. Now, she felt that her daily routine was 'boring beyond belief':

> *It's just the same jobs every day. You get up, make the fire, clean up, wash up, get breakfast. It's just all the same. I'm learning to drive and I came in the other day and just couldn't be bothered to do a thing. I could have done all the ironing, but you get in a rut. When you're working you do it because you know you're going out to work and you've got to do it. The days seem too long. I just wouldn't have left the pit. I couldn't have wished for a better job.*

While Mrs R's stress partly derived from having to cope with her husband's poor mental health after redundancy, to identify this as the primary cause would be misleading. At the root of her present depression and stress was the loss of important sources of social support and a meaningful identity at the pit canteen:

> *While I worked at the pit my dad died. He had cancer, and it was awful going through that, but all the men at the pit knew him, and they were really good, they helped me through it, and they helped me through [my husband's] heart attack and they were marvellous. Now I don't feel as though I've got anybody. If you've got troubles now, there's no-one to help you through them. Everything happened at once – my dad died, his mum died and then [my husband] had his heart attack – all at once. The men kept me*

going because they knew you, they know your life, they know your relations. You've still got friends but it's not the same. I'm not a loner. I like people. If they could open that canteen up again tomorrow, it would make my life worth living; but they're not going to. I wish it had never shut.

The friendships that she now found herself falling back on were no substitute for the primary relationships that sustained her at work. She had lost her job and its social contacts and was now required to cope with a husband debilitated by unemployed and ill health. However, the social support she could previously depend upon was no longer there to sustain her.

Her case endorses Coyle's (1984) findings, based on a study of redundant female textile workers in Harrogate and Castleford (a former mining town), that unemployment involves reduced autonomy and independence, restricted social interaction, fewer leisure opportunities, a diminution of self-esteem and financial hardship. It seems generally true of women in mining communities as elsewhere that they go to work 'at least as much to escape the confines of domestic life as to enjoy the inherent satisfactions of employment' (Cragg and Dawson 1984, p.71).

Wives of Working Miners

Interviews with the wives of working miners identified three sources of anxiety. A permanent one was the danger of the job. One Rossington housewife told us that 'I don't like them working down there. I think it's very dangerous and everyday he goes to work I live in fear' (Mrs T, Rossington). A second problem was uncertainty over the future of the pit:

They keep threatening it's going to close. I get a bit moody and me and him start to fall out. He shouts and gets right bad tempered. Then he shouts at the kids for the least little thing or storms out. (Mrs G, Hatfield)

Third were changes in status. Women showed an awareness of the new working conditions and relationships encountered by transferees. As contract workers found themselves in and out of work, this generated complicated procedures for claiming benefits:

The ins-and-outs are awful. We go on income support. It's better for us because that way they pay your interest on your mortgage and the little one will get free school dinners and clothing. Having said that, it's a nightmare. Whenever we've got the dinners and clothing through, he's gone and got a job, so we've never been able to use it. That really annoys me! Every time you do it, you have to go through that process. You can't go in and say, 'I filled this in a couple of months ago.' (Mrs H, Brodsworth)

Little research has been devoted to understanding the impact of male workers' job stressors on the emotional well-being of their female partners. One notable exception is a study by Rook et al. (1991) which found that the more the husband was experiencing problems at work, the greater was the propensity for his spouse to exhibit such symptoms of psychological distress as nervousness, restlessness and having 'frightening thoughts'.

Wives of Redeployed Miners

We also included in the interview sample women whose partners had found alternative employment. These men were almost universally described by their partners as happier in their new job than at the pit. Although, in the vast majority of cases, the replacement work found by the men was significantly inferior to pit work in terms of pay and conditions, all but one of the six women whose husbands were re-employed rated them more content in their current job. Mrs K (Askern), for example, was the wife of the self-employed kitchen fitter referred to in the previous chapter. She stated unequivocally:

> He loves it. I think to do something that he really, really enjoys, it becomes a pleasure as well as earning money. I think he likes it a lot better than going up and down the pit everyday. And I'm glad he's out of the pit.

Mrs S (Brodsworth), whose husband was now working as a labourer, also felt that her husband was happier now:

> He's out in the open now. He's always wanted to work outside, especially in the summer, when he can be out in the sun and not down there. He wasn't a faceworker but he did work down the pit, so it's just that he can work outdoors now. I think we're happier now. He is, and that means I am. I'm not worrying that he's down the pit.

In the case of re-employment, several factors coincide to reduce stress for women. First, the men are generally happier. Second, the partner's attainment of a new job has usually been preceded by a period of unemployment, the memories of which are still fresh in the women's minds. Third, there was not the kind of conflict over domestic matters we shall find to be typical during unemployment. For those whose husbands remained unemployed, such conflicts were ongoing.

Wives of Unemployed Men

In the survey we did not find that wives of unemployed men were any more or less likely to be employed than in other situations. Only rarely did the wife's employment cause marital tension. The financial problems of unemployment were talked about but they were regarded as inevitable and only at Brodsworth had these been long term. Even there, 40 per cent of those on benefits were still able to claim unemployment benefit and only a quarter had resorted to social security. Rather than money, wives were much more likely to discuss the problems of coping with their husbands' emotional reaction to being unemployed:

I've had a hell of a lot of pressure with Dennis. He was right depressed, and he was like a Jekyll and Hyde. You think, 'If I say that, he's going to go over the edge.' I was having to bite my tongue, which made me more angry than every – but I had to. I thought, 'It's either me biting my tongue, or he's going to explode.' It got to the point with that that I could have screamed. I could have just put my coat on and run. (Mrs M, Brodsworth)

Some men dealt with their emotional turmoil by withdrawing:

He misses going to work. He gets right down at the moment. He gets to the stage where he just withdraws. He say nothing's wrong but you can tell – because he goes withdrawn and he's so quiet and he doesn't want to do owt. He gets out of it again though. But it affects you all. If there's an atmosphere in the house, you can sense it. (Mrs R, Askern)

Significantly, the flashpoints for moodiness were often around housework. Husbands not only appeared as a permanent presence in the domestic sphere where they were normally absent, they also took it upon themselves to supervise their wives' housework. This was a not untypical complaint:

He wanders about. He follows you all over the house. He's terrible. I could smack him. If you're dusting something and you happen to miss a bit, he'll say, 'You haven't done that properly, you're wasting your time,' and I think, 'for God's sake get out'. We've come close to splitting up, actually. (Mrs C, Brodsworth)

Another woman, whose husband eventually found a job, recalled the stop-watch culture her husband had enforced whilst unemployed:

It was more that my routine got disrupted. Before, I fitted everything in but I did it when I wanted to. But then it would be 'Why are you sitting down?' or 'Do you have to hoover now?' or 'Why don't you have a drink instead?' Everything was all cockeyed. He'd lay in bed all morning, and then I'd go out, and he'd say, 'Where have you been? I thought you were going to be back by so-and-so.' I felt as though I was on the stop-watch all the time. (Mrs F, Askern)

Some felt that the man's apparent need to exert control over his wife decreased the time she had to herself:

I get less time to relax now, because he doesn't like me sewing. I know he doesn't particularly like me doing it at night. Whereas before I would sit, when he was on nights, every night until one o'clock in the morning if I wanted. I haven't done so much since he's been out of work. So I don't get as much time to myself as before. (Mrs F, Askern)

Just occasionally the issue was related to role reversal which the man would resent:

I used to come in and think, 'I've just done a seven-hour shift. He hasn't got up while eleven, he hasn't done a thing!' He hadn't hoovered up, there were not potatoes done; he wouldn't even go to the shops ... He just exploded. He said, 'If you can't keep up with your work at home, then you shouldn't be working. It's not my place to do housework!' (Mrs M, Brodsworth)

Even in the best cases, where the man showed willing, there were limits to what he was prepared to engage in. One woman recalled her husband's period of unemployment:

It was much easier for me when my husband wasn't working because he took on the extra jobs like hoovering. He didn't like to dust, though. He's never done things like ironing and that sort of thing, but he'd put a load of washing in and take it out. He didn't like housework and he wouldn't be content being a house husband. He did it because it helped me, and he didn't feel justified in doing nothing when I was working. He prefers it now that he's going out to work too. (Mrs W, Brodsworth)

Once re-employed, he had continued to offer more help than had been the case previously but the baseline was fairly low:

Even now, if it's a nice day and he's on afters, I'll put a load of towels in the washer in the morning and he'll take them out and hang them up before he goes off to work. He's quite good really. (Mrs W, Brodsworth)

The tension over domestic labour indicates the crisis in gender roles provoked by male unemployment. No longer able to fulfil their traditional role as main wage-earner, men tried to reassert control in other ways. When this extended to housework, which women traditionally controlled, conflict was inevitable.

Wives of unemployed ex-miners provided a variety of evidence to support the idea that 'unemployment affects not only individuals who lose their jobs but their spouses and families as well' (Liem and Liem 1990, p.200). McKee and Bell (1985) have previously reported on the patterns we found following unemployment. The constant presence of a male partner round the house becomes for the wife a threatening and unwelcome intrusion, especially in cases where the man insists on criticising or supervising her housework. It seems generally true that male participation in domestic chores increases only marginally, and encompasses only a narrow range of activities, during periods of unemployment (Binns and Mars 1984; Laite and Halfpenny 1987; Morris 1988; 1992). Indeed, as McKee and Bell (1985, p.396) point out, male unemployment implies 'an enlargement or magnification' of the woman's domestic role.

It did seem that traditional gender roles stayed resilient despite male unemployment. Men defined how much of what they were prepared to do:

The key tasks of child care and food preparation remain outside most men's ideas of appropriate male activity. Men also retain the option of deciding what to do, an option closed to most wives. (Binns and Mars 1984, p.684)

If challenged, the men fell back on rigid conceptions of the domestic division of labour which unemployment was not allowed to disrupt. However, we only rarely found that men directly objected to their wives working, as suggested by Popay (1985).

Overall, it seemed that the men set the tone of the marital relationship which the wives were required to inhabit. A study of the wives of redundant Pennsylvanian steelworkers came to a similar conclusion:

> *The effects of unemployment appear to be primarily indirect, or mediated, by the distress of the person actually experiencing job loss; the husband's level of psychological distress better predicted his wife's symptoms than did his employment status per se. (Dew et al. 1987, p.181)*

The wife, however, did not only have to cope with her husband's emotions. She also had to deal with the implications for the rest of the family.

Gender, Worry and the Family

In the previous chapter we discussed how survey respondents defined unemployment as less a source of stress than worry. This came from a battery of questions about worries in general. Not unexpectedly, there was a strong gender difference in the replies. For men, work-related problems (general problems, strike aftermath, unemployment) were more frequent than family-related problems (children, bereavement): 51 per cent as against 35 per cent. For women, the reverse was true: 33 per cent work-related as against 44 per cent family-related (table 3.5).

Our survey also indicated that a clear majority saw family life as having changed over the last five years (60 per cent) though this left a sizeable minority (40 per cent) who did not. Such changes were perceived as taking the forms of marital breakdown, problems with teenagers, poverty and less community spirit. Little importance was attached to a general breakdown of family values or to child neglect (table 3.6). Responses to a separate question reveals that, taking all the communities together, just over 80 per cent saw the future as getting harder, 17 per cent thought it would stay the same and just 3 per cent that it would get easier (table 3.7).

Here we concentrate on the ramifications of unemployment for family life. In one complicated case, the children had to get used to the family's new financial circumstances:

> *They don't get as many treats and that. They can't spend as much on clothes and stuff like that that we used to. They find that hard: they ask for things and they have to wait. The kids tend to want what other kids get and it's hard for them to accept that they can't have it when there's only one working. You're trying to get a uniform together for them going back to school because they've outgrown the other one. It's just hard. It just seems to be one vicious circle. You get a little bit and then you need to use it. There isn't a chance to*

TABLE 3.5 MOST WORRYING THING BY GENDER (EXCLUDING NOTHING): MAIN SAMPLE

	Men		Women	
	N	%	N	%
Work security	24		13	
Strike aftermath	12		12	
Unemployment	15		8	
All work-related		51		33
Child welfare	21		25	
Bereavement	14		19	
All family-related		35		44
Health	6		10	
Separation/divorce	4		4	
All personal		10		14
Other	5	5	9	9
Total	*129*		*130*	

TABLE 3.6a PERCEPTIONS OF CHANGES IN FAMILY BY AREA: MAIN SAMPLE

	Brodsworth %	Rossington %	Askern %	Hatfield %	Total %
Perceive changes	64	53	65	54	60
Perceive no changes	36	48	35	46	41

(*N* = 320)

TABLE 3.6b MAIN CHANGE IN FAMILY LIFE BY AREA: MAIN SAMPLE

	Brodsworth %	Rossington %	Askern %	Hatfield %	Total %
Marital breakdown	12	14	35	2	17
Child neglect	6	–	6	2	4
Poverty	24	14	8	21	17
Problems with teenagers	8	31	23	21	20
Less community spirit	24	26	8	19	19
Collapse of family values	8	–	–	14	5
Families better	4	–	2	–	2
Other change	16	14	20	21	18

(*N* = 198)

TABLE 3.7 FUTURE PROSPECTS FOR FAMILIES BY AREA: MAIN SAMPLE

	Brodsworth %	Rossington %	Askern %	Hatfield %	Total %
Get harder	79	80	83	83	81
Stay same	17	18	15	17	17
Get easier	4	3	1	–	2

(*N* = 320)

save anything because it's all spoken for. The kids find it hard but they adjusted a lot better than we did. (Mrs M, Brodsworth)

They also had to adjust to their father's new moods:

They didn't like their dad being at home all day. With him being moody and that, he would just fly off the handle and they couldn't get over him being like that. They found it a lot different. He's very moody and he'll snap at them but he's never hit them, he never has hit them only if they needed it. It's his different temperament. They daren't speak. It got to the point where they'd come in and say, 'What mood's my dad in?' If I said, 'I wouldn't talk to him for a bit if I was you,' then they'd be out. They wouldn't stop in the house and if they did have to stop in they used to go to their bedroom. They wouldn't sit down here with him.

Matters came to a head when their 15-year-old daughter took a drug overdose because she was being bullied at school. The need to go up to the school and sort it out had a good effect on the father. In his wife's words 'I know it sounds daft but it did, it sort of brought him to his senses.'

Such cases are compatible with studies and reviews of the general impact of unemployment on family life (cf. Jackson and Walsh 1987; Popay 1985) which indicate that, aside from suffering the deprivation of a reduced family income, the children of unemployed men often experience a sense of social stigma. Parents may feel guilty because of their inability to provide adequately for their offspring. Conflict may develop over the 'ownership' of social security benefits, and it is possible that the unemployed man's loss of breadwinner status or position as head of the family may result in domestic tension, even extending to divorce or child abuse (Elder and Caspi 1988). None of these are necessary consequences of unemployment. Everything depends upon the combination of circumstances, some which may make things worse, others which may make things better. To give some insight into this, we offer two case studies of families in apparently similar situations who handled them quite differently.

Compounding and Moderating Variables

As part of our sample of in-depth interviews we concentrated on six married couples, considered in close detail in a prior publication (Waddington et al. 1998a). Here, we focus on just two. The interviews were conducted simultaneously in different rooms of the couple's house. In both cases, the men had volunteered for redundancy from Hatfield Main on grounds of ill health in the late 1980s. Both were unemployed with working wives. Our particular focus is the female experience, though, as we shall now see, this was heavily structured by circumstances beyond their control.

The first couple, Mr and Mrs K, were in their late forties. They had three grown-up, married daughters and a primary school-age son. Though feeling pressurised into redundancy, it suited Mr K to take it, as a worsening neck injury would have made it difficult for him to carry on working for much longer. Mrs K worked part-time as a cook in a nearby social services day-care centre for the mentally impaired. She relished the responsibility involved in performing a socially useful role:

> *The kitchen is the heart of the building. It's hard work, it's like an eight hour job in four, so you haven't got a lot of time, but I enjoy my job and I've nobody telling me what to do. Here, you're the boss in the kitchen and it's up to you what people get. It's my domain, sort of thing. For most of the people there, that is their only meal of the day, so it's the satisfaction that they've had a good meal once they're there. You get some and you've never seen people eat like it! You do get attached to some of them.*

Mrs K was uneasy at the fact that she worked while her husband did not but he minded less. Indeed, he had found a role he clearly relished in caring for his infant granddaughter while his daughter worked part-time, and looking after his own son after school. None of this represented a serious challenge to his masculinity:

> *It fits in nice with both of us, there are no disadvantages. There's the advantage of her bringing in a bit more money. We share the house together – well, I do what I can. I do the washing for her, the ironing, the sink's always clean. I don't see why she should do it, when we're man and wife. You're a team and that's that. I've no qualms about doing women's work, none at all. (Mr K, Hatfield)*

Though generally active, Mrs K took an afternoon nap while her husband looked after the house and children.

The husband and wife also enjoyed the benefit of close, caring relationships within their extended family. They could rely upon their three grown-up children and their spouses to help out with shopping and gardening. With the help of her three sisters, Mrs K cared for her invalid mother and also kept an eye on an elderly neighbour.

Mrs K appreciated that her husband had an equitable temperament: 'He never worries you with anything'. As Mr K confirmed, 'I don't see why I should trouble anybody else.' Consequently, there was seldom any tension between them. This was in stark contrast to the experience of the second couple.

Mr and Mrs M were also in their late forties. One of their two sons was at primary school while the other, aged 21, still lived at home. Mr M had left the pit after contracting lymph cancer. Though fully recovered, he remained incensed by what he saw as the needless run-down of the industry and the lack of viable employment alternatives.

Mrs M was employed as a supermarket assistant, a job she found onerous and unrewarding because of her employers' unreasonable expectations:

> *What really annoys me is that I have to lift heavy boxes of soap powder and things like that, and I always think, 'I'm going into middle age and I shouldn't have to do this' and yet my employers are so tight-fisted it's more or less 'If you want the job, you work harder.' That annoys me. They shouldn't be allowed to take that attitude but they can because there's always someone there to take your job. (Mrs M, Hatfield)*

Mr M felt exasperated by, but powerless to prevent, this exploitation of his wife. Though keenly aware that he represented a burden to his wife, he would bridle indignantly whenever she mentioned his being out of work. Mrs M had to cope with her husband's emotional volatility, depressive tendencies and acute sense of boredom and isolation.

Mrs M acknowledged her husband's willingness to perform at least some housework in her absence:

> *If I'm at work he will do the housework for me. He'll dust and he'll wash the pots and when I come home he'll have me scrambled egg or a sandwich made and he'll say, 'I've hoovered up and I've dusted and I've made the beds.' It's not my standard sort of thing, but you don't say anything about it, just, 'Thank you, dear.'*

She reckoned that in any case she did three-quarters of the housework, though this was not appreciated in the household:

> *I've got less time now than I did have a few years ago because, when you're at work all day, you come home and sit for an hour and then think 'I'm going to have to get up and get the ironing done and the bedrooms want tidying round' and you can't tend to sit like you used to do. Before, when I cleaned, I finished at twelve and had all the afternoon to myself to do just what I liked, but now I don't get enough time, really. I'm outnumbered for a start. The eldest one will come in and say, 'Haven't you done this?' and I say to him, 'I've been at work all day! You do it! If you were in a flat on your own, you'd have to do it!' And Len will agree with me but then turn round and say 'Will you do so and so?' and I just can't win.*

Moreover, Mrs M was regularly obliged to intercede in the sporadic outbreaks of conflict between her husband and older son, often related to Mr M's exasperation at his son's decision to leave school after achieving ten 'O' levels.

Neither partner could depend upon their extended family for support. With the exception of her brother, Mrs M was not close to any of her living relatives. 'I've never had a good relationship with my mother, ever. I tend to tolerate her only because she's my mother.' Nor were there other close friends. As she explained, 'I more or less keep to myself.' Although Mr M used to have a close relationship with several male relatives, such closeness did not survive the onset of his lymph cancer.

Mrs M openly admitted to feeling stressed, evident in breathing difficulties, sweating and irritable bowel syndrome. Customarily, she would resort to a long soak in the bath with a book, a cigarette and a cup of tea. During her husband's illness she lost a considerable amount of weight, was tearful at work and, as she put it, 'used to cry into my whisky.'

There is more to these cases than simple variations in individual response. Though perhaps taken to extremes, the factors which affected their response to their situation were echoed in many of our interviews of individuals and couples. If we incorporate these into a summary table (table 3.8), we can see which emerge as crucial.

TABLE 3.8 TWO RELATIONSHIPS COMPARED: WIVES WORKING, HUSBANDS UNEMPLOYED

Moderating or compounding factor	Mr and Mrs 'K'	Mr and Mrs 'M'
Husband's attitude to unemployment	Resigned	Resentful
Husband's adoption of domestic role	Extensive	Minimal
Husband's temperament	Equitable	Volatile
Wife's attitude to job	Positive	Negative
Kinship network	Active	Attenuated

It is no accident that the husband's attitudes – to his unemployment, to domestic labour, to his wife's job – as well his general temperament, seem to be central. Though she may have resources of her own, in her job or kinship network, the wife has to inhabit the man's definition of the situation. This capacity of the man to set the agenda is our concluding point.

Conclusion: the Male Agenda

We have been trying to talk about women in four mining communities in the early 1990s but have ended up talking largely about men. No doubt there were aspects of their lives, around children and kin, which we did not ask about, where women felt they were in control. However, disruption of the normal pattern – of settled male work and women in part-time work or as housewives – seemed to erode women's limited control. Only by their own continued employment, or by their husbands finding new work, did women seem able to stabilise their experience of the contraction of male employment. Where men still worked in mining, they brought home their experiences of stress and insecurity. Where men were unemployed, women had to cope with financial problems, emotional burdens, family conflicts and, worst of all, the intrusion of men as a critical presence into the woman's world of domestic labour.

Even then, it was still possible to find a mutual way of coping by reforming family life around a new division of labour but the resources required were available to few. Our two case studies in particular suggested that Liem and Liem (1988; 1990) were correct to argue that it is the man who sets the agenda: it is his interpretation of and reaction to unemployment with which the wife is forced to cope. The brittleness of his feelings are fundamental to shaping her response. The prior nature of the marital relationship will provide mechanisms for conflict resolution or escalation. The woman's resources in coping also depend upon factors outside the couple. A rewarding job will sustain the woman's efforts but an unrewarding one will undermine them. Other sources of support may be a help or a hindrance. Jackson and Walsh (1987, p.207) cite earlier evidence that the wives of unemployed men feel an obligation to reassure and support their husbands but that no one necessarily reassures the wives.

What is therefore important is the extent to which other members of the immediate and extended family and the community as a whole support the woman in her efforts. Where there is already tension in the immediate family, for example between husband and son, coping with unemployment is more difficult since resentment becomes projected on to what is already a difficult relationship, so that the woman's role as mediator is under strain. Grown-up children can be supportive in practical and emotional ways or they can unintentionally compound stress where they present problems of their own. Ageing parents requiring care can be yet another source of strain or a welcome opportunity to keep busy. Finally, the community at large may offer a view of unemployment which supports or undermines attempts to preserve a sense of male identity.

So many variables are involved that abstract conceptions like coping capacity will not encompass the complexity of human response to unemployment. We agree that:

> *Understanding how a family handles an assault like unemployment requires not so much the correct classification of its relational or coping style. Instead, it entails the concrete exploration of the family's ongoing exchange with the relevant surrounding context, whether that be the kin network, the neighbourhood or the workplace. (Liem and Liem 1990, p.202).*

In traditional working-class communities the actual or imminent collapse of the main industry also threatens male identity, from which the community has historically drawn its concepts of the female role, of family life and of culture more generally. These wider effects are the subject of the next chapter.

4 The Impact on Community

INTRODUCTION

In the previous two chapters we looked at the effects of changes in the mining industry on individual men, their wives and families. In this chapter we take the broader view of mining communities as a whole: how their residents viewed community life, their experience of change and the specific effects of pit closure on community life. We begin by reviewing academic work on mining communities. We then draw on survey data and interview material to outline local perceptions of community, including the impact of pit closure and prospects for the future. The problems of young people, consistently identified by our respondents, are then discussed. The final empirical section reviews the findings of our attempt to measure stress levels across the four communities. We then conclude the chapter by comparing our 1992 study with other analyses of occupational communities experiencing de-industrialisation.

The Mining Community

The nature of Britain's mining communities has achieved mythological status, in which the real becomes difficult to distinguish from the sentimental. Bulmer (1975) has clarified the issue by using the sociological concept of an ideal type. The essential elements of the mining community are distilled into an ideal form that can then be used to analyse actual instances. In the ideal type, mining communities are both physically isolated and occupationally homogeneous. Arduous and dangerous working conditions promote solidarity amongst miners in opposition to the employer. Gender roles are markedly differentiated, with women leading a home-centred existence spent chiefly in the company of female kin and neighbours. The primary function of the miner's wife is to service the needs of her husband and family. By contrast, male leisure-time is spent in public places, notably the miners' welfare or working men's club, exclusively in the company of other men. Work, leisure, family and neighbourhood relations are therefore close-knit and interlocking (or 'multiplex') in form. Longevity of residence and dense kinship networks reinforce traditions of mutual aid.

Following the precise logic of the ideal type, Bulmer maintains that 'the interest lies in identifying and explaining *departures* from the ideal type, in the expectation that such discrepancies will be found to occur' (ibid., p.89, emphasis in original). Subsequent studies have identified the precise ways in which mining communities across the UK have deviated from his ideal type (Allen 1989; Allen and Measham 1994; Crow and Allan 1994).

Many of these differences are rooted in the experience of post-war change. The migration of mining families displaced by pit closures and the influx of 'green' labour (i.e. workers lacking a family tradition in mining) have given mining communities a far more cosmopolitan character (Coulter et al. 1984; Waddington et al. 1991).

The decision by the then National Coal Board (subsequently British Coal) to sell off its housing stock in 1978 to private purchasers or local councils has further diluted the indigenous mining populations as owner-occupiers or tenants with no mining connections have moved in. Conversely, due to better wages since the 1970s and the increasingly limited choice and availability of local rented accommodation, miners have migrated towards private housing estates beyond their village boundaries. Hence mining communities as a whole have become less homogeneous, with marked social and geographical divisions.

Such communities are not immune from general cultural changes. Divorce and single parenting, shifts in gender roles, more home-centred leisure – all of these were already impacting upon mining communities before large-scale pit closures. In a previous study (Waddington et al. 1991, p.169), we agreed with those (Gibbon 1988; Samuel et al. 1986) suggesting that the 1984–5 strike temporarily reversed a gradual decline in the traditional culture of mining communities.

The strength of tradition should not, however, be underestimated. As Warwick and Littlejohn (1992, p.15) point out, 'Communities may grow and they may disappear, though if a local culture has developed, it may provide the basis for a "historical community" despite a restructured economy, maybe even for a generation or so'. Their comparative study of four West Yorkshire communities – two of whose mines ceased operating in the 1960s and another in the 1980s, while the fourth had a colliery working close by – revealed that the 'social processes and institutions' synonymous with Bulmer's ideal type were 'now more a memory than a reality' (ibid., p.130). Nevertheless, there undoubtedly remained 'many echoes' of the local culture fashioned when mining was more staple to local economic life:

> *There is still a strong tendency to support the labour movement and there are still many reasons for political action to improve public facilities, health and education in the search for increased quality of living. The gregarious sociability of the old pit villages is still remembered and enjoyed in the contemporary pubs and clubs ... There is, however, much evidence of the penetration of a mass culture generated elsewhere, and the privatisation of entertainment through television and video viewing which has reduced participation in local social activities like church and chapel going, brass bands and other musical activities. There is a domestic division of labour which carries memories of the old male dominance, and changes have still not led very far down the road of gender equality in the home or in paid*

employment. Traditional social networks linking households with kin, friends and neighbours provide resources and constraints in a manner not unlike those of earlier communities, and a basis around which community identity is still maintained. The sense of the 'friendly' village or town is celebrated in numerous conversations wherever the researchers have gone, though not all are willing to concur. (ibid. 1992, p.131)

Since employment in coal has shaped such communities, its legacy remains long after the pit has closed. Studying attitudes to unemployment in the former coal-mining village of 'Cauldmoss' in central Scotland, Bostyn and Wight (1987) and Turner et al. (1985) identified strong remnants of a 'very conservative' cultural legacy. A powerful adherence to the work ethic and a related 'moral obligation' to sustain a 'respectable standard of living' remained. Despite a male unemployment rate of 30 per cent, there was every effort to maintain previous standards of family and community life.

It can therefore be seen that both processes – of continuity and change – are essential to our understanding of ongoing adjustments to industrial contraction in mining communities, whether the pit is closed or open. Social scientists and policy-makers must beware the tendency to see the demise of mining communities as cataclysmic or monolithic in its impact. The local character of any community is liable to have been shaped by varying patterns of tradition and dislocation. Knowledge of the nature and cultural development of mining communities will promote a better understanding of their social or psychological problems and capacities to cope, and facilitate a more effective regeneration strategy. For this reason we now move on to explore local perceptions of each of our four communities.

Perceptions of Community

Survey Results

Respondents were asked to rate as good, poor or average a total of eighteen aspects of local life: twelve services provided from external and local sources and six specific to the quality of local life. Another question asked them to assess their community as a place to live and to nominate its best and worst features.

As table 4.1 shows, externally provided services regarded as good by a clear majority of the main sample were transport and medical facilities. The verdict on schools was equally divided between good and average. Housing was rated good to average. Social services were regarded as average, though a third declined to rate them. The local council was perceived as average, though a substantial minority rated it as poor and a smaller group as good. Not surprisingly, the external service perceived as most inadequate was employment, with nine out of ten rating this as poor. However, almost as many cited provision for teenagers as poor. A half thought policing poor, while only a tenth rated it as good.

Of locally provided services, most people saw local pubs and clubs as good. More saw sports facilities as poor rather than average, though a sizeable minority saw them as good. Opinion on community groups was equally divided between poor and average, though one in six had no opinion to offer.

In terms of the quality of life, 'neighbourliness' was the most positively valued attribute. Social life was the next most valued. More rated 'community spirit' as average rather than good. Also into the 'average' category came people's health, though more felt it to be good than poor. Half felt the environment to be average with the rest evenly split between good and poor. On its own as an unequivocally poor aspect of the quality of life was law and order. Most rated this as poor, and fewer than one in ten as good.

TABLE 4.1 PERCEPTIONS OF COMMUNITY SERVICES: MAIN SAMPLE

Services rated as good	Brodsworth %	Rossington %	Askern %	Hatfield %	Total %
Pubs and clubs	54	69	83	33	60
Transport	54	71	66	35	57
Neighbourliness	60	56	61	53	57
Medical facilities	54	63	58	52	56
Schools	60	36	41	45	45
Social life	36	55	52	26	42
Housing	42	41	37	27	37
Community spirit	36	41	39	28	36
Health	31	32	26	32	30
Social services	43	36	21	18	30
Sport facilities	55	27	10	10	25
Local environment	28	32	25	9	23
Local council	25	23	18	11	20
Community groups	15	13	6	11	11
Police	3	12	8	11	9
Law and order	6	19	3	6	8
Provision for teenagers	5	4	4	0	3
Job prospects	0	9	0	1	3

(N = 320)

Perceptions of community revealed that respondents in the main sample had moderately positive views of their community generally (see table 4.2). Most classed it as average but most of the rest saw it as good. Asked to nominate the best thing about their community, respondents with roughly equal frequency chose friendliness, proximity to family or work, and peace and quiet. Asked to nominate the worst thing, a fifth said there was nothing bad and another fifth gave diffuse or unclassifiable answers. Most of the remaining three-fifths mentioned either nothing for teenagers to do or the absence of jobs.

Across the board and despite the pit having shut eighteen months before, the Brodsworth respondents had the most positive views of their community, with those from Rossington close behind. Then came Askern residents, with those from Hatfield the least enthusiastic of all. Against all expectations, the non-mining sample in Rossington appreciated the community more than the mining sample but then they had chosen to live there and were less likely to compare its present with its past.

These, then, were the general impressions of community revealed by our survey. Our in-depth interviews enabled us to draw more detailed and insightful impressions of residents' perceptions of each locality. In the remainder of the section we outline these 'self portraits' of the four communities, starting with Askern.

Interviews

Askern

Residents of Askern emphasised the friendliness of their village, a self-image in sharp contrast to its outside reputation:

> *I'd just say it was one of the friendliest places I've ever known in my life. I've never really been anywhere else that you can be so friendly with people, relaxed with them. If you live outside the village, you hear bad things about it and people think because you come from Askern you're either a trouble-causer or whatever. I've got friends that don't live in Askern and I've asked them to come round Askern for a night out and they won't come. Like I say, that's because you live outside the village and you don't know the people.*
> *(Mr S, Askern)*

The vibrant, sometimes rowdy, nature of the adult night-life was far removed from what was regarded as the most disappointing feature of the community – the absence of leisure opportunities for the young. One woman said, 'If they had as many facilities in Askern as there are pubs, it would be a brilliant place, particularly for the young' (Mrs K, Askern). Some young people were seen by her as antisocial and abusive: 'You can go out there and shout at somebody for sitting on your car or summat and all you get is a load of abuse.'

Older residents considered that the composition of the village had recently changed for the worse. A pre-strike influx of commuters on the Doncaster–London eastern line had gentrified some parts of the village, while the local council's policy of re-locating 'problem families' into former Coal Board housing stock had generated resentment among longer-term residents: 'But they've all changed now because people from outside have come, haven't they?' (Mr B, Askern).

In Askern there was a general perception that, whilst some residue of community spirit remained, it was not as strong as it used to be. A strong sense

TABLE 4.2 COMMUNITY AS A PLACE TO LIVE: MAIN SAMPLE COMPARED WITH OTHER SAMPLES

	Brodsworth	Rossington	Askern	Hatfield	All	Voluntary redundancy sample	Non-mining sample
	%	%	%	%	%	%	%
Type of community to live in							
Good	49	59	39	24	43	33	60
Average	48	39	54	60	50	46	38
Poor	3	3	8	16	7	22	3
Best thing about community							
Friendliness	39	12	41	18	27	44	29
Near work	14	32	5	38	22	10	13
Near family	11	25	26	23	21	30	18
Peace and quiet	22	23	17	12	18	13	30
Other	14	8	11	9	12	3	10
Worst thing about community							
Nothing for teenagers	3	38	33	20	24	19	25
No jobs	22	12	23	15	18	23	20
Traffic/pollution	13	3	9	5	7	0	9
Nosiness/gossip	12	8	7	3	8	8	9
Isolation	1	4	3	12	5	2	5
Other	18	13	14	31	19	36	17
Nothing bad	31	23	10	14	20	13	15
N	*80*	*80*	*80*	*80*	*320*	*80*	*80*

of camaraderie persisted among former workmates and friends, though in other aspects of village life a notable change was now apparent:

> *These were all pit houses so everybody who lived in these houses either worked at the pit or had retired from the pit and then their families went to the pit and they got a house so you all knew each other. Now you don't. It's different. You don't see your next door neighbours now from one day to the next. It's going down hill fast. No one seems to care any more. They used to keep the streets clean and that outside your houses and they don't care anymore. They're just dumping stuff all over the village. It's bad. If a house comes empty now they're not selling whereas you never saw empty houses before. They're just smashing all the windows up and nobody seems to bother. They don't stop them. I don't know what's up with everybody. It's wrong. They don't seem to take any pride in the village anymore. (Mrs R, Askern)*

Brodsworth

The views of Brodsworth residents had a very familiar ring. Here, too, the village was hailed as an exceptionally friendly place in which to live. 'I like it. The people are friendly. You can walk along the shops from one end to the other and everybody would speak to you' (Mr Wa, Brodsworth). If anything, local facilities were viewed more positively than in Askern. Such views were tempered by worries regarding the absence of employment opportunities, and a concern, especially among parents, over poor leisure facilities for the young, allied to growing vandalism among youths:

> *Then again there's not enough for the kids to do. They wait until the summer holidays to organise stuff like they're doing at the leisure centre now and the youth club for older kids. For Lynsey's age there's not much at all – nowt on the park. They come in and ask if they can go to the park on their own and I say no because you're worrying if they're alright, if they're safe, is anybody getting them. If they built the park back up again and put everything on them that used to be on them and get somebody there while ever the park's open to watch all the time, at least your kids would be safe and you could let them go but not now. Older kids go round wrecking it. (Mrs C, Brodsworth)*

In Brodsworth respondents acknowledged that community spirit now survived only in that part of the village known as 'the Squares', which harboured the traditional mining section of the community. Those moving out noticed the difference in their neighbours.

> *I don't think you get it much down here. I think you get it further up the other side and in the square. I couldn't say really that you notice the community spirit. Everybody more or less keeps themselves to themselves. (Mr S, Brodsworth)*

Those who had moved away from the Squares sensed the contrast in their new neighbours: 'It's different kettle of fish on this estate where everybody seems to keep themselves to themselves. It was a hard thing to adjust to' (Mr C, Brodsworth).

Rossington

In many respects, the views of our Rossington respondents echoed those of their Askern counterparts. By all accounts Rossington was a friendly community, albeit inhospitable to outsiders:

> *To a stranger, it's not very good because a stranger, maybe your age, coming out drinking at night would probably end up with a sore head. It's rough. I know a lot of people and I think its very friendly. I like it. (Mr M, Rossington)*

Once again the overriding complaint was of an absence of adequate facilities for local children. A swimming pool and a small play area were regarded as inadequate.

As in Askern, there was a strong perception that migration patterns had diluted the homogeneity of an erstwhile mining community:

> *There were more people moving into the village that aren't connected with mining. The new housing went up and things like that so a lot of people that we knew drifted away and a lot of people who had nothing to do with mining came in and I don't think you can call it a mining village any more. (Mrs B, Rossington)*

Community residents and local professionals tended to feel that this shift in the housing pattern had been to the detriment, and added to the instability, of the community. A local doctor referred to the 'feckless, homeless and single parents' who 'haven't integrated all that well'. Another emergent division was generational. A health visitor felt that whilst the old had managed to keep their sense of 'community and togetherness', they none the less felt 'very threatened' by the nature and pace of the changes occurring in the industry and were worried about their children's inability to cope.

New housing developments on the periphery of the old mining estates had diminished neighbourliness, causing a diminution of the erstwhile community spirit. Examples were given, such as: 'This street's a cul-de-sac and I've lived here seven years now and there's still people on the street who I don't know' (Mr M, Rossington) and 'Next door they've just gone away on holiday and they didn't even tell us they were going' (Mr S, Rossington).

Hatfield

Hatfield was portrayed as different from the three neighbouring villages because it was divided into three distinct parts. Two similar sections were divided by a railway bridge. The third was very different: 'Hatfield has always in a way been the snob area. Dunscroft is more down to earth and then Stainforth is a mining community' (Mr C, Hatfield).

More so than in the other three communities, residents of Hatfield remarked on the declining nature of local facilities:

It used to be a better place. There used to be a lot of shops you could go to but now they're closing them down and there's not many so if you want owt you've got to go into town. (Mr A, Hatfield)

Some applauded recent attempts to apply EU funds to the refurbishment of those parts of the village in greatest need of repair. However, local people and key informants alike felt that such improvements served only to disguise the dereliction of houses and poverty of families. Long-term residents objected to Doncaster Council's rehousing policy which was producing, in the words of a local police inspector, 'little concentrations of very difficult families'. Teenage boys were also apt to wreck any physical improvements:

You can see they're doing work round the houses and what have you but you get lads what just don't seem to be bothered and come and, no sooner they've finished, they start knocking it down. They're lads what live round here themselves but they just don't seem to be able to appreciate the work or what they're trying to do to update the place to make it look like something. They just don't seem to want it. (Mr A, Hatfield)

Overall, a gloomy portrait was painted by welfare officers responsible for Hatfield. As one of them told us:

I think that what's happened is that the area has lost any pride. There's no civic pride, no community pride and there's no individual pride and that's very difficult to achieve when you live in a house where there's water coming through the roof for so long the upstairs of the house is unusable. There are four children and they all live downstairs. Now I've been on to housing endlessly about this but they're a low priority so how do we engender pride in those parents, in those children and its tentacles spread outwards – there's no pride in the street, the street's a mess, the community's a mess.

Predictably, the older, working-class parts of Dunscroft and Stainforth were seen as having retained a strong sense of community solidarity. However, most residents still felt that people were becoming more circumspect and insular in their attitudes. Those moving to the more affluent Hatfield area remarked on the reserve of their new neighbours:

When we first came here one day people would talk to you and the next day you walk up and they turn round and completely ignore you. I can't do with that, I'd soon not talk and now I don't bother talking to them. (Mr C, Hatfield)

Members of these communities still had generally positive views of where they lived, its neighbourliness, friendliness and social life; but this way of life was threatened by changes in housing, social composition and divisions between young and old, rough and respectable. Previously self-contained and homogeneous communities could not protect themselves from social and economic change, even where the pit remained open. Where it had already shut or might conceivably do so soon, the process of change and deterioration were likely to be accelerated.

The Impact of Pit Closure on Communities

In addition to asking respondents for their impressions of their local communities we asked them to specify any particular effects of pit closure they may have been aware of. We already knew from previous research that the economic impacts of pit closure are always, immediately or in the long run, social impacts as well. The 'multiplier effect' on the local economy starts a process of gradual de-industrialisation and depopulation of the whole region:

> For every colliery that closes and every job that is lost, further jobs are lost elsewhere in the locality. The most immediate impact is on the industry's suppliers – engineering and haulage firms, and contractors, for example. Local shops and other consumer services also lose business because of loss of income in the community, even if in the short run the blow is eased by redundancy payments. In the longer term, areas that lose jobs suffer from out-migration, and as people leave to find work elsewhere, they add a further downward twist to local spending and the health of the local economy. Eventually, if population falls enough, even employment in public services (for example, schools and hospitals) adjust downwards. (Fothergill and Witt 1990, p.11)

The demoralising effects of pit closure on the wider mining communities are evident in the deterioration of the physical environment, control over young people and participation in community life. The closure of a mine and the redundancy or transfer of its employees fragment social cohesion. Pit closure brings the loss of such community facilities as recreation grounds and the withdrawal of a range of informal services, such as housing maintenance and snow clearance, which the pit and its men provided (Jones 1988).

Interview responses stressed immediate economic and social effects: the decline of rituals and focal points, housing and property decay, and internal divisions among the locals. In Askern, shops and pubs were the first to show signs of economic decline: 'I can't see the night life staying like it is because they're going to start shutting down pubs because they can't survive on the customers they're getting. It's the same with shops as well' (Mr S, Askern). Social relationships between men also suffered quickly:

> I think what it is since the pit closed you can see all your mates going different ways – there's some working on building sites and they've started to go out with their mates from their building sites or whatever. I can meet them now on the streets and it's: 'How are you going on? what are you doing now?' as if you've never bloody met them before. There's always that kind of

edge: they're trying to find out how you're doing, and you're trying to find out how they're faring. Some of us are earning more money than the others so you don't see them out anymore. Whereas you've got money to go out and sometimes when you do bump into them you can tell there's a bit of jealousy when they're talking to you. (Mr S, Askern)

As one former pit canteen worker had noticed, the former rituals of mining life had rapidly declined:

We had a gala the other week. There were hardly any stalls, nobody made an effort. They have a parade down the streets and there was nobody in it. We used to feel proud. When they used to come down with the NUM banner because mining's been my life. My dad was in the pit and my grandad and the same with my husband, its been in your family and we've not known anything different. You used to feel proud of that banner coming down and then they had the band and even that wasn't there this year. We didn't know the band had folded. (Mrs R, Askern)

Some of our respondents complained that they no longer felt they 'belonged' and had become detached from village affairs:

I don't know whether I'm in a cocoon or what but, like Monday morning, I was going out to the paper shop and a funeral car comes up and I had to ask, 'Whose funeral is it?' I didn't even know and I live here, and he only lived about four or five houses up on the other side of the street. (Mr G, Askern)

In Brodsworth, the process of decay had become even further entrenched. The miners' welfare and other clubs had become dilapidated. Houses could not be sold and local shops struggled for trade. For a wide section of the community, poverty had taken an even tighter stranglehold than in Askern and was influencing everyday community life:

You used to see all the men going to work through the fields and they'd all say 'Hello!' and things like that. People would be going into the shops, doing their shopping. They don't anymore because they haven't got the money to do it so you don't see half the people you used to see. I know they got their money for redundancy but a lot of them have spent it and they haven't got the money to go out and enjoy themselves anymore. (Mrs C, Brodsworth)

Even in Hatfield, where the pit remained open, derelict shops indicated the declining confidence in the local economy. In Rossington the general outlook was, if anything, less pessimistic than in Hatfield. This was possibly due to the fact that its mining workforce remained more substantial than Hatfield's and that here was a community now less reliant on coal-mining as its staple industry. Nevertheless, symptoms of ongoing decay were still visible in the form of boarded-up houses or entire terraces in need of redecoration or repair.

Future Prospects

Both survey data and interview material reflected considerable pessimism about the future for these communities. Asked for their views on the possible effects of pit closure, a clear majority of survey respondents thought that it would be detrimental to the community, though one in four thought it would have a mixed effect. Virtually no one thought that it would be beneficial, though one in ten thought closure would have little effect. The nature of the detrimental effects was defined quite precisely by our respondents: it would be economic (table 4.3). For every ten respondents, seven pointed to low incomes, two to the collapse of local business and one to depopulation. The most worrying effect of closure on their own family was clearly its impact on income, cited by three-quarters, though one seventh felt the anxiety caused by an uncertain future was the most worrying (table 4.4).

For some interviewees the shape of the future was indicated by villages nearby where the pit had been shut for longer:

> *There's a village just over the other side of the A1, Upton. That was a mining village and you drive through that place now and you can't stop because they'll nick your tyres. It's that kind of place. If you look at all the buildings – like the old Welfare, it's all boarded up and it's an old, disused building, same as all the other buildings round there. I can see Askern going the same way. There's nowt else can happen to it. It's got the woodyard down there but there's nowt else going for it. (Mr S, Askern)*

Nevertheless, people did not themselves want to move away. Fifty-three per cent thought they would definitely stay, 28 per cent that they would only leave reluctantly and 19 per cent that they would be glad to move away (table 4.5). In any case, the local housing market would soon prevent houses being sold, contributing to the spiral of economic decline:

> *A lot of people have said, 'Oh, I'll sell up and move and we'll go to a place where there's jobs.' Well, tell me where to move to and we'll go. But apart from that, once the pits do actually close, how are you going to sell your houses, because who's going to buy a house to come to a place where there's no work, no jobs? So then, the small businesses will take their trade to a more lucrative place and where there's people in employment, because nobody can afford to run a business when you've got a community on the dole, because all they do is run into bankruptcy. So they're out as well. So you've vacant offices to let, and shops to let, and everything else just runs down again, so there's going to be nothing. You end up with a ghost town. (Women Against Pit Closures representative)*

Yet, for all the anxiety reflected in our survey and interview material on the present and future of mining communities, there was clearly a dominant concern about the situation of young people. The survey indicated that the

TABLE 4.3 EFFECTS OF PIT CLOSURE ON COMMUNITY: THREE SAMPLES

Effect	Main sample %	Voluntary redundancy sample %	Non-mining sample %
Detrimental effect	62	76	66
Of whom specifying:			
Poverty	72	62	56
Business collapse	16	11	26
People moving away	13	23	11
Other	0	3	7
N	*320*	*80*	*80*

TABLE 4.4 MOST WORRYING EFFECT OF PIT CLOSURE ON OWN FAMILY:
THREE SAMPLES

Effect	Main sample %	Voluntary redundancy sample %	Non-mining sample %
Loss of income	74	72	64
Anxiety/uncertainty	14	6	3
No alternative employer	3	10	0
Having to leave area	2	0	0
Other	5	11	5
None	0	0	29
N	*320*	*80*	*80*

TABLE 4.5 FUTURE RESIDENCE: TWO SAMPLES ONLY

Future plan	Main sample %	Voluntary redundancy sample %
Will definitely stay	53	70
Would leave reluctantly	28	10
Would leave gladly	19	20
N	*320*	*80*

provision of facilities for young people was one of the most pressing priorities; the interviews told us why.

Problems Involving Young People

The accelerating decline of the British mining industry since the year-long miners' strike of 1984–5 has been associated with a host of social problems, ranging from drug misuse to theft, vandalism and truancy from school. For example, an unprecedented rise in crime (primarily, criminal damage and car theft) occurred in South Wales between 1985 and 1991, attributed by Baxter (1992) and Morgan and Price (1992) to a general loss of pride, and the breakdown of traditional bonds of family and community life. From our own communities we have only adult accounts of youth behaviour but the evidence is consistent. Young people were seen to be demotivated at school, prone to petty crime and resorting to drug use.

Schooling

Local schools had been affected by a twin legacy of industrial contraction: conflict within the family and declining employment prospects. Predictably, such difficulties had been most salient in Brodsworth, described by the chair of the governors of a primary school:

> If you've got a class of, say, thirty, twelve of those children are from split families, four of the children are in care, and one has just come back from a behavioural unit. That is a typical class for me in school now. When I first came six years ago, you would have probably had four children in the class from a split family; we may have had one or two under a social worker, but we'd never heard of the behavioural unit. So you can see the compounding of the problems.

The local comprehensive school headteacher explained that it was difficult to motivate pupils when even success at 'A' level would not produce local employment.

The greater levels of unemployment in Askern had effects noticeable to the local education and welfare officer:

> For every pupil I visit in Campsall, I'm visiting five in Askern. Nobody's working in the household and if they are I'm thinking, 'Thank God,' because it gives me something to relate to in terms of what the child can hope to work towards or look forward to. If there's nobody working in the house you're in a bit of a vacuum when you're trying to reinforce the rationale behind going to school.

As our key respondents noted, even where the pit remained open, the state of the local economy provided few prospects for school-leavers:

> Because unemployment has been around so long, the youngsters see no point in being in school, so we have quite a high percentage of non-attenders. Even parents taking the children to school, they see no point, if they're up late, in taking a child to school, so the child is kept off all day instead of getting there at ten o'clock or even having half a day. And by the time they reach fourteen, they see no reason to go to school, and what's the point of getting any exams because, 'I'm not going to get a job; I'm going to go on the dole.' (health visitor, Hatfield)

These observations are in close accord with theoretical work on the relationship between economic decline and poor motivation at school. Brown (1990) insists, for example, that pupils' orientations to schooling need to be explained in terms of the wider socio-economic context which structures perceptions of the opportunities and strategies available to them. He argues that it is 'the interplay between the pupils' collective understandings of being in school', and 'the institutional structures of opportunities in both school and the youth labour market', which best explain how pupils react to schooling (p.105).

Jackson (1998) argues that, as the contemporary crisis of global de-industrialisation has gathered pace, working-class young men experience 'the despair and pointlessness of the jobless men around them and the fragility of their own lives', for which they substitute other modes of power and status enhancement, such as 'a culture of aggressive, heterosexual manliness which deliberately rejects school learning as an unmanly activity' (p.89). As Reicher and Emler (1986, p.32) explain, the contract between young people and society which rewarded effort at school has collapsed:

> That bargain suggests that if they give up their time to study and accept the school regime, then they will be given the knowledge that will allow them to go on to a good job and a good life. Yet this is seen as no bargain but a con; for all that they might conform, they will remain poor and working class – so why should they conform?

The lack of opportunity was perceived to produce antisocial behaviour in the forms of drug-taking and crime.

Drugs

Substance abuse, ranging from the use of hard and soft drugs, to glue-sniffing and excessive or under-age drinking, appeared to have been increasing in each of our four communities. In Askern, adults – especially parents – were convinced that drug-use had now become widespread. The father of four teenage children told us of a recent occasion when:

> Two of my three sons just turned round and said, 'At Camps Mount school you can get anything and everything.' At the moment, touch wood, they've never been interested. Same as, my lads don't smoke and they don't drink at the moment but they're ten a penny and that does frighten me. I had to ship my other, 16-year-old, boy from Askern to my sister's at Bentley because he was mixing with the wrong sort. As young as 12, they're smoking and drinking on the corners and that's stressful for me because I'm watching her [his 13-year-old daughter] all the while. (Mr H, Askern)

In Brodsworth, the local comprehensive school headteacher thought drug-taking was confined to cannabis and other recreational drugs:

> There's quite a lot of cannabis round here. Cannabis is readily available at very low prices throughout the area and it's quite clear to us that at the weekends a significant number of school kids are smoking it. Quite a few of the older ones are into ecstasy and amphetamines. Interestingly enough, these are ex-pupils who have been unable to gain employment. Certainly, one or

two of the off-licences and supermarkets do a roaring trade and there's a fairly standard system up on Brodsworth shops where one of the older lads will go in and buy you four cans and give you three, so there's no problem in terms of getting drink. There is a certain amount of substance abuse: there's actually rather less glue-sniffing than I think would normally be expected. It just doesn't seem to be as fashionable in the area and therefore it's not picked up at all.

By contrast, a local doctor felt heroin use was growing amongst 16 to 24-year-olds. This observation was confirmed by a police officer:

At one school round here, we recovered fifty-four needles in the school playing fields. You can imagine what that can cause for kids. Two 4-year-old kids fell down last week and they had used needles actually stuck into their knees. (crime reduction officer)

This rising trend in substance misuse was not confined to communities affected by pit closure. Similar stories could be heard in Rossington and Hatfield where, once again, cannabis use was said to be endemic. Glue-sniffing was alleged to have become much more apparent amongst youth in Hatfield, whilst in Rossington, there were signs of heroin use in discarded syringes littering school fields and disused buildings. There was also an apparent rise in hard drinking:

These may not be ex-miners because they're too young but they'll be the children of miners or ex-miners. It's disproportionate for the surrounding villages. It's centred on them and I wonder if there is an element of boredom, of the macho image as well which comes into it. We're talking about 18–21-year-olds, T-shirts in winter, stripped down to the waist in summer, coming down the road at 11 o'clock at night full of beer – this macho thing – which 20-year-olds identify with so it's sort of surrounding that type of subculture. Certain areas of Rossington, certain areas of Hatfield certainly attract more than their fair proportion. (police inspector)

Perceptions of increased drug-use amongst young people need to be set in context. Men in mining communities have always placed a high value on a recreational drug, alcohol. As Coffield et al. (1986 p.132) found in a study of the young unemployed in a former mining community, 'The strongest tradition followed by the young adults we knew was drinking alcohol. The culture of drink was all around them and hard to avoid even if they wanted to.' Recreational drugs may only be an extension of this culture which, as we have seen, more than one adult male had taken up. Moreover, recreational drug-taking has increased throughout British youth culture (Miller and Plant 1996; Parker et al. 1995). Ecstasy would have arrived in mining communities with or without pit closures (Shapiro 1999).

Hard drug-taking is another matter. It has been correlated with unemployment. For example, Pearson (1987a; 1987b) sees heroin misuse arising from the loss of social esteem and identity, diminished social contact, and, above all, the destruction of habitual time structures resulting from unemployment. In this view, heroin misuse is less a form of escapism or search for oblivion than a highly rewarding and structured way of life which helps to compensate for problems associated with unemployment. There could be no better index of despair.

Crime

Our police respondents were convinced of an inseparable relationship between substance abuse, crime and industrial decay:

> *It seems to be linked with social deprivation. Going on from there, developing the question a bit more, because you've got a drug abuse problem you've then got acquisitive crime – theft, minor burglaries, if we can actually describe house burglaries as minor – the video, the television goes. It's something they can get £20 for which they can then immediately spend on drugs. (police inspector)*

The growing scale of the crime problem now affecting the two communities recently experiencing pit closure was spelled out by the police crime reduction officer responsible for both areas:

> *Crime in general has gone through the roof. Last year we got something like a 27 per cent increase. This year we're heading for a 35–40 per cent increase in reported crime but you've got to differentiate between reported crime and what actually happens, if you know what I mean. A lot of people here think it's a waste of time reporting things to the police so they won't tell them, so reported crime and actual crime is often totally different. I can provide you with the figures but off the top of my head we've probably had £75,000 worth of pedal cycles stolen in our sub-division in the last year. Petty crime, stupid things like theft from washing lines, criminal damage, people would never have dreamed of stealing washing a few years ago but nowadays its quite a common crime. We get a lot of vandalism at school. It's costing an absolute fortune vandalising schools. Another problem is with people driving away from petrol stations. You go to a petrol station, fill up your tank and drive away without paying.*

He felt most such crime was committed by 14 to 19-year-olds, which he attributed to a diminishing sense of community: 'There's no close-knitness, no sort of feeling that "I won't steal Mrs so-and-so's jeans because she's a neighbour or friend of my mam's." '

In both Askern and Brodsworth car crime was common:

> *There's a big problem with car theft. We've got what they call the Roman Ridge in Woodlands. It's like an old Roman road which runs at the top of Woodlands and from then on you've got like wasteland at the back and*

there's loads and loads of cars just taken up for joy rides. They're taken up there and just abandoned, set fire to, burnt out, do anything to. I think that is a big problem in Woodlands. There's nothing else for people to do. (crime reduction officer)

Even in the two villages with open pits crime had risen substantially:

Last year I think we were looking at about 20 per cent rise in crime compared nationally to 17 per cent. Now, we've got a 38 per cent rise in crime but, again, it's small time. It isn't small time if it's your house that's been broken into! It's videos, push bikes. I expect we lose push bikes six at a time. A mountain bike's worth £300; if you can nick it and get £50, it's a good weekend's work. So, somebody hires a van, nicks six mountain bikes and makes £300 because he whips them down to Lincoln or somewhere like that where there's loads of bikes and he disappears into the dishonest society. (police inspector)

In Hatfield, in particular, this trend had been accompanied by growing incivilities among local youths. The local Chief Superintendent explained how,

In the morning when I come to work, I get a print-out of what we call the one-liners: it's an index, if you like, and it's of every incident that we've dealt with over the last 24 hours. And I look at it and it reads: 'Youths – nuisance, nuisance – youths, youths on school roof, youths on bus shelter, youths on motor bikes'. All 'youth'.

Here, as in Brodsworth, car crime was of paramount concern, with stolen cars from surrounding areas being abandoned like trophies on the village margins.

In Rossington we were told of a familiar catalogue of problems. For example, the local village doctor lived on a peripheral housing estate which was regularly afflicted by vandalism, burglary and theft:

When I first came to Rossington I never locked my garage door. I suppose it's come on gradually over the past five years; and nowadays, if you're out at night, you see youths in motor cars tearing up and down the streets, rushing up to road ends and slamming on the brakes, and screeching tyres and revving up. You didn't used to get that sort of thing here. (local GP, Rossington)

A minority of the residents we interviewed in all four communities referred to the influx of single-parent families as likely causes of the growing crime rates. However, the majority of interviewees felt that poverty and the lack of employment prospects were the underlying causes of youth delinquency. As one community constable informed us:

The thing in my mind is that kids are leaving school now and they can't claim dole until they're 17 so one of the feedbacks that we get is that they see

that as slavery to them – they're just cheap labour to be discarded after their twelve-month period and a lot of them won't accept it because they're getting a good education at comprehensive schools and they're leaving bright intelligent kids, and I think they think that there's a con trick out there and they're not going to fall for it. They think 'I'm not going to go and work for a tenner more than I can get on the dole,' so for a lot of them there's nothing and that's why we're seeing an increase in things like theft of clothes from washing lines. We never saw that before, did we?

Possibly linked to this was the perception that other local institutions, such as the NUM, could no longer exercise their former authority over local youths. As one Hatfield NUM official informed us, 'The authority of the NUM in the village to hold things together has gone. Miners have a lot of say, they dictate the social values – what's acceptable and unacceptable – in their village. Take away the pit and you take away all that.'

Campbell's arguments about the car crime underlying the 1991 and 1992 youth riots on working-class estates may be extended to mining communities. She rejects simplistic explanations in terms of single-parent families and moral decline, insisting that:

neither manners nor mothers are to blame, but that there is an economic emergency in many neighbourhoods where the difference between what women and men do with their troubles and their anger shapes their strategies of solidarity and survival on the one hand, danger and destruction on the other. (1993, pp.302–3)

According to this viewpoint, the theft and flaunting of high-performance cars was a bid to appropriate the one arena left available to young men for asserting their masculinity – the street:

Mass unemployment changed the men's relationship to space because when their means of making a legitimate living was destroyed, then their licensed means of episodic escape – waged work – was withdrawn. They were stuck at home. The lads, on the other hand, stuck to the streets. (ibid., p.320)

Driving a stolen car at high speeds along communal streets is a perverse expression of a masculinity thwarted in its traditional outlet of waged work and leisure consumption. For other members of the community it was another symptom of decline.

Stress and Community

Although it is virtually impossible to quantify the stressful impact of long-term changes and those produced by the recent contraction of mining on residents of our community, the results of our survey none the less provide some tentative insights into where symptoms of stress are most manifest and why this should be the case.

Table 4.6 summarises the average (mean and median) stress scores for miners and their female partners in each of our four communities. It is apparent from the table that, while there appears to be some polarisation between the average stress scores for the 'closed' (Askern and Brodsworth) and 'working' (Hatfield and Rossington) communities, such differences are only significant at the 9 per cent level and, therefore, cannot be regarded as conclusive. However, when we consider tables 4.7 and 4.8 a more interesting picture gradually begins to emerge.

It can be seen from table 4.7 that, while there is no significant difference between the stress scores of residents in the closed communities (Askern and Brodsworth), or between those where the mine is still operating (Rossington and Hatfield), the most apparent level of difference occurs between members of our long-term unemployed and 'safe' working communities (Brodsworth and Rossington, respectively). This comparison is statistically different at the 5 per cent level. Other interesting differences are to be found between Brodsworth and Hatfield, the second of our working communities (significant at the 8 per cent level), and between Askern (short-term closed) and Rossington (significant at the 6 per cent level) and Askern and Hatfield (significant at the 9 per cent level). With the exception of the outcome between Brodsworth and Rossington, these levels of significance are below 10 per cent and should, therefore, be regarded as inconclusive. They none the less point to a weak relationship between stress and the status of the local mine – something that is more strongly emphasised in table 4.8.

What table 4.8 reveals quite markedly is that the simple criterion of whether the local colliery is open or closed appears to be a crucial determinant of community stress levels. The aggregated scores for Askern and Brodsworth (closed) versus Hatfield and Rossington (open) reveal that mining residents in the former communities experienced relatively higher stress levels. This difference is significant at the 1 per cent level. When analysed according to gender of respondents, such differences are not so readily apparent for men, but remain significantly the case for women. This suggests that pit closure is an outcome which impacts more greatly on women than on men.

The final table in this series (table 4.9) reveals an interesting comparison between the stress scores of mining and non-mining residents from Rossington. The fact that the mean and median scores for these sub-samples of our survey are virtually indistinguishable suggests that it is factors inherent to the community itself, rather than specific employment background, that generate symptoms of stress. Taken together, the results of this particular section of our survey seem to suggest that while the psychological well-being of mining families is linked to the status of the local mine, particularly where women are concerned, the levels of stress experienced by miners (or ex-miners) and their partners may be felt to a similar degree by the non-mining segment of the community.

TABLE 4.6 STRESS SCORES BY COMMUNITY

Community	All				Men				Women			
	N	Mean	Median	Standard deviation	N	Mean	Median	Standard deviation	N	Mean	Median	Standard deviation
Askern	80	8.5	8.0	5.3	40	7.6	7.0	5.7	40	9.5	9.0	5.1
Brodsworth	80	8.6	7.0	5.3	40	7.6	7.0	5.2	40	9.6	8.5	5.4
Hatfield	80	7.1	6.0	4.9	40	7.3	6.0	5.1	40	7.0	7.0	4.8
Rossington	80	7.2	6.0	5.2	40	6.1	5.0	4.4	80	8.3	6.5	5.7
	Kruskal-Wallis (H test):[†] $H = 6.6$; $p = 0.086$				Kruskal-Wallis (H test): $H = 2.84$; $p = 0.42$				Kruskal-Wallis (H test): $H = 5.96$; $p = 0.11$			

Note: maximum individual stress = 42 (see appendix for details of calculation).

[†] The Kruskal-Wallis (or H test) is a non-parametric test for the difference in the means of several samples (cf. Daniel 1978).

TABLE 4.7 STRESS SCORES: COMMUNITY COMPARISONS

Community comparison	N	Mean	Median	Mann-Whitney test of differences – All	Mann-Whitney test of differences – Men
Askern	80	8.6	8.0	W = 6426	W = 1615
Brodsworth	80	8.6	7.0	p = 0.96	p = 0.96
Askern	80	8.5	8.0	W = 6937	W = 1652
Hatfield	80	7.1	6.0	p = 0.09	p = 0.76
Askern	80	8.5	8.0	W = 6982	W = 1768
Rossington	80	7.2	6.0	p = 0.06	p = 0.15
Brodsworth	80	8.6	7.0	W = 6954	W = 1664
Hatfield	80	7.1	6.0	p = 0.08	p = 0.67
Brodsworth	80	8.6	7.0	W = 7009	W = 1774
Rossington	80	7.2	6.0	p = 0.05*	p = 0.13
Hatfield	80	7.1	6.0	W = 6460	W = 1729
Rossington	80	7.2	6.0	p = 0.95	p = 0.29

Note: maximum individual stress = 42 (see appendix for details of calculation).
* = significant at 5% level.

Conclusions

The effects of pit closure or its prospect on mining communities is not unique. There are striking parallels with agricultural communities devastated by the American 'farm crisis' of the mid-1980s, caused by a decline in world markets. Though not living together, farmers constituted an occupational community defined as much by their long-standing relationship to the land as miners were by theirs with the pit. Farm families confronted by the crisis found it difficult to come to terms with their loss of independence and self-reliance; they virtually withdrew from community life in preference to coming into contact with their erstwhile friends, neighbours and creditors (Van Hooke 1990). Farmer (1986, p.61) reports how the adult males in particular suffered 'a loss of their fundamental sense of identity'. Wives observed their husbands to be incapable of opening up and talking through their problems, as if too ashamed to acknowledge anything which might be interpreted as weakness or failure. As Lempers and Clark-Lempers (1990) discovered in their study of adolescent boys and girls in a Midwestern farm community, the economic crisis had the effect of generating higher levels of depressive symptoms, drug-abuse and delinquency. Despite the apparent collapse of the local economy, there was strong resistance to moving away. 'The psychological tie to place is so compelling that even unsatisfying work is preferable to leaving the community' (Farmer 1986, p.61).

TABLE 4.8 STRESS SCORES BY PIT STATUS

Pit status	All				Men				Women			
	N	Mean	Median	Standard deviation	N	Mean	Median	Standard deviation	N	Mean	Median	Standard deviation
Pit closed	160	8.6	7.5	5.3	80	7.6	7.0	5.2	80	9.5	9.0	5.2
Pit open	160	7.2	6.0	5.0	80	6.7	5.0	4.8	80	7.6	7.0	5.3
	Mann-Whitney test: W = 27802; p = 0.01**				Mann-Whitney test: W = 6819; p = 0.19				Mann-Whitney test: W = 7100; p = 0.024*			

Note: maximum individual stress = 42 (see appendix for details of calculation).

** = significant at 1% level.
* = significant at 5% level.

TABLE 4.9 STRESS SCORES BY MINING/NON-MINING

Type of work	All				Men				Women			
	N	Mean	Median	Standard deviation	N	Mean	Median	Standard deviation	N	Mean	Median	Standard deviation
Mining	80	7.2	6.0	5.2	40	6.1	5.0	4.4	40	8.3	6.5	5.4
Non-mining	80	7.3	7.0	5.0	40	6.4	5.0	4.6	40	8.3	8.5	5.7
	Mann-Whitney test: W = 2654; p = 0.89				Mann-Whitney test: W = 1386; p = 0.94				Mann-Whitney test: W = 1312; p = 0.95			

Note: maximum individual stress = 42 (see appendix for details of calculation).

A plethora of recent structural changes, most notably in employment and housing, had ensured that the populations of each of our four communities had become markedly more cosmopolitan than Bulmer's 'ideal type'. Nevertheless, many aspects of local culture still represented a throwback to the days when all four villages were decidedly 'mining' in character. As in the American farm crisis, it was the dismantling of established relationships, lost traditions and fractured daily routines which formed the root cause of current social difficulties. People now felt more isolated and detached from community affairs; one-time colleagues were now perceived as rivals and the social rituals that once reinforced a sense of common identity had suddenly disappeared. The erosion of employment prospects was palpably affecting the outlook of young people. Demotivated at school, teenage boys especially were turning to drugs and car crimes in a search for exciting validation of male identity. Consequently, social divisions between young and old were emerging.

It was far from apparent to residents or professionals in these communities what could be done to restore or reform a sense of pride in the community. They felt powerless in the face of economic and social forces that seemed way beyond their control. How far the difficulties confronting them were common to other UK mining localities is a question tackled in the following chapter.

5 The Experience of Other Mining Communities

INTRODUCTION

This chapter has two objectives. First, we establish how far the findings of the last three chapters transfer to other mining localities affected by pit closure. Second, we explore social consequences of industrial contraction under-emphasised in our Doncaster research. We draw on two studies by others – Turner and Gregory (1995) and Guy (1994) – and two of our own, one published as Critcher, Parry and Waddington (1995) and one not previously published.

Turner and Gregory (1995) traced the employment histories of redundant miners from two closed pits: Brodsworth (1991) and Markham Main (1993), both in Doncaster. The former belonged, of course, to one of the four communities included in our own comparative study. These authors were also concerned with assessing the career advice and training on offer to ex-miners. Guy (1994) asked similar questions of a larger sample. He conducted a postal survey of miners made redundant at five of the ten collieries closed in October 1992: Grimethorpe (South Yorkshire), Parkside (North-West), Silverhill (Nottinghamshire), Taff Merthyr (South Wales) and Vane Tempest (North-East).

Our own case studies, commissioned after the Doncaster project, examined mining communities affected by long-term pit closure. A study of Thurcroft, near Rotherham in South Yorkshire, was carried out two and a half years after the closure of the colliery. A survey of former mineworkers and their female partners and some in-depth interviews were commissioned by Rotherham Metropolitan Borough Council and Rotherham Training and Enterprise Council, with supplementary funding from the Rural Development Commission. Our general research brief was: 'To investigate and report on the social, economic and psychological impact of the closure of the Thurcroft colliery on the miners, their families and the community as a whole' (Critcher, Parry and Waddington 1995, p.1).

A study of Warsop Vale, in west Nottinghamshire, was undertaken as part of a broader study of social problems and regeneration strategies in the Barnsley and Meden Valley coalfields, by Sheffield Hallam University researchers for the Government's Coalfields Task Force (see chapter 8). In-depth interviews were conducted with local residents and key informants (e.g. community workers and local authority development workers). Undertaken in February/March 1998, nine years after the pit shut, it provides the strongest evidence about the cumulative effects of closure. The location in Nottinghamshire, with its differing political and trade union traditions, contrasts with our South Yorkshire examples. Together, these case studies extend the generalisability of our Doncaster findings and explore the context for regeneration initiatives discussed in chapter 8.

Turner and Gregory: Brodsworth and Markham Main

This research focused on the experience of two separate samples of miners. Initially, 77 mineworkers from Markham Main colliery were interviewed between June and October 1992, when the colliery, though still open, faced the prospect of closure. Follow-up interviews were then carried out between June and September 1993, soon after closure, with 70 of the 77 original respondents. A separate survey was carried out of 176 former Brodsworth miners, between July 1992 and January 1993, around two years after closure.

By the time of their second interview only 39 per cent of the Markham Main men were in paid employment, a third with private mining contractors. Ten per cent were in training or further education; 26 per cent were unemployed, while a 'staggering' 23 per cent classified themselves as long-term sick. At Brodsworth the situation was even worse: 32 per cent were employed, 46 per cent unemployed and 19 per cent unfit for work. The sickness statistics were not attributable to age alone:

> They become even more significant when the age of the mineworkers is taken into consideration: the Markham Main men had a mean age of 39 at the second interview. It is hardly an age with which long-term sickness would be associated. The former Brodsworth workers were a little older – 43 – but it is scarcely old. It is more than 20 years to the official retirement age. (Turner and Gregory 1995, p.154)

Such findings confirm the view of academics like Beatty and Fothergill (1998) and Fieldhouse and Hollywood (1999) that 'official' unemployment rates for mining areas tend to disguise substantial underlying additional (or 'hidden') levels of unemployment in the form of permanent sickness.

For the minority of Turner and Gregory's respondents who had been fortunate enough to find jobs, levels of pay had fallen markedly compared with amounts they had formerly received at the pit. Most ex-Brodsworth employees reported wage reductions of at least £100 per week. Only two respondents had maintained their previous level of earnings. No one had exceeded it.

Turner and Gregory argue that both communities were actually better placed to recover from pit closure than other South Yorkshire pit villages:

> Markham Main and Brodsworth ... are in significant contrast to many other coalfield localities, where individuals and communities are

disadvantaged through either a poor road infrastructure, or through geographical remoteness ... Markham Main and Brodsworth had none of these problems. This begs an important question. If success in gaining alternative employment at Markham Main and Brodsworth is still so difficult to achieve, what chance have redundant mineworkers in areas with none of their advantages? (ibid., p.159)

If this argument stands, then even higher rates of unemployment and withdrawal from the labour force on grounds of ill health might be anticipated elsewhere. The CCC survey throws some light on this.

The CCC Survey of Five Pits

The Coalfield Communities Campaign survey was carried out between December 1993 and April 1994. Postal questionnaires produced 878 replies, a 30 per cent response rate, comprising 166 replies from Grimethorpe, 252 from Parkside, 188 from Silverhill, 98 from Taff Merthyr and 174 from Vane Tempest.

Almost half of the ex-miners (46 per cent) remained without work a year after pit closure, four-fifths of whom had been continuously unemployed. Unemployment was worst at Vane Tempest (50 per cent) and Silverhill (48 per cent). Since, overall, 9 per cent of respondents were in training or full-time education, well over half were not in paid employment. The level of sickness was again striking:

For the sample as a whole [of those classing themselves as 'unemployed' in this survey], the proportion was nearly 30 per cent. In Taff Merthyr it reached as high as 55 per cent. This means that the number of men not working and on benefit-level income is much higher in mining areas than it appears from simply looking at registered unemployment. If the figures from this survey were repeated in other coalfield areas, the proportion of miners out of work in Britain could be up to twice as high as official figures suggest. (Guy 1994, p.26)

One per cent had officially retired. Thus 44 per cent were currently in paid work, including the 3 per cent (28 men) who had become self-employed. The average wage in new jobs was £173 per week, but lower for those re-employed outside mining at £161 – £74 per week less than the weekly average at British Coal. Of the 28 men who had become self-employed since leaving the mines only 3 had managed to improve their weekly pay. Guy concluded that 89 per cent of the men in the overall sample were financially worse off than before.

Such findings are consistent with those of Turner and Gregory. We can put this simply. Of every ten ex-miners four would be re-employed, three unemployed, two would have withdrawn from the workforce on the grounds of ill health and one would be in training or education. These figures appear to change little over time, as we can see at a glance from table 5.1, which summarises the levels of unemployment/permanent illness uncovered by the above surveys and by our Doncaster research. Though it is just possible that ex-miners' unemployment will have declined recently, as it has nationally, such local economies tend to be slower to respond to upturns in the economy as a whole. Even those in work experience severe decreases in earnings, work longer hours and have less security and generally poorer conditions compared with mining employment. These common experiences clearly impact on whole communities, as we have seen in Doncaster. We now consider two other examples of ex-mining communities to see if the decline of community is evident there as well.

TABLE 5.1 LEVELS OF UNEMPLOYMENT AND PERMANENT SICKNESS: EX-MINERS FROM SELECTED COLLIERIES

Colliery	Approximate time since closure	Unemployment/ permanent sickness %
Markham Main	'Soon after'	49
Askern	6 months	48
Grimethorpe	12–18 months	44
Parkside	12–18 months	45
Silverhill	12–18 months	49
Taff Merthyr	12–18 months	45
Vane Tempest	12–18 months	52
Brodsworth	18 months	58
Thurcroft	2 years	60
Brodsworth	2 years	64

Sources: Critcher, Parry and Waddington (1995); Guy (1994); Turner and Gregory (1995); and the present study.

The Thurcroft Study

Background and Methodology

Thurcroft colliery was sunk in 1911. For seventy years the village expanded with the pit. By 1981 Thurcroft's population was almost 5,500, with roughly 400 local men (29 per cent of male workers) employed by the colliery (People of Thurcroft 1986). At the onset of the 1984–5 strike, the pit employed 850 men, producing coking coal, mainly for the British Steel Corporation plant at Scunthorpe. Following the strike the workforce was reduced to 500 by a redundancy programme involving men over 50 but gradually increased back up to 568 between 1985 and 1991, as men transferred from pits closed nearby. By 1991 only a quarter of the colliery workforce lived in the village, yet the pit remained the focus of community life, such as social and sports activity.

However, in November 1991 local managers and trade union officials were told by the Area Director that, owing to overcapacity in the Electricity Supply Industry (ESI), sector, the main recipient of Thurcroft coal, the pit would cease production in eight days' time. Since the Modified Colliery Review Procedure required three months' notice of any decision to close, management needed to obtain the consent of its employees. Faced with a threat to withdraw the £10,000 redundancy supplement the workforce voted to accept closure and the pit ceased production on 6 December 1991, though salvage work continued until September 1992. (The story of the pit's closure will be returned to in chapter 7, where we discuss an abortive attempt to reopen it as a worker take-over.) Our study took place in 1994, two years after closure, during which time the former mineworkers and their families had to adjust to Thurcroft village without a pit.

Our survey sample was designed to include 40 Thurcroft ex-miners from Thurcroft; 40 Thurcroft ex-miners from the Rotherham area; and 40 partners/wives of ex-miners from Thurcroft. In the event, we managed 35, 37 and 35 respectively, a total of 107 instead of 120. This was mainly due to difficulties in obtaining reliable address lists. British Coal would not disclose them and NUM records were patchy. Some of the initial sample had moved, some did not respond and others declined. Nevertheless, the eventual sample was adequate and reflected the various skill levels of jobs at the pit.

The survey was conducted in the summer of 1994. A trained interviewer undertook fifteen in-depth interviews (five from each of the three sub-groups) in the autumn. There were particular problems finding Thurcroft women willing to participate in a follow-up interview because they regarded the subject as irrelevant, belonging to the past, itself an indicative attitude. It also meant, as in most surveys and interviews, that we had the views of only those available and willing to talk to us. We cannot be sure that their circumstances and experiences were the same as those unavailable or unwilling to talk to us.

Employment and Unemployment

Employment status was divided into three: those in full-time 'permanent' employment (thirty-six men or 34 per cent); those in temporary or part-time employment (twenty men or 19 per cent); and the unemployed (fifty-one men or 48 per cent). Of those officially classed as unemployed, almost half were receiving unemployment benefit (30 per cent) or income support (18 per cent). Twenty-two per cent classed themselves as permanently sick, whilst 12 per cent were undergoing training, with or without benefits and just five of the employed worked for themselves.

In new jobs, forty hours was the usual basic working week. A third habitually worked overtime, normally between seven and twelve hours a week. Rates of basic pay were generally low, with just under a half earning less than £150 per week. Overall, 70 per cent earned less than at the colliery, the difference usually being somewhere between £41 and £80 a week. Compared with their old mining jobs, most men appreciated better working conditions and some improvement in job satisfaction; but pay, hours of work, job security and trade union representation were criticised.

We asked those in work how they had obtained their jobs. By far the most frequent method used (by 55 per cent) was through informal channels such as family and friends. Answering an advert or applying at the factory gate accounted for another 16 per cent. Thus only 18 per cent – ten out of fifty-six men – had found a job through one of the formal agencies like British Coal Enterprise or the Employment Service. The role of private employment agencies caused particular controversy. One unemployed man told us:

> *I know I'll get a job but it ain't gonna be an agency. I don't want to work for an agency again 'cos you don't get shift allowance or owt like that. I mean, you're doing the same job – in fact, you're doing more work than them that work at the place – and they're getting double what you're getting. Because agency workers are there they think, 'Oh, we'll do less, let them do more.' Why should we? I worked at an electronics firm, eight, nine months nearly, and I asked them to set me on and they said, 'There's no jobs.' So I said, 'Well, I've been working nine months.' But there's no jobs full time, know what I mean? So, when the holidays came, I said, 'I've had enough,' because you don't get holiday money either. So when the August holiday came, I told 'em to stick it. Well I know I've suffered for it but it were just the principle of it. (Critcher, Parry and Waddington 1995, p.24)*

Only 6 out of 101 men had been continuously employed since pit closure. The majority of the rest (52 per cent) had experienced one period of unemployment, while almost a quarter (23 per cent) had been unemployed for less than six months and over a third (36 per cent) for a total of two years or more. Amongst the kinds of job being looked for, the most favoured were driving (25 per cent), labouring (14 per cent) and engineering (14 per cent). Nineteen per cent said they would take anything, while 11 per cent had given up looking entirely.

Despite this apparently flexible and realistic approach to job search there were still some minimum conditions to be met. Nominating three main reasons why they had been put off applying for jobs, ex-miners gave two kinds of answer. A third of all reasons cited unacceptable conditions: low pay (23 per cent) and too far to travel (12 per cent). However, they were much more likely to feel that they would not be acceptable to the jobs. Two-thirds of reasons were of this type: lacking the right skills (20 per cent), not the right age (15 per cent), lacking appropriate experience (15 per cent), too many applicants (8 per cent) and a presumption that the employer would prefer not to employ ex-miners (7 per cent). Respondents suspected or had discovered that employers regarded ex-miners as expensive or difficult to re-train.

Interviews with unemployed ex-miners highlighted feelings of unhappiness and depression. As in the Doncaster study, inability to pay their way in family and social life and a general sense of uselessness pervaded their comments. Dependency on the wife's wage was another source of humiliation.

Women's own relationship to work was explored in the survey and interviews. We asked both men and women questions about whether female partners worked, what jobs they did, their hours, pay and conditions, and how they obtained their jobs. Overall, 54 per cent of miners' partners were economically active. Pit closure does not seem to have encouraged more women to find work: as many women had stopped work as had started it since the pit closed. Women's employment rates did not seem to depend on the employment status of their husbands, though many men expressed opposition to their wives working and disgust at their low levels of pay.

Female employment was concentrated in the distributive and catering services (41 per cent combined), although almost as many were in miscellaneous services (33 per cent). Over three-quarters of women, compared to just half of men, worked in the service sector. A narrow majority (52 per cent) of these jobs were part-time. Unlike many of the men's new jobs, most of the women's jobs were viewed as permanent. Nearly all the part-timers worked between eleven and twenty-two hours per week. The great variety in the nature of women's work was reflected in their take-home pay. While nearly a half (45 per cent) earned less than £80, over a quarter (29 per cent) earned over £120. Many women were clearly content with part-time jobs. Despite low levels of skills and pay, they were compatible with family responsibilities, got them out of the house and provided much-needed extra income.

Income, Children and Community

Three-quarters of miners had received redundancy payments of between £11,000 and £30,000, with a median range of £21,000 to £25,000. Over half of the sample (54 per cent) had either nothing or less than a quarter left. Only 5 per cent had managed to retain all, and 9 per cent at least three-quarters, of their redundancy money.

A clear majority said that they were 'a lot worse off' than before (52 per cent) and another 17 per cent that they were 'a bit worse off', though 19 per cent claimed to be 'a bit' or 'a lot' better off. Often, families' points of financial comparison had ceased to be their income when the pit was open. Of greater concern now was the marginal difference between living on benefits and having a low-paid job. Overall, 19 per cent (20 of the 107) claimed some current worry over finance. Interviews indicated concern about the future, with the effects on children being a primary source of worry.

Most (63 per cent) felt that pit closure had not affected their children. The remainder were evenly split between 'a little bit' or 'quite a lot' of effect. The effects nearly all related to the family having less money (75 per cent). There was, again, a clear majority (58 per cent) believing that pit closure would have no effect on their children staying on at school, though just over a third (37 per cent) felt it would make them more likely to stay on. Asked if pit closure made them worry more about their children's future, a slim majority thought not (53 per cent) compared with those who thought it did (43 per cent). Invited to nominate two things which would improve their children's future, most opted only for one: better prospects in jobs (40 per cent).

Views of the local community were generally very positive, with almost half seeing it as a 'good' or 'very good' place in which to live, compared with one in five viewing it as 'poor' or 'very poor'. Asked to nominate the 'best thing' about the community, close on half (46 per cent) nominated friendliness and closeness. The worst things were lack of recreation facilities and crime (24 per cent each).

Asked to characterise the effects of pit closure on the local community, a surprisingly low number (19 per cent) referred to 'less money around', while 36 per cent nominated a decline in social life. Other perceived effects, such as crime, the closure of shops and declining morale, were each nominated by less than 6 per cent. Hence the main impact was seen to be cultural – on the common life of the community – rather than economic, on how much money people have.

While approximately half (49 per cent) thought that the future prospects for Thurcroft were likely to remain the same, almost a third (31 per cent) forecast that they would get bleaker. Even so, most expected to stay in the community; the minority who would contemplate leaving would do so with reluctance.

The Thurcroft findings confirm the profile of ex-miners in previous surveys (see table 5.1): one half employed, the other half unemployed, a significant minority of whom have withdrawn from the workforce. They also add some detail such as the part-time nature of much employment, the movement in and out of work and the controversial role of private employment agencies. To ascertain the percentage of unemployed is too crude a measure to encompass the poor quality of such work as can be found. It also demonstrated the static rate of female employment, its largely part-time nature and the low levels of skill and pay. To that extent, its findings were all too predictable. So was the decline in the community. While most were still loyal to Thurcroft, the village was perceived to be deteriorating, most obviously evident in levels of crime but also in a sense of dislocation and decay.

Having been asked to provide a list of recommendations for action, we listed a range of services which local people appeared to need: access to financial and employment advice, the provision of training and education, facilities for childcare and play. We concluded:

> We make no apology for the fact that all this sounds very much like what used to be called community action. That seems to us to be what Thurcroft needs. Such a programme could not in itself meet the needs for a reasonably paid job and a secure income. But it could improve the level of skills, provide relevant and expert advice on training, benefits and finances, inaugurate short courses and instigate community recreation projects. The alternative, as one of our respondents put it, is that Thurcroft will become a 'ghost town'. (Critcher, Parry and Waddington 1995, p.151)

In the event, there have been few subsequent initiatives in Thurcroft. The level of local activism and local authority intervention has remained low. Local economic development has been concentrated on other pit sites and the trading estate adjacent to the M18 motorway a few miles away. The colliery site itself is being turned over to municipal waste landfill. In our second community case study, much worse conditions had produced some response inside and toward a community whose experience of pit closure was longer and had been compounded by its greater isolation and environmental decay.

The Warsop Vale Study

Background and Methodology

Situated at the outer perimeter of west Nottinghamshire, Warsop Vale was built at the start of the 20th century to accommodate the families of miners working at Warsop Main colliery. The village is tiny: 220 terraced homes in 5 streets, with a population of around 650 people. The 1991 Census revealed that 25 per cent of the population was less than 16 years old and 19 per cent fell within the 16–24 age range; 11 per cent of adults were of pensionable age, while 15 per cent were unemployed and 17 per cent were suffering a long-term limiting illness (compared with the county average of 8 per cent). Just over half the households had no car.

Historically a traditional, tight-knit mining community, Warsop Vale's links to the coal industry have gradually eroded. Warsop Main's total workforce of 1,465 in 1980 fell to 1,009 by 1986, and again to 849 by its closure in 1989. As of March 1998, three-fifths of local houses were owner-occupied with virtually all the rest privately rented. A single landlord owned most of these, thirty of which were unoccupied. All his houses were severely dilapidated. New families had moved in as some ex-mining families had moved out.

Apart from a single general store incorporating the post office, a small central play area for young children, a set of garden allotments and a solitary public house, Warsop Vale lacked basic amenities. There was no longer a miners' welfare and, in the absence of a local primary school, younger children were bussed to Church Warsop. There was a small community centre and adjoining playing-field, with limited facilities: main hall, small kitchen and a sports changing-room.

Recent employment, housing and population trends had adversely affected the physical, economic and social condition of Warsop Vale. Even by 1992 it was apparent that, 'Since the closure of Warsop Main Colliery, the effects on Warsop Vale have been extreme and deeply damaging, leaving local people depressed and unsure of the future' (CTRU [Civic Trust Regeneration Unit] 1992, p.11). However, escalating concern over the condition of local housing and the general decline of the community provoked the formation in 1994 of the Warsop Vale Residents' Action Group, prominent since in campaigns to rejuvenate the village.

We were asked to produce a qualitative portrait of the social problems besetting the community, especially former mineworkers. In 1998 32 local residents and 8 key informants from local authority agencies were interviewed. Two residents' meetings were attended and a range of reports on the area, produced between 1992 and 1997, consulted. The aim was less to provide a statistical snapshot of the area, as had been the case at Thurcroft, than to analyse perceptions of and reactions to long-term decline. As elsewhere, employment was a key factor.

Employment and Unemployment

The demise of the local colliery removed the staple source of local male employment. Warsop Vale men re-entering employment had a diversity of jobs. Only a few clusters of men worked for the same employer. For example, four worked at Johnson's Controls (car seat-cover manufacturers) in Mansfield, and another four at WH Davies 1984 (Engineering), three miles away. A gang of local men went crop-picking in Lincolnshire. Other jobs were with small employers, such as a welder for a car-exhaust fitter, an assistant supervisor for a small tyre-manufacturer, a residential careworker, a hospital porter, a garden centre assistant and a barman. Local jobs were characterised by low pay, insecurity of tenure, poor working conditions and non-unionism.

Working respondents also stressed the loss of camaraderie and autonomy compared with mining. Some enjoyed the work but several told stories of sharp practices about safety and short-term contracts and of general hostility to trade unions. The conditions for the crop-pickers were the most extreme:

> *It's a bit like the old butty system in the pits when somebody would get a team together. Off they go to the fields of Spalding, picking vegetables and packing them so that they get back about 8 o'clock at night – for £3 an hour! They work extra hours to pay £25 each to the bloke who's got the transit van. If there's eight in the van, that's £200 they're paying him. So, technically, they're supposed to be free of the stress of unemployment, but there's all these other strings to the fact that they are in a job: working them hours, in them conditions, and being ripped off for travelling to and from it. (community development officer)*

Warsop Vale women had restricted employment opportunities. A local small business employed mostly female staff, making plastic surrounds and curtains for bathrooms. Most of the thirty women lived outside the village. Pay was low – less than £4 an hour – but working relations in a family firm were good. Generally, employed women were hard to find, though there was some demand for part-time cleaners.

Many local people were too ill to work and poor as a consequence:

> *There are a high number of people with limiting long-term illness so any unemployment figure wouldn't necessarily include them. And what does hit you in the face about Warsop Vale is that there's an awful lot of poverty*

around and with that poverty goes a lack of self-esteem, an apathy and loss of all expectation for the future. (community development worker)

The cost of public transport hindered travel. A bus ride to Mansfield cost £1.40 for a single ticket with discounts unavailable before 9 a.m.:

To sign on for a course at West Notts Technical College, for instance, it would cost you £4.10 return bus fare to get there and back. Who's got that kind of money if you're on benefits? Somebody with a job, we worked it out that you'd be looking at about £28 gross if you got a job at Oakham Business Park. We either have to look at providing affordable transport for people or bringing jobs and training to where they are. (community development worker)

The Civic Trust Regeneration Unit's report pointed to a reluctance to travel far to work: 'This attitude may reflect the insular character of communities, a lack of confidence amongst local people in seeking work, and the fact that a large sector of the community has traditionally not needed to travel out of the Warsop Area' (CTRU 1992, p.26).

Housing and Environment

Two of the most striking problems at Warsop Vale were the state of the housing and environmental despoliation. When the National Coal Board decided in 1984 to sell off the Warsop Vale estate, those properties not purchased by existing tenants at the knocked-down price of £2,000–£3,000 were sold on even more cheaply to local landlords. Intense controversy surrounded allegations that the landlord now owning most of the rented properties had left many empty and failed to repair the others. As the chair of Warsop Vale Residents' Action Group explained:

I've been in folks' housing and thought, you know, 'That cannot be right!' One particular old woman was sleeping downstairs on the couch instead of going upstairs because her bedroom's full of damp. Seventy-odd-year-old. That, to me, is not acceptable.

As long-term residents began to move away, jobs disappeared and the village acquired an unsavoury reputation. Vacant properties were vandalised. New tenants were poor, often transient, welfare-dependent families. Long-term residents regularly accused such tenants of moonlight flits and encouraging crime. According to one 30-year-old man:

You see, they move out and he doesn't board them up or nowt. Then you get somebody coming from Shirebrook or Warsop and they're nicking radiators, they're nicking gas fires, floorboards, toilet windows; even the copper tank in the loft. All the water just drains through. There's not one house in this village that hasn't got damp. Next door to the shop, there were maggots coming out of the wall – hundreds of them. The bottom road they call 'the

Arab Sector' after Bosnia. If you walk down there at night, you're a brave fucking man.

Such problems were highlighted by a housing survey of the village, commissioned by Nottinghamshire County Council and the Rural Development Agency in 1996. The report, 'Stopping the Rot' (County Homelessness and Housing Team 1996), revealed findings based on internal and external inspections of 120 houses. Assessment was made of rising or penetrating dampness, condensation problems, poor safety, inadequate facilities or miscellaneous forms of disrepair. Thirty-six of the thirty-nine properties internally inspected were declared unfit for human habitation.

Hitherto, little action had been taken against the errant landlords. Residents on fixed-term 'assured shorthold tenancies' were reluctant to take legal action against their landlord, fearing their tenancies would not be renewed. Even families of ex-miners with long-term protected tenancies lacked financial resources to take action. The local council had been reluctant to serve repair notices to private landlords because of their obligation to provide mandatory grants towards the cost of repairs.

The 1996 Housing Act made such grants discretionary. Subsequently, the council began to serve repair notices against the main landlord. He responded by seeking a judicial review of the council's actions, arguing that it was unreasonable for the council to bring unoccupied houses up to the required standard when the village itself did not constitute a 'viable economic unit', and that the council's hidden agenda was to drive him out of the village. The issue was therefore deadlocked until the case was heard. This inertia compounded the basic problem, as the chair of the Action Group pointed out:

> *If the housing is sorted out, then we could stand a chance of bringing in inward investment. But nobody's going to invest in a village that looks like a bomb's dropped.*

The general environment was as run-down as the housing. A depressing air of neglect pervaded sections of the built-up community and its surrounding landscape. Aside from derelict housing, neglected sites about the village attracted household refuse. The colliery tip and railway sidings went unreclaimed. The colliery was developed on land leased from the Fitzherbert Estate. As these leases do not expire until well into this century, the estate was under no obligation to recover the land and environmentally improve it. British Coal was doing little, local opinion suspecting that the Warsop Main tip contained coal reserves which could be profitably washed out, and that there was extractable limestone elsewhere on the site.

Social Problems

Despite the wide range of physical and socio-economic problems currently besetting it, Warsop Vale exhibited traces of the community spirit and neighbourliness from its days as a mining community. However, indigenous residents had become increasingly apathetic, fatalistic and demoralised. The resulting void in popular village activism had been filled by a small number of relatively new inhabitants who, with a few longer-term residents, became the nucleus of the Warsop Vale Residents' Action Group. This small group of committed village residents had become a driving force behind initiatives and campaigns to regenerate the entire community.

Nevertheless, Warsop Vale was beset by a host of social problems. Divisions existed between the young and old, and between older and newer residents. Resentment towards the transient occupants of privately rented houses was common. A local man in his thirties and a woman in her mid-forties voiced these views:

We're being injected with undesirables! I've lived here all my life and I walked up today past two empty houses and there were people in 'em two days ago who I'd never see before. They move in, run their bills up, and then move out.

They've turned us into a dump. They're dirty, scruffy, they just don't care. They're making the place stink ... Why should decent people who've paid for their houses have that to put up with?

Others living or working in the community gave a different account:

What's a shame about it really is that they've had eighteen years of 'look after yourself' and being encouraged to buy your own home – a little corner of England, as they put it. And for them that have, you're then looking for somebody to blame if you've invested your life savings in somewhere and it comes under attack. And after all, it's the private landlords who are really letting the place down. (community development worker)

As far back as 1992, there was evidence of a growing social division between older residents and local youths:

Older people in the area remember a thriving and supportive mining community, while younger people have known only its decline, unemployment and despair. This has not only led to frustration and disillusionment, but alienation between young and old based on a misapprehension that they have different problems. (CTRU 1992, pp.11–12)

This schism had grown wider in more recent years. Local youths gathered on street corners and kicked footballs against end terraces, a practice that enraged older people. When young people were barred from the community centre, activities of older users, such as bingo and dancing, were deliberately disrupted.

A perceived rise in crime exacerbated social divisions. A Community Safety Survey undertaken by Nottinghamshire County Council Social Services Department in January 1997 (Community Support Unit 1997) suggested that fear of crime, as much as its actual amount, was the issue. One hundred and twenty-three questionnaires disclosed that significant minorities of the village population had had their home broken into and property damaged (24 respondents), their vehicle stolen (21) or the contents of their vehicle taken (19). More than a quarter (37) had suffered theft from garden sheds. Both actual and vicarious experiences of crime generated a high fear of crime. Asked whether they felt that crime was 'a problem in this area', only 4 respondents replied that it was 'no problem', 47 thought it was 'a bit of a problem', 29 'a problem' and 43 'a big problem'. With no local police station and delays in the response time of Warsop police, even the purchase of a single police motorcycle was regarded as an improvement.

Young people, women and the elderly expressed disillusionment in different ways. Prominent amongst problems affecting young people was an apparent lack of motivation and ambition at school. In their submission to the Task Force, the Warsop Vale Residents' Association pointed out how:

> The local secondary school has identified that there are a disproportionate number of children with problems from the village. A unique subculture exists. There is a lack of expectation by pupil, teacher and parent.

Key informants emphasised how young people were reacting to their general environment.

> If you look around at the housing and general environment you get the obvious impression that nobody seems to care. What worries me is the kind of message that sends out, especially to young people. That if they're left to live like that and accept that as a norm, what values does it give them? If we as adults and authorities allow this, what are we telling them about their future lives and what they can expect if they're living in a place like this? (community development worker)

There was anecdotal evidence of increased drug-use in the village, though participants in a focus group of fourteen 12 to 18-year-olds meeting as part of the Community Safety Survey denied this.

Women respondents expressed anxiety about the future of the village, the lack of prospects for local children, poverty and low incomes, and the perilous nature of vacant houses where children played. They bemoaned the lack of a village focal point. Relative newcomers in particular suffered isolation, loneliness and rejection. Women wanting to work complained of a lack of childcare but also recognised that they lack the skills, qualifications or confidence to find a job. For the elderly, the foremost problem was the absence of local facilities, apart from a weekly lunch club. They would have to move away to find sheltered housing.

Political Exclusion

Divided amongst themselves, such groups also felt neglected by outside agencies. In its 1992 report the CTRU referred to local feelings of 'scepticism about the commitment of agencies, including the local authorities, to do anything' (1992, p.87). Smaller villages resented the concentration of District Council resources in Market Warsop:

> They feel that nobody bothers about them, nobody will do anything, and there's very little that they can do for themselves. Things are being done piecemeal, but not being built on. Differences are not seen across the whole community; there is no sense of progressive development. They've got a feeling of being discarded: 'Oh, we've done all this before. People come and then they go away.' (enabler, Nottinghamshire Rural Community Council)

Warsop Vale's geographical isolation and small population reduced its political importance for local authorities. There was a general sense of official indifference:

> I mean, at the moment, if you go into The Park, there's somebody moved in a couple of months ago with three horses. They just arrived one day – whop! That would never happen on a council estate, for God's sake. Yet, Warsop Vale? Nobody gives a toss. I'm surprised actually, that we haven't been out before with baseball bats and stuff like that because, I mean, by the time the police get here, you can rip a tank out and the water'll be running down the street. And people honestly feel now they can get away with it. But if that was in the middle of Warsop, that wouldn't happen – wouldn't be allowed to happen. (chair, Warsop Vale Residents' Action Group)

In this climate of humiliation and despair villagers felt powerless to control or shape their own destinies. Proposals to start up a limestone quarry on the village's periphery had exacerbated these feelings:

> The quarry will be at the back of North Street. They're gonna come up and go out the back of The Park, apparently, straight through the centre of the village. I think that, eventually, if the quarry did come, there would be no reason to stay. I mean, it's not going to attract investors. People are just going to get up and go into council houses. So, at the end of the day, you're just going to end up with a ghost town. So what do we do? Just hope and pray that there's not gonna be a quarry? Like we did a couple of years ago – hope and pray that Warsop Vale would become a Renewal Area. You know, all we seem to be doing is hoping and praying and getting kicked in the sodding teeth for it. (chair, Warsop Vale Residents' Action Group)

At a meeting called by the Warsop Vale Residents' Action Group in January 1998 the chair expressed anger and frustration that more positive developments were constantly delayed. While acknowledging that funding applications were unavoidably slow to process, she protested that three years' continuous agitation had produced few tangible benefits. Across the community as a whole, optimism was dissipating and being replaced by feelings of futility and resentment, as exemplified by the following comments of a disabled ex-miner:

Getting anything done for this village off of Mansfield District Council or
Notts County Council is like plaiting sawdust. Short of a couple of F-15
fighters to bomb the place there's bugger all to be done. We can't even sell up
and move. Nobody wants to buy a house here. Next door, they've just taken it
off the market after two years. Gas central heating, all windows and doors
double glazed, Adams fireplace, the lot. Dropped it from £23,000 to
£17,000; still, nobody will touch it. So, you tell me, what are we to do?

Warsop Vale was an extreme case of an ex-mining community in decline.
Its problems were compounded by its small size and geographical remoteness.
Both men and women had restricted employment opportunities. In the nine
years since pit closure there had been a sharp deterioration in the standard of
housing and the physical environment. A shifting population had provoked
internal divisions. Crime was seen as a major problem. In the face of such
burgeoning problems local political institutions seemed paralysed. With their
few allies the Action Group set out to attract attention and funding to their
area. Such activity indicated the scope, but also limitations, of regenerative
self-help.

Regeneration Initiatives

In 1992, after the pit was closed but before the Action Group was formed,
came one early initiative. Following consultations with local tenants an
application was submitted via Nottinghamshire County Council for European
Regional Development Funding to upgrade the village roads and pavements
and introduce street lighting. Previously, the road surface had been a rough
mixture of tarmac patches and broken cobbles. Lighting had come from the
colliery's generator rather than the local authority network and had stopped
when the pit shut. With the success of the application these problems were
remedied.

In 1996 the Rural Development Commission granted £15,000 to provide
a play area for young children. A large part of the responsibility for flattening
and clearing the area was taken by local residents, a group of seven or eight of
whom (mainly women) worked day and night on the project, with machinery
and personnel from Welbeck Colliery.

The 'Stopping the Rot' report of 1996 led to a 'Planning For Real' exercise
in which Warsop Vale residents were invited to consider what needed most
improvement in the village and how it might be achieved. Funding of £5,000
was raised by Nottinghamshire County Council and the Rural Development
Agency to commission the Neighbourhood Initiatives Foundation to facilitate
consultation. However, this process was eventually suspended, largely because
participants objected to some of the methods of consultation, such as sticking
paper or cardboard objects on to a model of the village. There was also a view
that the project was a waste of money: £5,000 would have been better spent
on house repairs.

Another initiative stemming from the survey was an approach to the Groundwork Trust agency for assistance in the environmental improvement of the village. The agency agreed to use full-time workers and local volunteers to grass over areas of the village and plant a small wood to screen off the old pit site. After a year-long delay the agency reported to a meeting called by the Warsop Vale Residents' Action Group in January 1998. A representative for Groundwork Trust informed the meeting that, whilst the agency had been able to secure European funding of £120,000 and an equivalent sum of council money for coalfield land reclamation, ownership issues were now impeding progress. Much of the derelict village space was owned by local landlords and negotiations were having to be carried out to secure it for public ownership. The only publicly owned land was the community centre car-park. Work on this was scheduled to start in the spring of 1998.

Unhappy with the lack of progress, the Action Group had decided, a month earlier, to proceed with its own clean-up campaign. With the help of the local Rotary Club they disregarded the question of ownership to set about clearing and replanting an area of land adjacent to the main road. According to the group's vice-chair this had an immediate effect on village morale:

> I saw a man smile a rare smile a dozen weeks ago, all because [the Chair of the Action Group], the Rotary Club and myself were digging in a few daffodil bulbs. It might seem like nothing, but at least it's progress that people can see.

The 'Community Safety Survey' also produced some results. Nottinghamshire County Council provided seventy-five burglar alarms and thirty-five dummy boxes. A further £27,000 was set aside for the provision of two youth workers for the area.

Finally, the Warsop Vale Residents' Action Group submitted a bid, in November 1997, for £99,000 of ERDF (European Regional Development Fund) 'Objective 2' money (see chapter 8 for a full explanation of this funding regime) to develop the existing community centre with a project management and development worker. There would be an initial six-month period of consultation with local residents to develop an agenda for action as well as feasibility studies for the provision of adequate childcare and transport. The centre itself would be open on a twice-weekly basis, providing access to IT and photocopying facilities, voluntary and statutory agencies and job-search information and guidance. It would also host a minimum of four training courses per annum. Amongst other proposals were a regular newsletter, annual village events, a furniture project and a food co-operative. The centre manager would focus on 'capacity building', developing the necessary skills and resources to ensure the project's continuation beyond three years. This bid was unsuccessful because it scored thirteen fewer than the 45 points threshold. However, the Action Group aimed to resubmit this bid in April 1998 under 'Priority 4' of the Single Regeneration Budget (SRB), a UK funding regime.

Matched funding would be required from elsewhere, possibly from the district and county councils. North Nottinghamshire Training and Enterprise Council had already pledged support.

A month before the Objective 2 application, the Warsop Vale Residents' Action Group also submitted an application for £200,000 of lottery money. A more ambitious project, this involved the renovation of two vacant shops and their transformation into a community resource centre. Locally trained workers would be employed to carry out the renovation work. The resource centre would act as a focal point for community regeneration, providing childcare, training and education, employment and welfare advice, and such practical facilities as a telephone, photocopier, launderette and furniture recycling project. The centre would have its community worker and administrative support. The application aimed at 'giving people a desire to stay, providing a focal point and improving the fabric of the community, and an opportunity to get to know your next door neighbour'.

Also pending at this time was the outcome of another Priority 4 (SRB4) bid put forward on behalf of Warsop Vale by the local community development worker, which aimed to alleviate youth disaffection, drug-taking and educational under-motivation in the village:

> *That's focusing on disaffected youth. One of the things we have done is to put in a bid – not that they want bids yet! – for education support in the community centre so that every night we could run a homework club. We could link into primary and secondary schools and offer somebody for kids to come and read to, assuming their parents aren't prepared to do it. We could have a community award scheme to encourage the kids. We could have a couple of computers, CD-ROMs, reference books, so that them as wants to move into education can do so. And a big part of that is to challenge the culture that exists at the moment and the lack of expectation and do it in a non-threatening environment. (community development worker)*

All these initiatives were within existing legal and funding structures and involved local residents or community workers applying directly for projects. There was also a perceived need for other statutory agencies to take action. Mansfield District Council was criticised by some key informants for its inaction over the particular problem of the recalcitrant local landlord:

> *Given that a lot of people are simply too scared to take action against the landlords, what ought to be happening is that the council should be doing an annual inspection. The legislation's there to say there should be an annual tour of accommodation. (community development worker)*

If the council acquired the properties they could be redeveloped, perhaps to include housing for the elderly. The council also has responsibility for planning permission for the proposed quarry. Intervention to prevent it would indicate a sensitivity to the views of local residents.

As advocated in our Thurcroft report and in the lottery application, the most obvious community need was for a focal point for social, educational and generic advice activities. These exist elsewhere in mining communities, such as at Bilsthorpe, Newstead and Grimethorpe. Whilst this would need substantial external funding, the county and district councils could at least help in acquiring property or land.

Transport was another area where some imaginative interventions were needed:

> *It needs investment in schemes that are not necessarily putting buses on. The hiring of mopeds could be set up as a small enterprise, linked to teaching young people how to drive them and getting them through their test. And then there's the joint transport service: the Post Office do what they call the 'post bus' – while they're going out with the post, they use the van as a bus as well. (enabler, Nottinghamshire Rural Community Council)*

Key informants shared the view that a major and dramatic development – an immediate sign of progress – is necessary to revitalise the residents. There were repeated references to the need for some sort of 'political catalyst' or 'champion' to act as a symbolic figurehead in the promotion and regeneration of the area.

Some of the proposed schemes were ambitious, others more modest. All would contribute to giving the residents of Warsop Vale some hope, especially if planned with their involvement. In 1992 the Civic Regeneration Trust had commented that 'Warsop Vale has the spirit of a beleaguered settlement' (1992, p.87). In view of the range and pervasiveness of the problems that they faced it is remarkable that there remained a vast reservoir of community spirit, determination and dynamism. Without knowing it at the time, these qualities were about to yield rich dividends. In the two years following our research Warsop Vale was successful in two out of its three submissions, with the third application also proving successful on resubmission. Whilst exemplifying the type of potential for self-help that could be harnessed in the general process of regeneration in mining communities, the recent experience of Warsop Vale is an object lesson in the institutional and democratic deficits currently impeding the effective revitalisation of former mining localities. Such themes will be revisited in greater detail in chapter 8 – after we have taken a brief pause to consider how Britain's miners and the trade unions who represent them have been affected by, and responded to, the privatisation of their industry.

PART III:
THE RESTRUCTURED INDUSTRY

6 Privatisation and its Consequences

INTRODUCTION

Our concern here is with the possible effects of privatisation on industrial relations, working conditions and practices, and health and safety within the deep mines.[1] We are especially interested in the extent to which trade unionism may have been marginalised and employee solidarity undermined, both in the majority of pits owned by RJB Mining and other, single ownership mines.

Much of the industrial relations in the privatised coal industry perpetuated the tough management style formerly exercised by British Coal, itself part of a more general tendency of capital in the 1980s to 'ring-fence the power of the trade union voice – particularly the national union organisation' (Blyton and Turnbull 1994, p.298). Crouch (1990) and Smith and Morton (1993; 1994), have also argued that employers took advantage of Conservative government strategies to reduce union power. Employment laws prohibiting strikes and secondary action undermined trade union resistance and made 'union exclusion policies legal and feasible' (Crouch 1990, p.361). Smith and Morton explain how this erosion of union power was achieved by either 'total exclusion', involving the de-recognition or refusal to recognise trade unions, or by 'partial exclusion', entailing restricting and circumventing trade unions through joint consultation, direct communication, performance-related pay and the use of contract labour. This was not a universal trend. Some employers continued to see unions as necessary to secure the 'active co-operation of the workforce' (Blyton and Turnbull 1994, p.299).

In recently privatised industries other than coal, union power was systematically eroded – for example, in the electricity supply industry (Colling 1991), shipbuilding (McKinlay and Taylor 1994) and the water industry (Ogden 1994). The rationale was the need to become more efficient in newly competitive markets (Pendleton and Winterton 1993). However, Ferner and Colling (1991) use the case of the gas industry to deny that privatisation is inevitably linked to harder-line management. The privatised companies did not always continue the hardline policies of the state sector. Quality of service and investor confidence were more important priorities in some privatised sectors than shows of political strength. In some cases privatisation even enhanced union influence. In a study of three privatised utilities – telecommunications, gas and water – Fairbrother (1994) outlines two possible trade union responses: adaptation within traditional forms, or a 'process of renewal, broadening their bases of union concern and activity' (ibid. p.339).

In his view, the latter response in particular invariably results in more representative and participative forms of trade unionism.

In privatised industries as a whole, the pattern is unlikely to be uniform across sectors and regions. In mining, such variation is even more predictable because of differences in ownership and control, exposure to different product markets, variations in managerial styles, distinctive local trade union history and each colliery's particular experience of the transition from nationalisation to privatisation.

The range of collieries included in our study (table 6.1) was chosen to explore such potential variations: a management buy-out, a private-sector consortium supported by labour movement organisations, and four collieries belonging to RJB Mining. Of the four RJB mines, Rossington was reopened on a lease-and-licence basis and its workforce re-employed on different terms and conditions.[2] At Harworth the Union of Democratic Mineworkers (UDM) had sole recognition rights, the other three being dominated by the National Union of Mineworkers (NUM). Kellingley remained open in the transition to privatisation, whereas Maltby was reduced to development-only status. The management buy-out of the Betws colliery in Wales involved reopening a closed mine. Another privatised colliery, the worker take-over at Tower in South Wales, was also included in this study but will be discussed separately in the next chapter.

At each colliery we intended to interview representatives of mine management, the main trade unions (i.e. NUM or UDM and National Association of Colliery Overmen, Deputies and Shotfirers [NACODS]) and a minimum of three surface and three underground workers from each pit, encountered in the pit canteen during shift interchanges. This was mostly achieved except at Betws (see table 6.1). Key informants from a range of relevant institutions were also interviewed: RJB's head of mining, the NACODS general secretary, the UDM national president, and from the NUM the national vice-president and area general secretaries for Nottinghamshire and South Wales. We discuss in turn the immediate prelude to privatisation, aspects of industrial relations at all four RJB pits, then the same issues at Longannet and Betws separately.

The Prelude to Privatisation: Resistance and Accommodation

In the three years before privatisation in January 1995 potential buyers and trade unions manoeuvred for position. UDM reaction was to seek private-sector funding to enable them to buy their own pits. Following unproductive attempts to forge commercial partnerships with a local electricity distributor and American deep-mine corporation, the UDM eventually found a partner in Coal Investments Limited, owned by Malcolm Edwards, a former commercial director of British Coal. Rejected by the Government in the main bid the company picked up six pits under lease and licence between 1992 and 1994.

TABLE 6.1 FEATURED COLLIERIES AND INTERVIEW RESPONDENTS

Colliery	Operator	Majority union	Interviews	Core employees (approx.)	Contract workers (approx.)	Features
Harworth	RJB Mining	UDM	18	490	380	Core pit – 'seamless' transition
Kellingley	RJB Mining	NUM	10	450	200	Core pit – 'seamless' transition
Maltby	RJB Mining	NUM	11	100	700	Core pit – 'difficult' transition
Rossington	RJB Mining	NUM	10	300	0	Closed, then lease and licence
Longannet	Mining (Scotland)	NUM	10	750	250	New company with TUC, NUM and worker involvement
Betws	Betws Anthracite	NUM	4	114	0	Closed, then management buy-out

Note: At all collieries, interviews were conducted with representatives of the majority union (NUM or UDM). NACODS officials were also interviewed at all pits, except for Betws, Rossington and Longannet. At the last-mentioned colliery, interviews were obtained with representatives of SCEBTA (Scottish Colliery Enginemen, Boiler-firemen and Tradesmen's Association) and COSA (Colliery Overmen and Staff Association). With the exception of the Betws colliery manager, Harworth's personnel manager and RJB Mining's head of mining, we were not permitted to interview management representatives.

By contrast, the NUM continued to advocate industrial action to oppose privatisation. At its annual conference in 1992 NUM delegates voted unanimously to reaffirm their opposition to privatisation by multinationals, management buy-outs, or worker co-operatives on the grounds that each would erode safety standards, wage rates and conditions of employment (National Union of Mineworkers 1992a). The NUM's national president Arthur Scargill condemned co-operatives for their 'disastrous results' unable to operate in 'a hostile capitalist environment' (National Union of Mineworkers 1992b, pp.9–10). There was some dissent within the union. In advocating a worker buy-out at Thurcroft, in Rotherham, that pit's former NUM delegate argued at the conference that:

> If it is better for Rio Tinto Zinc or Hanson or Cons Gold or Anglo American to own Thurcroft Colliery, tell me and I will go and ask them tomorrow if they want to but, at this moment in time, I thought it would be a better idea if the workforce had more control. (National Union of Mineworkers 1992a, pp.22–4)

Elsewhere, NUM branches at collieries surviving only on a care and maintenance basis were talking to potential buyers, like RJB Mining and Coal Investments, who were keen to obtain former BC mines under lease and licence. Branch officials at Markham Main and Rossington, interviewed in the autumn of 1993, endorsed the sentiments of an official at Trentham near Stoke-on-Trent:

> We are there to represent our members but the bottom line is we cannot represent our members by simply saying the pit should stop in the public sector – and bump! The shafts are gone.

All had talked at length to representatives of RJB Mining and Coal Investments. At Trentham, there was a preference for the pit to be taken over by Coal Investments because of Malcolm Edwards's superior knowledge of the markets. By contrast, the Armthorpe and Rossington respondents objected to Edwards's prerequisite that ex-miners take out shares in any new company to demonstrate their commitment to potential financial backers. Doncaster officials were more impressed by Richard Budge's more traditional attitude to trade unions:

> He had no objections to the NUM or UDM. He felt it was better to have unions who he could negotiate with on behalf of the workforce, rather than potential problems all the time. I think he'd been up front with us and we hadn't got this problem of share ownership schemes. (Rossington NUM official)

In the event, Rossington went to RJB Mining and Markham Main and Trentham to Coal Investments. Miners had done little to affect the outcome but this was not the case elsewhere. At Maltby, a South Yorkshire colliery remaining open only for development work following the publication of the Heseltine pit-closure list, a hundred NUM members resisted management's attempts to persuade or coerce them into taking redundancy, believing that British Coal would otherwise permanently close rather than privatise the mine. At two Welsh pits where miners had vainly tried to prevent closure, attempts were made to reopen them. Betws colliery closed in January 1993 but by April 1994 a management buy-out team, backed by former miners, raised enough capital to reopen the mine on a lease-and-licence basis. Tower colliery, South Wales's only remaining deep coal-mine, had closed in April 1994. The general secretary of the Welsh area NUM had long suspected that preparations were under-way for a lucrative management buy-out:

> *From what I understand, there's belting going in and being stored underground, chocks going in and being stored, machinery which you normally wouldn't get and you are paying for now ... In the event of it being privatised, I would say it wouldn't become a coal mine, it could become a* gold *mine because all the capital expenditure has already been carried out.*
> *(general secretary, Wales Area NUM)*

Consequently, 150 Tower Lodge members each committed £8,000 personally to a proposed worker take-over of the colliery. In the autumn of 1994 the 'Tower Employee Buy-out Team' submitted a successful bid to the Department of Trade and Industry for ownership of the mine.

At the rest of our sample – Longannet, Kellingley and Harworth – production continued through to privatisation. At the latter two, workers again suspected capital investment and workforce reduction to be preparations for a management buy-out. In April 1994 British Coal abandoned its enhanced redundancy scheme. Miners were offered a £6,000 lump sum as an inducement to work weekends and extend the length of shifts from seven and a quarter hours to twelve hours. Kellingley and Maltby were among a minority of Yorkshire pits to reject the deal, while Harworth was among the majority of Nottinghamshire pits accepting it.

The New Year of 1995 dawned with a coal industry in private hands (see table 6.2). In England, RJB Mining now operated twenty of the best collieries and added a significant part of British Coal opencast sites to its own operations. Coal Investments owned a handful of pits previously closed by British Coal that required significant development. Hatfield colliery in South Yorkshire continued under a management buy-out. In Scotland, Mining (Scotland) operated just one deep mine with a sizeable number of large opencast sites. Monktonhall struggled on, first as a mineworkers' consortium then as a more conventional company. In Wales, all the significant opencast sites were taken over by Celtic Energy. Betws was now run by a management team and the small mine at Cwmgwilli also went to Coal Investments. The last remaining deep mine of any size, Tower colliery, was taken over by its workforce.

TABLE 6.2 COLLIERIES WHEN PRIVATISED, JANUARY 1995

Area/mine	Operator	Additional information
Scotland		
Longannet	Mining (Scotland)	Consortium involving input from Scottish TUC and NUM
Monktonhall	Monktonhall Mineworkers	Worker take-over bought out by Waverley Mining; closed 1997
North-East		
Ellington	RJB Mining	Lease and licence
Blenkinsopp	RJB Mining	Former private small mine
Yorkshire		
Kellingley	RJB Mining	
Prince of Wales	RJB Mining	
North Selby	RJB Mining	Merged with Stillingfleet
Riccall	RJB Mining	
Stillingfleet	RJB Mining	
Whitemoor	RJB Mining	Merged with Riccall
Wistow	RJB Mining	
Maltby	RJB Mining	
Thorne	RJB Mining	Mothballed
Rossington	RJB Mining	Lease and licence
Hatfield	Hatfield Coal	Management buy-out
Markham Main	Coal Investments	No buyer found after Coal Investments collapse; closed 1996
East Midlands		
Asfordby	RJB Mining	Newest mine but major geological problems; closed 1997
Bilsthorpe	RJB Mining	Closed 1997
Harworth	RJB Mining	
Thoresby	RJB Mining	
Welbeck	RJB Mining	
Calverton	RJB Mining	Lease and licence; closed 1999
Clipstone	RJB Mining	Lease and licence
Annesly/Bentinck	Coal Investments	Taken over by Midland Mining 1996; closed 1999
West Midlands		
Daw Mill	RJB Mining	
Coventry	Coal Investments	Closed after Coal Investments collapse 1996
Hem Heath (formerly Trentham)†	Coal Investments	Closed after Coal Investments collapse 1996
Silverdale	Coal Investments	Taken over by Midland Mining 1996; closed 1999
Wales		
Point of Ayr	RJB Mining	North Wales; closed 1996
Tower	Tower Goitre Anthracite	Worker take-over
Betws	Betws Anthracite	Management buy-out
Cwmgwilli	Coal Investments	Small mine – care and maintenance only after Coal Investments collapse 1996, then closed

† Trentham was renamed when taken over by Coal Investments.

Privatisation Under RJB Mining

In the first year of operation RJB Mining reported pre-tax profits of £173 million. This success was nearly marred by an all-out strike by its NUM members. In February 1995 Richard Budge wrote to his employees, asking for their agreement to a three-year wage freeze until 31 March 1998 because coal sales to power stations were likely to fall over the next three years (*Financial Times* 20 February 1995). Three months later 83 per cent of the NUM vote favoured strike action in support of a basic pay-rise. The company took out an injunction against the NUM because it had exceeded the 28 days by which action must have taken place following a ballot. Nevertheless, RJB Mining took the threatened action seriously. Immediately after the injunction the men received a £250 one-off compensation payment for bonuses lost during holidays. RJB then conceded a 3.2 per cent across-the-board pay-rise. In a second ballot of NUM members in February 1996, 65 per cent voted against strike action on pay. The NUM had forced RJB Mining's hands on wages but had not achieved its more important long-term goal of securing negotiating rights. The subtlety of RJB's approach was also evident in its industrial relations practices: the dominant management style, working practices, technology, pay and conditions, employee participation, health and safety and relationships with unions.

Management Style

All our respondents commented on the open and direct communicative style of RJB management. The company's head of mining explained their approach as follows:

> *Richard and I visited every single colliery in the first few weeks. We went out and met them, and got a good feel for what was happening, and said, 'Here we are: we are open, we are honest; what we tell you, you can believe. If you have any problems or complaints, get in touch with us.' People have phoned Richard and got straight through and had their problems answered ... So we tried to create an atmosphere of trust to get away from the rather macho-style of management that existed in certain parts of British Coal.*

At all four pits, miners commented on the chief executive's good-natured, easy-going style, his acceptance and speedy resolution of specific grievances:

> *It's a lot better place to work, now. It's the way management are with you, the way they talk to you. Before, they used to talk to you like dirt, whereas now, it's a, 'Good morning, how are you going on?'... When he first took over we thought, 'Well, he'll give us a couple of months and treat us right and then he'll start coming the upper hand,' but it just hasn't materialised. (Kellingley miner)*

Working Practices

After privatisation RJB Mining maintained existing working practices. Legally, they were constrained by the Transfer of Undertakings (Protection of Employment) Regulations 1981 (TUPE),[3] which protects the jobs and conditions of employers when companies change hands, but this was not the main motivation:

> *The people we took on 31 December 1994 were quite well traumatised, but believed that they had survived the holocaust and were looking for some stability and we determined that there should be as seamless a transition as there possibly could and we set out our stall to do that. (head of mining, RJB Mining)*

The emphasis on multi-skilling, first promoted by British Coal, was continued above and below ground. Any given surface worker might find himself alternating between jobs in the medical centre, baths or lamp room, or else driving a fork-lift machine: 'Well, it started about three or four years ago. Keeping the machines running: it all affects your bonus. If you break down, you don't get paid anyway [so] the fitter and electrician help out' (Kellingley miner).

The £6,000 deal requiring workers to perform more flexible hours had caused few problems at our sample of pits, though sharp practices were cited at Selby where employees were alleged to be routinely working flexible shift patterns: 'I've got a lot of mates there. They are trying it on: they are doing different shifts, bringing them on at all different times to cover all the way round without having to pay them overtime' (Kellingley miner).

Unlike British Coal, RJB Mining was committed to reducing reliance on contract workers. During our visit to Harworth, contractors were being paid off in order to accommodate transferees from RJB Mining's Bilsthorpe operation. The company claimed that contractors constituted 47 per cent of the underground workforce in 1995, though as table 6.1 shows, the proportion varied between pits.[4]

Technology

Little technological change had occurred at any of our pits. RJB Mining inherited British Coal's investment in proven, highly mechanised mining systems. Union leaders had serious doubts about roof-bolting techniques but miners welcomed its potential to speed things up in pursuit of higher bonuses: 'Everything is geared up now to get coal. In the headings where everything used to be steel, now we have roof bolts which are lighter and cheaper and we can go faster' (Kellingley NACODS official).

Payment Systems

Bonuses were central to RJB's incentive strategy and delivered tangible benefits to workers: 'Our basic wage has just gone up by about £4, that's all – and that's the first pay rise that we've had in seven years! But our bonus has never been as good for as long. We never had a consistently high bonus before' (Kellingley miner).

At Rossington, a lease-and-licence pit where miners were re-employed on different terms and conditions, earnings were less impressive. Standard shifts were increased from seven and a quarter hours to eight hours and miners' incentives were based on monthly targets rather than lineage cut. Miners experienced no reduction in earnings, though bonuses were lower than at other RJB collieries. Sickness entitlements and concessionary coal allowances available at other mines were only agreed after lengthy negotiation.

The high bonus earnings enjoyed by face and development workers caused some divisions. Deputies felt they had been misled about the terms of a quarterly 'efficiency payment', awarded on the basis of every official's work performance in such key areas as safety, and interpersonal and report-writing skills. At Kellingley, deputies had been led to believe that, unless any of them committed a 'serious misdemeanour', the bonus would be rubber-stamped. However, in the first round of assessments, only fourteen of seventy-two received the payment.

Health and Safety

The February 1996 edition of RJB Mining's in-house publication *NewScene* reported that the level of accidents in its first full year of operation was the industry's lowest ever. The rate – 8.79 accidents for every 100,000 manshifts worked – represented a 34 per cent improvement over the last year under British Coal. There had, however, been an increase in the rate of serious accidents, rising from 2.92 per cent to 3.22 per cent annually. Three fatalities occurred in the first year of privatisation, two at RJB Mining's pits in Thoresby (Nottinghamshire) and Kellingley (Yorkshire).

The company's head of mining dispelled the suggestion that safety standards were deteriorating, since government, shareholders, unions and the workforce all expected safety to be a priority. Some men complained that the reporting of accidents was discouraged, especially by contractors, but general opinion confirmed that RJB Mining was enforcing stringent safety standards. Employees received strict reminders to check all equipment before operation as part of the company's commitment to risk assessment procedures:

> *Before you attempt any jobs, it's making you stand back and think about it: look at something, identify all the dangers and then say what you're going to do to stop them happening. I think he [Richard Budge] is very much into training. He's been unfortunate in having the number of fatalities that he's had. I don't see how they wouldn't have happened under British Coal. (Maltby NACODS official)*

The NACODS general secretary suggested that firmer resistance to compensation claims depressed the level of accident reporting, which some men endorsed: 'What it is now, if anything goes wrong, you're to blame. They are trying to get out of paying compensation claims or anything like that. That's what it's mainly about' (Kellingley miner).

For the NUM, roof-bolting remained contentious. In August 1993, seventeen months before privatisation, three men were killed at Bilsthorpe Colliery (Nottinghamshire) in a roof fall. An interim report by the Health and Safety Executive concluded that the cause lay in deficiencies in the roof-bolted support system (*The Guardian*, 25 January 1994). The NUM vice-president felt his members were complacent about roof-bolting techniques:

> *When I speak to branch officials about it, one of the problems they have got is that the men have got used to just sticking roof bolts in. They don't want to set anything else: 'Why do I want to set girders in here? It's all right as it is. This is the fourth face we've had and there's been no problem.' ... I can't support roof-bolting as sole means of support. (NUM national vice-president)*

Employee Ownership and Participation

When RJB Mining took over from British Coal, all employees were given fifty free shares then worth £2.54 each. If opting to buy a further 100 shares for £3.20 outright or on a save-as-you-earn scheme, they received 200 extra free shares. Under new government rules on profit-related pay schemes, employees were to be awarded a further £500 worth of shares as part of the wage deal of March 1996. The company intended employees to own up to 10 per cent of shares.

Only at the UDM colliery were there any signs of greater employee commitment being generated by the scheme:

> *I think the workforce have got a different approach as regards being shareholders, because the amount of men that you hear talking, 'Oh, the shares have gone up.' So they're keeping an eye on it. It's created an interest, summat else to talk about. (Harworth UDM branch official)*

Elsewhere, the share option was regarded as a good financial deal not requiring identification with the company:

> *Your money does not go to RJB Mining, it goes to the Halifax Building Society in an account in your name. Any time you wish to stop it you just draw your money out. If, at the end of the day, he goes bankrupt, the Halifax Building Society has got your money, not him. At the end of five years, you have got a choice: either buy shares or not buy shares. It is actually a decent offer to make some money. (Maltby NUM branch official)*

Nevertheless, most respondents appreciated the more settled and co-operative atmosphere than the one experienced under British Coal, partly because political interference had ceased: 'The problem before was that we were used as a political football. But it's a business now and, to be quite honest, we are all fed up with it. We don't want any hassle' (Kellingley miner).

Union–Management Relations

Whatever was said before privatisation afterwards RJB Mining had a clear intention to exclude trade unions from all but the local level:

When it comes to communicating with the workforce, we do it directly ... We don't recognise the trade unions for the purpose of negotiation and I think that is clearly understood by everybody now. They are not happy with it. What we have said is that we will discuss any proposals we have with them ... We are more than happy to consult with them, communicate with them, but as I have said in the past, if we go to consult trade unions on something, that doesn't necessarily mean we are looking for their consent. As an employer, I don't need their consent to do anything, but I would like to have their understanding. I don't need their permission, but understanding, yes, I would like that. (head of mining, RJB Mining)

The company saw three functions for its trade unions: to educate their members on such everyday issues as safety, to lobby politically on the coal industry's behalf, and provide representation for employees within the company's grievance procedure.

Accordingly, there were no formal consultation or conciliation agreements with unions except for six-monthly safety meetings with the NUM and UDM separately. NUM national officers were excluded from even informal consultation. The UDM national president emphasised that RJB Mining were prepared to consult him only when it suited them:

What he don't agree to is collective bargaining. Although, when he's been prepared to offer or give wage increases he's always had a meeting with me and said: 'What do you think about it?' without actually negotiating. (UDM national president)

Branch officials appreciated a new system where problems could be speedily resolved at a local level but they were aware that the unions were being excluded:

I mean, as an individual workman, I can go and see the manager more or less any time I like, but in my capacity as a union representative, it's a different matter. I mean, at the end of the day, we've had to work hard at getting into a majority situation with the workforce, because [management] could always sit back and say, 'Well, you don't represent anybody here, anyway.' (Rossington NUM branch official)

Increasingly, unions operated with a workforce divided by whether they had ever accepted redundancy payments, currently enjoyed large bonuses or were working for contractors. Individualism was replacing collectivism:

I'll be honest, if you're on over £100 a shift and you were on nothing eighteen months ago and you're working, the feeling among some is, 'Look after Number One, now.' (Maltby NUM branch official)

The biggest problem for the unions appeared to be the growing indifference of their members. Even at their own pits NUM membership rarely exceeded 50 per cent. Respondents agreed it would take an especially controversial turn of events (e.g. the imposition of longer hours, a wage cut or the curtailment of bonus payments) to provoke industrial action. In the spring of 2000 Rossington miners imposed an overtime ban for over three months demanding improvements in bonus payments. The dispute remained localised because Rossington was on a different payments system from other Yorkshire pits.

Privatisation Under Independent Ownership

We discuss similar issues at the two independent collieries separately.

Longannet Mining (Scotland)

At Longannet, which continued operating during the transition to privatisation, there were no significant changes in coal-cutting methods and techniques. All workers had been awarded a basic pay-rise of 3.5 per cent and bonus payments were the equivalent of RJB Mining's. A share option scheme operated, though by union estimations only around a quarter of the workforce had subscribed to it. Members of COSA (Colliery Overmen and Staff Association – an affiliated body of the NUM) had accepted the £6,000 flexibility offer because it guaranteed their superannuation entitlements at age 50.

Greater flexibility in working practices had occurred since privatisation. The company's determination to depress production costs required a restructuring of the workforce and the adoption of a less compromising style of management. During the first year of trading management had asked for and obtained fifty voluntary redundancies as part of a cost-cutting drive. On the day of our visit (22 April 1996) branch officers returned from a meeting where the company had requested seventy further redundancies. Contractors supplied a quarter of the total workforce of a thousand.

The NUM was recognised at all bargaining levels (local, area and national). Union officials welcomed the opportunity to approach line managers directly: 'I mean we can go and speak to them, it's an open door policy. We feel from the trade union point of view that it's alleviated a lot of problems. It's alleviated a lot of nonsensical walk-outs' (Longannet NUM branch official).

Safety concerns had been re-established:

It's become more of a concern. Speaking truthfully, there's more involvement from management, more involvement from the government inspector ... There's a lot of education, a lot of teach-ins. The likes of risk assessment involves not only officials but the general workforce. So I think there has been a good emphasis put on the question of safety, from the trade union side as well as the management side. (Longannet NUM branch official)

However, management style was seen to be hardening. Despite the fact that the company was formed with support from the Scottish TUC and the Scottish Area NUM, and that one worker-director was always present at board meetings, managers were seen as less inclined to act on employees' suggestions or routinely consult the workforce:

We have come to this position now where I can see traits of the old British Coal in this company. They tend to do a lot of things now without consulting us. I think they just tolerate us, just put up with you because you're there. (Longannet SCEBTA official) [5]

Betws

At Betws, dramatic changes had occurred in the management and operation of the mine, with a reversion to old-fashioned, hand-got pillar and stall techniques. The increased dangers of such methods were offset by a clear management commitment to safety and the offering of inducements to employees:

We report the accidents and we pay the men here a safety bonus: if there are no accidents or reportable injuries in a month, I think everybody gets on average about £35. It raises awareness; if anybody has an accident, he is made to feel bad because he's cost everybody their bonus and that is right enough. (Betws manager)

The company also had an unorthodox wage structure. A weekly production target was set but a standard weekly wage plus a pre-determined bonus was paid, whether or not the target was met. If production exceeded the weekly target the surplus went into a 'pool', used to supplement weeks when production fell short. If this was insufficient an extended shift had to be worked:

If I add into the pool more frequently than I subtract from it, the pool will grow and, when it grows to a certain figure, they get a share out of extra money at the end of the month. If they take out from the pool more frequently than they add to it, the pool starts to shrink and, when it shrinks to a given level, or the overdraft disappears, then I invoke the extended shift ... which is very unpopular. (Betws manager)

Although the manager had advised his employees to join a trade union – principally for the legal protection – in practice there was only partial recognition:

We recognise both the NUM and NACODS but only at the local level. It's too risky for me to recognise them at area or senior level. Both of them come and negotiate – no 'negotiate' is the wrong word. We don't negotiate here. We meet every Wednesday like clockwork to discuss any issue and the boys are kept up to date on how the business is doing.

The tough line was accepted because it was seen to be in everybody's interests:

The manager is tough: straight talking but his word is good. There's 114 men here and what we are looking for is employment for as many years as we can, and sometimes he has got to take tough decisions we don't like. But at the end of the day, if we are below tonnage, you know you have to work that extra hour to get the tonnage back up. We are a team effort and it's the only way we can operate and be successful. (Betws NUM branch official)

General Discussion

The process of trade union marginalisation, achieved by British Coal, had been continued in the newly privatised mining industry. 'Partial exclusion policies' included talking to employees 'over the heads' of their union, promoting a share option scheme to encourage greater identification with the company, and deliberately ensuring that directors and managers were more responsive and approachable than their British Coal predecessors.

RJB Mining only dealt with unions at a local level. The company was prepared to *consult* the major unions – but only to foster understanding, not to elicit consent. Basic pay-rises, share options and bonus schemes discouraged union militancy. Innovations in working practices were claimed to involve no diminution in safety standards, though disincentives to report accidents may have disguised the real rate.

Trade union power within RJB Mining had now been nullified: senior NUM officials were debarred from entering RJB mines and the UDM national president was consulted only by occasional invitation. Management maintained that the unions' role should be limited to education, lobbying and representation of grievances. RJB Mining had maintained the schism between the NUM and UDM by granting recognition only to the union demonstrating majority membership at branch level. The workforce was internally divided by conditions of employment.

In carrying out such policies RJB Mining enjoyed two important advantages. First, its management style compared favourably with that of British Coal. Second, it had the luxury of captive markets for its coal. Huge profits were being achieved without prior investment and development:

I mean, he had all the interest charges wiped out, which meant he could sell coal for £5–6 a tonne cheaper without doing anything. Everything was gotten ready for him: all the headings and machinery were in place just to get going and make some money. (NUM Nottinghamshire area secretary)

In such a context, further reform of industrial relations was not expedient. The fragmentation of ownership in the privatised industry further marginalised the unions. Employees of different owners were now competitors rather than colleagues. At Longannet and Betws managers who were, in principle, more supportive of trade union activity none the less strove to limit their influence.

Across the privatised mining industry as a whole there was little prima-facie evidence to support Fairbrother's suggestion that privatisation can encourage the development of more participatory forms of trade unionism. At Longannet, and all the RJB Mining's collieries except Rossington, local union officials enjoyed greater autonomy and a newfound capacity to achieve immediate results. However, this was a precarious position of influence, subject to the informal goodwill of local management and the vagaries of market forces, exemplified by the uncertainty surrounding RJB Mining's relationship to the power generators.

The conclusions of our research have been largely confirmed by another recent study. Using a research design similar to ours, Wallis (2000) presents case studies of seven recently privatised collieries. Four of these ('Nottston' and 'Mansthorpe' from Nottinghamshire, and 'Donborough' and 'Dearnley' from Yorkshire) are owned by RJB Mining, given the pseudonym of Coal UK (CUK). Two others, 'Workham' (Nottinghamshire) and 'Abergoed' (South Wales), are management buy-outs. The last, 'Cwmpridd' (South Wales), is a co-operative venture.

There is a considerable degree of overlap in the focus, findings and conclusions of this study and our own. Wallis generally endorses our main argument that RJB Mining ('CUK') has continued the process of trade union marginalisation begun by British Coal. She concludes that the company has taken 'a more robust approach' in its dealings with the trade unions at collieries unprotected by TUPE, 'where the legal framework has restricted managerial objectives to a lesser degree' (ibid., p.201).

Wallis agrees that at 'Abergoed' (actually, Betws), 'managerial prerogative' was asserted most decisively, with the union role having been relegated to that of the manager's 'mouthpiece'. Management respondents freely acknowledged their view that the unions' role should be confined to communication and representation.

Her inclusion of 'Workham' colliery, a Nottinghamshire mine acquired by 'English Mining' (actually, Midland Mining) in 1996 following the collapse of Coal Investments, provides a more extreme case than any we encountered. Here more than anywhere else was to be found a management who 'sought not only to consolidate those patterns of industrial relations developed by British Coal between 1984 and 1994, but also to intensify them' (ibid., p.130). The company had withdrawn trade union recognition and refused to co-operate with, or provide facilities for, local branch officials. It had also striven to undermine trade union organisation in other ways. Workers from Yorkshire, who would be disinclined to join the majority UDM, had been recruited. A free accident insurance scheme had also been promoted to usurp one of the main trade union functions.

The assessment by Wallis of health and safety is harsher than our own. She maintains that only Cwmpridd (Tower) had health and safety standards comparable with those of British Coal. This she attributes to the more favourable climate for industrial relations established by worker ownership. Clearly, more evidence is required to clarify this issue.

Wallis takes a contingent approach to explaining variations in industrial practice, emphasising the presence or absence of TUPE legislation as a key determinant of industrial relations at any given colliery. However, she also suggests that variations in the residual solidarity of NUM and UDM branches, resulting from the miners' strike, may also help to account for managerial attitudes. Since Nottinghamshire miners did not directly experience the demoralising effect of the 1984–5 strike defeat, they generally retained a more enhanced 'commitment to solidaristic behaviour' than their Yorkshire and Welsh counterparts. Thus:

> *Management at Workham, Mansthorpe and Nottston may therefore have embraced policies designed to undermine collective organisation, because the position of organised labour at these collieries remained relatively strong. By the same token, because organised labour had already been significantly weakened at Donborough and Abergoed as a result of the defeat of the 1984–85 strike and the post-strike restructuring of industrial relations, management may not have considered it necessary to erode collective organisation at these collieries. (ibid., p.209)*

This is an interesting, though not entirely plausible, piece of speculation. Its central premise, that solidaristic commitment had dissipated outside the UDM heartland, is difficult to sustain when applied to the attitude of, say, the Maltby 'NUM die-hards' referred to in an earlier section.

Wallis is decidedly more sceptical about the possibility of national strike action. She considers that the high proportion of non-unionism within the industry, combined with the ongoing NUM–UDM schism and the fact that RJB Mining utilises such a high complement of contract workers employed by outside companies, makes such a likelihood remote. In any case, local bargaining has taken priority since privatisation; but even here, branch officials know that local industrial action in the climate of economic uncertainty constantly besetting the industry may be seized upon by management as a justification for pit closure. Wallis refers to recent strike action at 'Workham' to substantiate her view that it is the smaller, independent companies that remain most vulnerable to trade union sanctions.

On the basis of our own case studies it seems to us that employees in other smaller companies would not readily follow Workham's example, since they are conscious of the need to guarantee the ongoing viability of their collieries by maintaining output and profitability. Against this, we are persuaded by the arguments of full-time NUM officials that RJB Mining is more vulnerable to sanctions than was British Coal. The privatised coal industry is now more concentrated and capital-intensive than its state predecessor. Stoppages on just one face could rapidly inflict financial damage, and a private company could not expect the Government to finance sustained confrontation as they did with British Coal. The trade union leaders we consulted felt certain that their members' loyalties had not been compromised by the company's share-ownership scheme, and were confident of their capacity to seriously harm the employer through strike action. However, they fully recognised the difficulty involved in unifying a membership which welcomed the respite from confrontation and had been placated by unprecedented earnings.

What is so far indisputable is that the marginalisation of the mining trade unions has run parallel with the run-down of the industry. Key underlying reasons are the catastrophic reduction in the size of the industry and its increasingly precarious future. Such factors have been compounded by the post-strike schism between the NUM and UDM and the political exclusion of their leaders. If there is little evidence from the coal industry to justify Fairbrother's optimism that trade unions can successfully adapt to privatisation, this may well be primarily because the NUM leadership has steadfastly adhered to a traditional trade union view and rejected both adaptation and renewal through a broadening of activity. Despite a drastic reduction in membership, proposals to realign themselves or join up with other unions have long been shelved. The miners' unions are greatly diminished and divided. It remains to be seen whether market pressures on the owners will provoke a resurgence of solidarity.

NOTES

1. Although not considered in detail in this chapter, the opencast sector was an important constituent of privatisation. In 1999–2000, over 40 per cent of UK mined coal came from opencast.

2. 'Lease and licence' refers to a system whereby individual collieries are granted a *licence* to mine specified areas of coal under *lease* (i.e. for a predefined period).

3. Terms and conditions could be changed if the employer gave sufficient notice or gained the consent of the workforce. However, interpretations of this and its European equivalent – the Acquired Rights Directive 1977 – were the source of ongoing legal wrangles in the European Court of Justice (*Financial Times* 26 September 1995).

4. Trade union officials said they were unaware of the extent of union membership among contractors.

5. Scottish Colliery Enginemen, Boiler-firemen and Tradesmen's Association.

7   Worker Take-overs

In the dreary Hills above Hirwaun, where the low clouds meet the moorland mist, the pit-head tower emerges from the post-Christmas gloom like a sepulchre. Tower Colliery is not a ghost from the past of Britain's rich mining history but a vibrant business, a unique example of worker-capitalism reborn ... when 239 miners marched back up the mountain to reclaim as their own the last deep mine in Wales. (Finance section, The Guardian *3 January 1998)*

INTRODUCTION

On 2 January 1995, 239 miners and more than 1,000 supporters and well-wishers gathered at the pit-head to celebrate the revitalisation of a mine closed only eight months earlier as part of British Coal's rationalisation plan. Despite facing seemingly insurmountable obstacles, Tower's former employees had succeeded in their singular attempt to reopen the mine as a worker take-over in the newly privatised British coal industry.

Those playing central roles in the buy-out interpreted its significance differently. A senior representative of the accountancy firm Price-Waterhouse, which had acted as financial advisers to the Tower men, said: 'This whole occasion has a wider dimension; it shows the resurgence of the entrepreneurial spirit in Wales' (*The Guardian* 3 January 1995). Having ceremoniously cut a red ribbon to release 239 red balloons into the air, Ann Clwyd, Labour MP for the Cynon Valley, drew a rather different lesson:

> *Today is better than 1947 when the industry was nationalised. Now it's a people's pit. The miners and the community have shown the way – when you are prepared to fight you can win. (*The Independent *3 January 1995)*

Tyrone O'Sullivan, then NUM lodge secretary and new worker-director of the company, argued that:

> *We've got the knowledge and the will to make Tower profitable and the profits will go back to the community through our wage-packets. We're going to make a success which others might well copy. (ibid.)*

Such optimism has been vindicated. In its first year of operation the worker take-over achieved post-tax profits of over £2 million (*The Independent* 4 December 1995). Since 1995 the enterprise has perennially been in profit and over £6 million has been invested in new equipment. An extra fifty-seven workers have been recruited. Annual turnover of £18 million in 1995 had increased to £24 million by 2000. As befits a latter-day fairy-tale the Tower story had already been transformed into an opera, with plans to make it the basis of a £6 million feature film (Weekend Magazine, *Financial Times* 22 July 2000).

Tower's success contrasts markedly with other attempted worker take-overs in the mining industry – at Monktonhall, in the Lothian region of Scotland, and at Thurcroft in Rotherham, South Yorkshire. In 1992 workers at Monktonhall also succeeded in reopening a disused mine, only for it soon to experience financial difficulties, necessitating an eventual rescue by a 'conventional' company before its final closure in 1997. The Rotherham initiative, instigated by representatives of the local metropolitan borough council and ex-Thurcroft miners, was thwarted by British Coal's decision to cease paying the care and maintenance costs of the pit while negotiations were in progress. Worker-shareholders decided it would be too risky to pay for the continued upkeep of the pit themselves without any guarantee that they would be awarded the lease and licence to run the mine.

All three initiatives contradicted the official policy of the National Union of Mineworkers. Nevertheless, as the Conservative Government's pit-closure programme of the 1990s paved the way for privatisation NUM branches sought means of protecting or salvaging their jobs as an alternative to the apparently futile strategy of direct industrial action advocated by their national leaders. The attempted worker take-overs of Monktonhall, Thurcroft and Tower offered such an alternative.

This chapter reviews the three examples in order to examine which factors affected the very different outcomes and the extent to which each found a balance between political ideals and economic realities. We have used both secondary and primary data. Secondary data included a wide range of documentation: minutes of meetings, reports and informal correspondence, and media coverage. Primary data was obtained by a series of in-depth, semi-structured interviews with worker-shareholders and directors, non-shareholder ex-miners, and other key informants such as trade union officials, local government officers and professional advisors. Twenty interviews were carried out at Thurcroft in the autumn of 1992, twenty-three at Monktonhall in May 1993, and seventeen at Tower, mainly in January 1994. A few follow-up interviews were conducted at Monktonhall in 1995 and 1996. Categories and numbers of respondents are detailed in table 7.1.

We begin our overall argument by addressing the relevant literature on worker take-overs (WTOs). Its objectives are to provide a working definition of WTOs, outline the key factors generally considered relevant to their chances of survival and prosperity, and establish a basis for assessing them in terms of social ideals of ownership rather than economic indicators of performance. A presentation of our comparative cases then follows, outlining the key developments and analysing variables responsible for commercial success or failure. We also assess the political principles of each and how these were converted into practice. We end with a specification of the conditions most favourable to a successful worker take-over of a mine.

TABLE 7.1 INTERVIEW RESPONDENTS BY CATEGORY

Respondents	Thurcroft	Monktonhall	Tower
Participant ex-miners	5	9	12*
Non-participant ex-miners	5	6	–
NUM officials	4	2	3
Company directors	3	2	2**
Management	–	2	–
Local authority officials	1	3	–
Professional advisors	2	–	–
Total	**20**	**24**	**17**

Key:
* = includes one canteen worker and two outside contractors.
** = directors, also management.

Worker Take-overs: Definitions and Principles

A Working Definition

We adopt Paton's (1989, p.16) definition of a worker take-over as 'a case in which a business is continued, or created, on the basis of the assets of an endangered or bankrupt enterprise, by the workforce, or part of it' – either within a co-operative structure, or within an ownership framework which ensures that 'ultimate control resides with the workforce'. Paton distinguishes three contrasting contexts in which WTOs occur:

- *conversions*, which take place when a conventional business is still viably trading;
- *rescues*, which arise when the enterprise is in crisis but has not ceased operating; and
- *phoenixes*, which involve a marked interruption in production and trading.

Other discussions of WTOs have examined reasons for their success or failure.

Factors Contributing to the Success or Failure of WTOs

Analyses of WTO success and failure have been undertaken by North American researchers, e.g. Stern and Hammer (1978) and Gunderson et al. (1995), and British authors like Bate and Carter (1986), Cornforth (1983) and Paton himself. European studies include some in Austria (Wieser et al. 1997) and Turkey (Yildirim 1999).

Based on a study of six attempted employee buy-outs (four successes and two failures), Stern and Hammer highlight the particular influence of two categories of primary determinant:

Parties to the bargain recognises the importance of two factors:

(a) 'entrepreneurial and managerial leadership', which refers to the crucial political, organisational and representative activities undertaken by individuals at the preliminary stage of the buy-out; and (b) 'the parent company response', which concerns the extent to which current owners perceive their interests to lie in negotiation with its former employees.

Political, social and economic resources incorporates:

(a) the extent of institutional support available from such agencies as the relevant trade union(s), financiers, government departments or 'free professionals' (e.g. sympathetic lawyers or accountants); (b) the degree of 'environmental pressure' from political lobbying, media publicity and community fund-raising; and (c) the likelihood that the new firm will be able to achieve or maintain commercial competitiveness.

Gunderson et al. (1995) endorse the significance of strong and credible leadership and the availability of adequate expertise. They also emphasise how the support of all the relevant actors – employees and union, parent company, government, current debt-holders, financiers, and the local community – is an essential ingredient of a successful take-over. Ideally, all parties should stand to gain from the venture.

The importance of such variables is emphasised by Yildirim's (1999) study of an employee buy-out of a state-owned Turkish steel mill which had been shut down in 1994. Fundamental to the re-opening of this loss-making operation, whose closure cost 6,000 jobs in a region otherwise devoid of re-employment possibilities, was a determined seven-month campaign. Instigated by the steelworkers' union and local community the campaign was supported by the mayor, chamber of commerce and local politicians. A series of well-attended mass demonstrations and marches eventually 'embarrassed the government into making a sympathetic response and brought the plight of the workers and community to the public's attention' (ibid., p.567). In any case, selling the mill back to its former employees was seen as one of the best political options available to the Turkish Government. Union officials enlisted the support of academics and managers to draw up a purchase plan which won financial backing from the local chamber of industry and commerce and the Shopkeepers' and Artisans' Association.

Local political and practical support are clearly crucial factors. However, Gunderson et al. further stipulate that any proposed restructuring under employee ownership 'must involve *real change, not just cosmetic modifications*' (ibid. p.428, their emphasis). External support is more likely to be volunteered where employees can pinpoint concessions over wages or jobs, alongside proposed changes in (say) supervision or training as evidence of the new company's enhanced viability. Finally, it is imperative that the take-over group has adequate time in which to plan and prepare its bid.

Paton (1989, pp.44–5) contends that both the immediate and long-term success of any WTO may depend on whether the enterprise was acquired as a conversion, rescue or phoenix strategy. He limits his discussion to the rescue and phoenix strategies. The rescue strategy has the advantages of maintaining existing customers and retaining key workers. Disadvantages include time constraints on business appraisal, jeopardising redundancy entitlements and the high price of current assets. The phoenix strategy has the advantages of more time to plan, cheaper purchase of assets and a workforce committed to the enterprise. Disadvantages include loss of jobs, waning custom and key workers drifting away. How an enterprise is acquired affects its long-term viability. Three influential factors are identified: 'the efforts of a cohesive homogeneous group of skilled workers'; leadership by an individual or group 'which is competently committed to both social and commercial objectives and which can balance short- and long-term considerations'; and effective external support, especially from other WTOs (ibid., p.125).

Bate and Carter (1986, pp.60–1) attribute the success or failure of co-operatives to the presence or absence of key 'internal' or 'external' conditions, where:

> *Internal factors include: levels of conflict; discipline; worker commitment, motivation and satisfaction; flexibility; and skill levels. External conditions, in addition to the availability of a support structure, relate to the security of the market, the appropriateness of the product, competitiveness, and the existence of discrimination (positive or negative) towards the co-operative.*

The need for flexibility, adaptability and innovation are stressed by Yildirim (1999). In the Turkish steel mill, the relaxation of job demarcation made a vital contribution to improved productivity and profitability. Even more importantly, the mainly engineering experience of existing managers was quickly supplemented by new managers with marketing and financial expertise. The plant had previously operated a highly centralised system of decision-making, replaced by an emphasis on local autonomy, transforming the plant's 'operational culture' from that of 'subservience and passivity' to one of 'innovation and creativity' (Yildirim 1999, p.570).

In a study of twenty-two management or employee buy-outs recently occurring in Austria, Wieser et al. (1997) emphasise the relationship between commercial effectiveness and a greater flexibility of decision-making, which enables restructured companies to explore and develop new markets. However, despite the fact three-quarters of the companies achieved increases in turnover and productivity almost all admitted to serious financial concerns. This had occurred because the buy-outs were operating in the 'lower performing' stratum of the Austrian economy.

In a comprehensive review of these and other relevant variables, Cornforth (1983) confirms Wieser et al.'s point that a principal reason why many co-operatives fail to survive is that they are often established in adverse commercial conditions, involving industrial decline, cut-throat competition, and recent histories of poor management or investment. Doomed co-operatives are further characterised by inappropriate management skills, under-capitalisation and under-investment and inadequate training. The prioritising of social objectives, such as maximising jobs, can inhibit commercial strategy. Generally, a co-operative benefits from the advice and assistance of co-operative development agencies for feasibility studies, initial management support and the facilitation of loan arrangements.

Alternative Criteria for Evaluating WTOs

The effectiveness of WTOs can be measured according to such objective yardsticks as productive efficiency and profitability. However, as Mellor et al. point out, a commitment to 'maximising quantity and quality at the lowest price' is often incompatible with co-operative objectives: 'Many are in business precisely because they do not want to exploit other workers and natural resources' (1988, p.109). The performance of worker take-overs can be assessed against such social and idealistic criteria.

Interviews with co-operative employees by Cornforth et al. (1988) emphasise how workers' evaluations of their own enterprises dwell on precisely these types of criteria, such as: the opportunity to work alongside socially and politically compatible colleagues; pride in owning the company and working for themselves; having control and discretion over their work; egalitarian working and commercial practices; and imparting knowledge and values to the wider community. Negative evaluations cited the company's failure to adhere to its underlying ideals; low pay; the stress of involvement in decision-making; the requirement to monitor under-performing colleagues; and sheer physical and mental fatigue.

Such evaluations echo trade union and labour movement critiques of WTOs. On the one hand, they are seen as serving such important functions as: helping to oppose closures and protect jobs; enhancing industrial democracy and challenging managerial prerogatives; promoting work reform; and extending the influence of the labour movement in the small business sector. Alleged deficiencies are that they: distract workers from the class struggle and encourage collaboration with opposing interest groups; absolve government of its responsibility to retrain employees; undermine opposition to privatisation; fragment union power and reduce bargaining strength; involve financial risk to workers; entail collaboration in job losses; violate trade union principles concerning craft skills and demarcation; induce tendencies towards self-exploitation by the workers; reduce safety; and encourage low wages and poor terms and conditions (Paton 1989, pp.128–34).

Two concepts are crucial in this critique. The first, the *degeneration thesis* (cf. Cornforth et al. 1988), asserts that, regardless of their original ideals and socialist aspirations, workers will be forced by market imperatives to adopt a progressively more capitalist style of managing their enterprise (e.g. hiring non-owner employees and devolving full control to managers). The second, *sweat equity* (Thomas 1988, p.309), refers to unpaid overtime or very low wage rates deemed necessary to remain competitive. Partial support for this position is provided by Yildirim's study of the Turkish steel mill. Despite undoubted improvements in safety and perceived job security a clear majority of employees (over 70 per cent) claimed that they were working much harder now than they had worked before. They distrusted the union as inseparable from management, condemning it for approving redundancies caused by new technologies. Most of all, they objected to below-average wages.

Cornforth et al. (1988, p.4) do not regard the dilemmas of WTOs as insoluble: 'While economic forces are an important constraint they do not completely determine the organisation and management of an enterprise or the goals that it pursues'. This argument is validated by Pendleton et al.'s (1995) study of the impact of employee ownership on trade unions and collective bargaining in the passenger transport industry. Research on thirteen employee-owned and twenty-six conventional bus firms demonstrated that there typically existed 'a complementary rather than competitive relationship between new forms of representation and prior existing union structures' (ibid., p.598). The union's role was often expanded and strengthened. Trade union and management representatives followed through a commitment to representative and participative structures which protected their traditional roles and functions (ibid., p.601). This is entirely consistent with Cornforth et al.'s assertion that, 'A new position is required which does not regard democracy within co-operatives as either impossible or inevitable, but instead as subject to *choice* and *restraint*' (1988, p.4, emphasis in original).

Such analyses provide a conceptual perspective for our three case studies.

Case study 1: Monktonhall

Overview

Monktonhall started production in 1965. It is located next to Danderhall, a small village in East Lothian, fifteen minutes' drive from Edinburgh. Only a minority of the workforce have ever lived locally. Despite the pit's modern infrastructure, its huge reserves and apparently competitive production costs of £36 per tonne (1,000 kilos) it last made a profit in 1982. After the 1984–5 strike British Coal planned drastic reductions in its 'peripheral' coalfields of Scotland and South Wales. In 1986 the majority of Monktonhall employees were made redundant and less than a third re-employed as private contractors.

The workforce was reduced from 1,141 to 267, face production ceased and the pit continued on a 'development-only' basis. The Scottish Area of the NUM had the option of placing the pit in the Modified Colliery Review Procedure. Since no pit had ever survived a review (cf. Beynon et al. 1991) they argued for it to be mothballed, anticipating a Labour victory at the imminent general election. With no remaining pits in the Lothians Monktonhall had become the natural water sump for a large geological area. Despite the excessive pumping and other care and maintenance costs British Coal agreed to mothball the pit until June 1991, at which point the situation would be reviewed.

Two separate campaigns emerged to rescue the mine. In April 1989 a proposal was put together by an ex-British Coal mining engineer, Jim Parker, and a group of local ex-miners including Jackie Aitchison, a former NUM branch secretary of Bilston Glen colliery who had been sacked in the strike. This Monktonhall Consortium was intent on forming a mineworkers' company to resume the running of the mine. To this end Parker produced a report claiming that the pit could viably employ 187 miners on £320 per week, mining 200,000 tonnes per annum. Each miner would be asked to invest £2,000, the remainder to be provided by financial and commercial institutions.

Lothian district and regional councillors and the NUM developed an alternative proposal based on a commissioned feasibility study by Coal Industry Consultancy Services. They argued that £10 million of investment was needed which British Coal should provide. The two groups were in open conflict. Local authorities and the NUM argued that the Consortium would never find adequate capital, citing the Consortium's decision to raise each worker-shareholder's stake to £10,000. Nevertheless, British Coal offered the Consortium the lease in 1992, despite a rival bid from an established company, Caledonian Mining. The new operators found the mine had been stripped of most of its equipment and spent much of 1992 scouring the coalfields for second-hand machinery. They were three months late in developing their first advanced face.[1] Early in 1993 the men voted to work for seven weeks without wages to avert a cash crisis and prevent a take-over by Caledonian Mining. By May the company reported debts of £1.8 million.

The local authorities commissioned another feasibility study, by Quayle-Munro, who concluded that a further £3 million was needed to start another face. The mining entrepreneur RJ Budge intervened, signing a letter of intent in September and guaranteeing the men's wages. He offered to make the required £3 million investment and pay back each miner £1,000 for his individual stake of £10,000, or allow them to leave with £3,000 in severance pay. With the hopes of a firm backer for the company the local authority and the Department of Trade and Industry also promised to contribute. However, this offer was rejected in November 1993 by a ballot of the shareholders and Budge withdrew his offer.

Within weeks a new backer was found in Waverley Asset Management, who offered to invest £3.5 million in return for a 49 per cent share. The company was restructured: 'A' shares (comprising a controlling stakeholding of 51 per cent) were held by those workers who originally invested £10,000; while 'B' shares represented Waverley's ownership of the remaining 49 per cent of the company. With the injection of capital the Monktonhall company was able to buy new equipment, develop a second face and increase its workforce from 167 to 260. New miners were employed but not offered shares.

Scottish Power remained the colliery's major market. A Monktonhall director told us in April 1995 that he was satisfied with the progress the company had made but maintained that a change in UK energy policy was the only guarantee of a long-term future. Accounts filed at Companies House in February 1994 for the period ended 31 May 1993 showed that the company had made a post-tax loss of £3,726,800 and that its liabilities currently exceeded its assets by £2,056,800. The company continued to mine and trade coal but was unable to generate sufficient revenue to invest in the development and machinery required to realise the colliery's potential. At their annual general meeting in December 1995 shareholders accepted the inevitable: the company was taken over completely by Waverley, although each original worker-investor retained his £10,000 shares. This proved only a temporary respite for the beleaguered workforce. In 23 April 1997, after a serious flooding of workings, the colliery went into liquidation and was closed down two months later.

Analysing Monktonhall's Economic Performance

The feasibility study carried out by Coal Industry Consultancy Services on behalf of the NUM and Lothian Regional and District Councils emphasised the availability of 8 million tonnes of good-quality accessible coal reserves. No one doubted Monktonhall's huge potential:

> *We've always believed – and that's why we have fought so hard to save Monktonhall – that there is a vast potential there ... a vast coal reserve. The quality of coal that Monktonhall produces is good quality: it's not just steam coal for power stations, it would be good for industrial and domestic markets as well. (Scotland Area NUM officer)*

Mined at 500,000 tonnes per annum, the colliery's life expectancy was fifteen years. A comparatively large pit, Monktonhall had high operating costs and needed new seams developing. For some we interviewed the problem caused by the incessant build-up of water was insuperable: 'I worked in that shaft for ten years. We injected that shaft at the cost of £1 million per shaft and we still couldn't beat the water' (former Monktonhall miner). This problem proved decisive in the last few weeks of the pit's life. Consideration of such factors underlay the feasibility study's argument that 400 men working retreat mining methods could be employed at the pit but that only British Coal could provide the £10 million of required investment.[2] Despite the opening of the Peterhead natural gas-fired power station in 1992 markets could be found with Scottish Power in the absence of competition for the supply of low-sulphur coal. All this depended on the initial injection of capital.

The Consortium had to play down these problems to project an image of a competent and financially sound company. Claims to have secured external investment and agreements with British Coal to salvage machinery were discredited by newspaper reports. Capital remained a problem: 'We knew the enterprise was under-capitalised and therefore was going to meet serious problems in the future' (Lothian regional councillor).

The lack of capital necessitating the use of cheap, unreliable equipment, disrupted production:

> *The finances would never be enough to handle it. British Coal had great difficulties even with endless supplies of money and endless supply of spares ... They [Monktonhall] have not got the back up ... They have got to pay through the nose. (former Monktonhall miner)*

A serious consequence of the company's under-capitalisation was that new, more productive, faces could not be developed. Excessively optimistic projections did not help:

> *It was three months' lost production before we ever started and that was Jim Parker's fault. He was living in cloud-cuckoo land. If he had listened to the miners down there developing: they were telling him that there was no way the pit would coal until December or January at the earliest, and he's been away telling the banks that we'd be coaling by the beginning of November. (Monktonhall miner)*

A lack of management experience adversely influenced key strategic decisions:

> *The trouble was those that sat as board members at Monktonhall, their mining experience was very limited ... I mean, Jackie had never worked on a coal face in his life, so his input to a coal production face was nil. Now, he could talk about production but he couldn't come up with any answers. (Monktonhall NUM delegate)*

Consortium members, clearly aware of the risks, were driven on, partly by the encouragement of local politicians from such diverse parties as the Conservatives and the Scottish Nationalists, and partly by their own desperation, a word used frequently by outside observers. Less clear were the motives of British Coal in preferring the Consortium bid over that of Caledonian Mining. Local councillors and NUM officers suspected BC of selecting the weaker bid to jeopardise the future competitiveness of the pit. Such suspicions may have been well-founded.

A Social Critique of Monktonhall

The primary motive for the Monktonhall initiative was to save the pit from closure or privatisation. The company chairperson told us: 'The alternatives are multinationals or bulldozers'. The buy-out contributed little to the local economy, since most of the workforce, over four-fifths, commuted in. But the lack of local jobs for redundant miners was a motivating factor, as one case history demonstrates:

> *The pit was mothballed and there was no other pits to go to. I landed quite lucky because I got a wee job in a fruit wholesalers which I worked at for four years. I had a wee spell in insurance but I didn't like that. In August last year, I made up my mind and came down and spoke to a couple of representatives at Monktonhall. I spoke to my wife who was a bit concerned because it was £10,000 that we didn't have and would have to borrow on the strength of my house. That's the big worry: if it goes down the tubes, I'll lose my house. (Monktonhall miner)*

Most miners had their immediate economic interests at heart:

> *Let me stress something very clearly: it's a business and we all have to change our ideas or forget it. It's a new rethinking process. You must change your attitude to the project you are going into. It is not an exercise in social engineering, it's a business – a world business – with all the problems that appertain to it. (chair, Monktonhall Consortium)*

Management was conceded the right to manage within collectively agreed policy. Initial attempts at democratic management were soon abandoned:

> *It's one thing that we have learned: you've got to give management their head and let them take care of operations. But if it is a matter of policy, then that has to be put to the men. (Monktonhall miner)*

Miners had changed their attitude to work: it had become less instrumental. The work was harder but more satisfying:

> *I like the atmosphere here because it's totally different from working for the Coal Board ... I can speak to the manager here on equal terms ... he's trying to be constructive and not to bring you down, 'cos he knows you are trying hard – that's the difference. (Monktonhall miner)*

A more egalitarian ethos now prevailed, albeit at the expense of long-standing trade union practices. Absenteeism and strict demarcation were discouraged. The danger, that working harder and more flexibly for the common good might shade off into self-exploitation, became apparent in the decision, made in March 1993, to work for eight weeks without wages:

> *It was work for nothing and the pit still goes, or take a wage from someone else. So we said we'd work for nothing. We got the highest production that week. (Monktonhall miner)*

Though one fatality had occurred, all denied that safety standards had deteriorated. There had clearly been a decline in insurance and pension provision. Compensation for injury was much less than that formerly provided by British Coal. Some men injured underground accepted light duties rather than sick pay and compensation. However, the new conditions were agreed by the men who retained the right to call an emergency general meeting to raise any issues of safety, discipline, pay or conditions.

Union membership was regarded as an irrelevance in a self-managed concern:

> *You can't have a union when you are talking about your own money. It doesn't make sense. If you had invested £10,000 and there was a picket out there, what would you tell him to do? 'Get to fuck!' that's what.*
> *(Monktonhall miner)*

This attitude changed dramatically in the process of Waverley's two-stage take-over. After six months of protracted negotiations involving the Advisory, Conciliation, and Arbitration Service (ACAS) a conciliation procedure was set up with the NUM branch in late 1994. By 1996 the pit was 90 per cent unionised. The colliery's prevailing ethos had been dramatically transformed:

> *It's just like everywhere else – it's just a job ... you're a worker with shares in the company, that's all. At the end of the day, you are just a number on a board. You don't have a say in how the company is run although you can have some input, suggestions-wise. (NUM delegate, Monktonhall)*

Case study 2: Thurcroft

Overview

A brief description of Thurcroft village and the circumstances leading up to the closure of its local mine was given in chapter 5. In this section we concentrate on the three months after closure. With underground salvage still in progress over 200 miners turned up at a mass meeting to discuss taking over the pit. Local authority officers involved in the Coalfield Communities Campaign had prompted the NUM branch to take action. Lothian councillors and the head of the Monktonhall Consortium addressed meetings.

The campaigns to reopen the Monktonhall and Thurcroft collieries were initially backed by the NUM at both area and national level. Following the re-election of the Conservative Government the NUM redefined both initiatives as inimical to its basic strategy of outright opposition to privatisation and withdrew support at its annual conference. Thurcroft Colliery (1992) Ltd was nevertheless formed and attracted 161 potential shareholders. Each made the company an initial loan of £4,000, to be converted into shares at a later date. British Coal were initially persuaded to continue with the care and maintenance of the pit, meeting the cost of £20,000 per week. However, their stance soon changed:

> *Negotiations between the miners' company and British Coal went well initially. As it became clear to British Coal that the miners' buy-out plan had a serious chance of success, however, British Coal's pace slowed dramatically. It began to question points that it had been thought by the miners had already been agreed. British Coal refused to meet the care and maintenance costs, arguing that were it to bear such costs that would lessen the chances of survival of other collieries in the region. Declaring that it deserved an 'Olympic medal for patience' in its dealings with Thurcroft (1992) Ltd, it closed the pit for good in August 1992. (Turner and Gladstone 1993, p.354)*

By the following December the pit had been bulldozed out of existence.

Analysing Thurcroft's Demise

Most of Thurcroft colliery's best coal reserves had already been extracted prior to 1991. Twenty million tonnes remained, suitable for the electricity supply and steel industries. Thurcroft was unaffected by water problems though there was some convergence (the crushing of roadways due to shifting strata which is unavoidable in deep mines). Otherwise the infrastructure was sound. New coal faces had been in an advanced stage of development and machinery was in place.

A small colliery, Thurcroft's fixed operational costs were relatively modest. The business plan projected sales in the first year of 85,000 tonnes of coking coal: 200,000 tonnes to the ESI, 5,000 tonnes to domestic consumers and 35,000 tonnes for industrial use. National Power and the British Steel Corporation had each expressed an interest in purchasing Thurcroft coal.

Thurcroft worker-directors were less successful in attracting financial backing for the venture. Two private mining companies, Ryan Mining (often referred to as Ryan's) and AF Budge (owned by the brother of Richard Budge, the head of RJB Mining), each expressed a commercial interest which was quickly discouraged because they expected total control. British Coal's former commercial director Malcolm Edwards provided contacts but no financial backing. The confidence of potential backers was undermined by two factors: the absence of a credible management team and the weakness of the company's business plan.

To enhance its credibility the company needed a managerial figure of proven stature as a figurehead. British Coal's former managers were reluctant to jeopardise their superannuation entitlements by joining the Thurcroft initiative. The ex-manager of a closed Nottinghamshire colliery emerged too late as a candidate. Additionally, legal advisors lacked expertise in mining, which delayed negotiations with British Coal.

The Thurcroft initiative crucially lacked strong leadership, capable of organising discrepant factions and focusing the attention of shareholders. There was insufficient time to affect cultural change, as the Sheffield Co-op Development Group representative noted:

> *The transition from one form of organisation, i.e. a struggle in the political field, to save a pit, to an effort to be a credible business organisation able to run a pit, is quite a big transition. At first, it was run very much like a union branch. The level of argument at the big meetings was always confrontational. The transition from being a group of workers to being people aware of what is needed to be done to run a business inevitably takes time. In the circumstances that prevailed at Thurcroft, there was not the time to make that transition.*

The mine plan, drafted by an ex-National Coal Board manager working for a small licensed mine, developed out of the original feasibility study. This advocated introducing American 'intermediate' mining techniques in the long term. This preference for using 'in-seam continuous miners' (low-profile machines that cut a multitude of roadways rather than the total extraction of long-wall methods) along with roof-bolting had the advantage of requiring lower capital investment and was more suited to either smaller-scale mining or thicker seam sections. Such techniques were considered risky and unsafe by the Thurcroft miners, who preferred more conventional retreat and part-retreat methods. A plan lacking credibility with the workforce could scarcely be sold to potential investors. Few believed it was possible to mine 300,000 tonnes with 210 men, as stipulated by the plan, when they had only mined 510,000 tonnes with 637 men.

Practical assistance came from two principal sources: the Sheffield Co-op Development Group and Rotherham Metropolitan Borough Council. The Co-op group distributed a leaflet amongst steering committee members, asking such questions as:

> *How is the business going to be run? How is the project going to be managed in the meantime? What is the future role of the workforce? What needs doing now to prepare the ground?*

No answers were forthcoming.

Rotherham Council made concerted efforts to support the plan. They were instrumental in persuading British Coal originally to delay outright closure. They commissioned the expert feasibility study and appointed legal and financial advisors. They promised to commit £47,000 through a wages subsidy scheme and to lobby politically for grants and investment. They could not, however, prevent British Coal's ultimatum.

Some saw this decision as politically motivated, others as primarily economic:

> *It was in the interests of British Coal, which at the time was scheduled for an early privatisation, to use its control of the national coal resource to prevent future competitors from gaining a foothold in British mines capable of making profits. (Turner and Gladstone 1993, p.355)*

Having announced their ultimatum British Coal amassed hundreds of tonnes of hard-core and rubble on the pit surface ready for shaft-filling. This was the final deterrent to the worker take-over.

Case study 3: Tower

Overview

Situated between the Cynon and Rhondda valleys of Mid-Glamorgan, Tower colliery is South Wales's sole surviving deep coal mine. The present mine shaft was sunk in the early 1930s. Tower produced high-quality anthracite and dry steam coal for the coal-fired power station at Aberthawe.

The first major uncertainty about Tower's future occurred late in 1993 when a package of voluntary redundancies reduced the 600-strong workforce by a third and the number of permanently employed miners to 250. Local NUM opposition, including a march by 2,000 supporters through nearby Aberdare, proved futile. In April 1994 British Coal announced the imminent closure of the colliery. Ignoring Tower's £28 million in profits in the preceding three years management argued for closure, since power-station demand for its coal was declining (*The Independent* 7 April 1994).

A determined anti-closure campaign ensued, including a 280-mile protest march on the Department of Trade and Industry and a 27-hour underground sit-in by Ann Clwyd MP. The Tower lodge voted to resist closure by placing the pit's future in the colliery review procedure. British Coal immediately rescinded its closure decision, 'in light of the strength of the NUM's feeling and the union's optimism for the future of the colliery' (*Financial Times* 16 April 1994). Production and development would be continued until privatisation.

British Coal subsequently disclosed that this reprieve was conditional on employees accepting substantial wage cuts and the forfeiture of redundancy payments. Placed in this dilemma the workforce voted to accept closure. However, following the public outcry against closures in October 1992 the Government decided that all condemned collieries would be kept running on a 'care and maintenance basis', pending their transfer into private ownership.

Believing that the colliery had been closed primarily to enable a management buy-out and convinced that the pit had a viable future Tower lodge officials investigated the feasibility of a worker take-over. Within two weeks of the pit's closure lodge officials had solicited the advice of Fairwater Consultants, a TUC-sponsored support agency for worker co-operatives. Meetings of redundant miners endorsed the idea of a take-over. At Fairwater's recommendation would-be participants were asked for an initial investment of £2,000 – to demonstrate the strength of their commitment to potential financial backers – and £364,000 was raised as preliminary capital.

Working from a makeshift 'office' alongside the post office in Aberdare, a five-man team of former lodge officials, TEBO (Tower Employee Buy-Out), began to prepare their bid for submission to the Department of Trade and

Industry. TEBO surprisingly engaged as their accountants Price-Waterhouse, who had administered the sequestration of the NUM's funds during the national miners' strike of 1984–5. They then secured financial backing from Barclays Bank on the basis of two important conditions: first, each would-be shareholder should increase his or her investment in the project to £8,000; second, the five-person board of company should comprise three management- and only two worker-directors. TEBO accepted both conditions and eventually submitted their bid. In November 1994 the Government announced that 'Goitre Tower Anthracite Limited' had been chosen as its 'preferred bidder' for the mine. Tower employees returned to work on 2 January 1996.

With 239 employee shareholders and five director-shareholders Tower reported post-tax profits of more than £2 million for its first twelve months of operation. In December 1995 each employee was awarded a 'Christmas bonus' in the form of an interim dividend of £500, after tax, with a further share dividend to come in March 1996. One month later basic wages were increased by £23 per week and £1 million was reinvested on a state-of-the-art coal-face shearer. At this point Tower's economic viability was indisputable.

Analysing Tower's Economic Performance

Union officials believed that Tower's performance had been misrepresented by BC:

> *A lot of our coal stopped going to Aberthawe, and we all knew it wasn't the price or the quality. We knew it was a tactical move to close the mine: one minute British Coal said that the mine was unviable, and the next minute we heard there was a management buy-out team wanting to buy the pit themselves. (Tower NUM surface representative)*

New equipment, installed just before Tower's closure, confirmed these suspicions. Tower shareholders eventually came to own a colliery geared up for work with an intact infrastructure and a skilled workforce readily available.

Tower workers decided to pursue a different market strategy from that of British Coal:

> *All they ever spoke about was power generation. We had 70 per cent power station and 30 per cent other products. I mean, just in money value alone, the price of industrial and house coal is double that of power stations, so why didn't they sell it? (Tower materials officer/NACODS member)*

Only a quarter of the new market was found in power stations, all the rest in domestic wholesalers and industrial consumers. Contracts were agreed, covering four-fifths of output over five years. The remaining one-fifth was deliberately held back:

> *We wanted it that way because I still believe today that the price of anthracite will go up – not by a lot, it might be 5–10p – so I wanted to keep some coal back for the fourth year. (personnel manager/worker-director)*

Tower had a better strategy than Monktonhall. Enlisting the services of Fairwater Consultants and Price-Waterhouse provided expert and credible financial and strategic advice. They were paid for by the Department of Trade and Industry who had agreed to subsidise small bidders.

Tower's advisors quickly impressed upon the TEBO team that it was imperative to assemble a credible group of mine management personnel. In addition to an experienced mine manager (who had recently resigned at nearby Betws colliery) and the ex-director of the National Coal Board in South Wales – who had resigned ten years earlier in protest over the Government's pit-closure programme – as chairperson, TEBO also employed a number of trusted and experienced people in other key managerial positions. The inclusion of such an able and experienced pool of talent, already familiar with Tower's structure and geology, not only helped to inspire the confidence of financial institutions and, ultimately, the Department of Trade and Industry (DTI), but also added expertise to TEBO's strategic bid.

The TEBO team acted unconventionally in securing the talents of a financial director from outside the mining industry. The logic of the decision not to appoint a former colliery accountant was explained by a management director:

> *Any decision on marketing, or any financial decision, was always dealt with at area or national level. The result was that the accounting people at the collieries were almost always completely naive in the ways of the world and didn't have the necessary contacts or confidence. And what we said was, 'Look, if we're going to be dealing in the market, there's no way we can be using inexperienced British Coal people.'*

TEBO showed themselves willing and able to adapt to the demands of strategic players such as Barclays Bank. Tower representatives also insisted that the mining and business plans should be based on realistic assessments of their potential. The mining plan was predicated on the most conservative rather than the most optimistic estimate of reserves. Projections of sales and revenue were based on 'world' (i.e. baseline) coal prices rather than the most optimistic of available 'guesstimates'. This careful and calculated approach to organisation and strategy ultimately served to impress Rothschilds, the Government's merchant bankers, and the DTI. But political factors were also important.

In the absence of NUM support TEBO cast their net wider. They conducted a massive lobbying operation, writing to every Conservative Association. This campaign was supported by entertainers and performers, such as Billy Bragg and Screaming Lord Sutch; newspapers (most notably the *Daily Mirror*); local politicians, like Ann Clwyd; and local councillors who provided office premises and secretarial assistance. John Redwood, the Secretary of State for Wales, also lent his tacit support:

Tyrone went down to meet him and persuaded him to support us. He couldn't say outright, 'I support the Tower miners,' but what he did do, he came out with a local paper which was supporting Tower miners and walked on to the steps of the Welsh Office in Cardiff with Tyrone and Phil and the cameras, holding that in his hand. We understand he did a lot of hard work behind the scenes. (Tower NUM lodge secretary)

Faced with such an alliance commercial competitors Celtic Energy withdrew their bid. Still, the final government decision remained a puzzle:

They'd given a hell of a lot of pits to Budge, and due to the fact that we'd always been a very militant pit and the last in South Wales, perhaps they felt, 'Ah, well, we'll give 'em the one to appease them,' I suppose. (Tower NUM surface representative)

A Social Critique of Tower

The Tower employee buy-out aimed not only to restore jobs but to improve employment conditions. TEBO undertook to prioritise basic wages over bonuses, which they made clear to their advisors:

We said, 'There'll be no arguments. If you don't agree with it, so be it. Just don't give us the pit.' ... And if the day comes when the price of coal is so low, and it never will, that our guys go underground for £100 a week, that's the time when we all walk away. We don't mine coal like bloody slaves any more. (Tower personnel manager/worker-director)

Short-term expansion was to be rejected in favour of long-term viability:

The moment you say to us, 'Okay, you can do 800,000 tonnes a year,' the first thing that does is shorten the life of the pit ... Not only that, you've got to start chasing the markets now and for what? The aim of the company, as set out on day one, was to create as many jobs as we can and maintain those jobs for as long as we can – not to rip the coal out quick for a quick buck. (Tower management director)

Workers at Tower colliery were well aware how this would work to their advantage:

We've got a target to hit and we hit that every week and they aren't pushing us to get the extra like they were with British Coal. The targets are more comfortable. (Tower faceworker)

More generous compensation for sickness and illness was provided, yet absenteeism fell dramatically. Indeed, managers saw workers as almost too willing to do whatever was necessary to keep the concern going. As the management director put it, 'You've got to be ever so careful that you're not overworking a very willing horse'. Monktonhall miners were forced by circumstance to work unpaid for a two-month period, whereas Tower employees were requested to work, at basic rates of overtime, in order to maintain the company's schedule.

Relations between workers and mine management had become more egalitarian and relaxed than under British Coal:

> *There's a different atmosphere to it. It isn't cut-throat anymore ... I mean, only a week or two ago, I was sat down talking to the manager here. You couldn't have done that under British Coal. They'll tell you what's planned and isn't planned all the way up. Never had that before. But as it stands, I've put my 8,000 [pounds] in, he's put his 8,000 in: he may be manager, I may be a face-worker but we're still equal at the end of the day. (Tower face-worker)*

There was a fine line to be drawn between democracy and discipline. The lodge secretary cited instances of inappropriate conduct by both absentee men and hectoring managers, who had to be reminded of priorities and principles. Specific issues remained sensitive. Demarcation was relaxed but only up to a point:

> *I've said, 'Look, if there's a job regularly filling in for absenteeism, let's create a job and have done with it,' but at the end of the day, that's where you've got to put your company hat on as well; you've got to look at what's viable for the company. What I say to the company on flexibility is that that's, again, got to be done safely. People can't just fill one job and train in it for a week and then pretend that they know it because you're creating room for accidents with things like that. (Tower NUM surface representative)*

Differentials remained a source of resentment. As one NUM surface representative put it, 'I think we're all on a decent living wage, here, but you'll always get one group of workers saying, "How come we're only on this while they're getting that?"' Contractors had to be retained, to the embarrassment of NUM officials, because they allowed adjustments to the size of the workforce without affecting core jobs. Commercial logic thus required a dilution of trade union principles.

There were no serious disputes in the early years. In January 2000 the Tower WTO experienced its first-ever strike – so unexpected as to be 'reported everywhere as a matter of high comedy' (Weekend Magazine, *Financial Times* 22 July 2000). The dispute occurred after a small earthquake prevented access to the coal-face for three months. Once the men returned to work management pressure was applied to make up for lost time. This resulted in a 24-hour strike. As the personnel manager/worker-director ruefully remarked, 'I taught these boys how to go on strike so I can't be surprised when they turn it against me.'

Few of the workers interviewed had or wanted any great say in the day-to-day management of the mine. A mature trade union structure represented their interests instead. Quarterly meetings of shareholders provided opportunities to receive and request information:

If anybody has any questions to ask, they can either be tabled before in a formal letter on the day or you can raise your hand. Ordinarily, we have full and frank discussions in these meetings. It's never that they're without a bit of controversy but we are in the mining industry after all! (Tower NUM surface representative)

An inescapable sense of pride pervaded the whole enterprise, reflecting the belief that Tower was bringing something genuinely innovative to a hostile marketplace:

In an industry in which we're dealing with capitalism every day as far as our markets are concerned, what we've done from a socialist point of view is consider more carefully what should be done with the profits and provide better conditions of employment. So we have actually blended them both together. I also think this: that we've taken principles of honesty and integrity out there into capitalism and have not been kicked in the teeth because of it ... We've given people hope who felt there were no victories left in the working-class movement, because they do see a group of people fighting back and winning against the odds. (Tower personnel manager/worker-director)

Despite the opposition of the labour movement and the credibility given to the Government's nationalisation programme this sense of achievement was widespread.

Discussion

Our case studies point to a series of conclusions about success and failure in WTOs, with clear implications for future projects.

A Summary of Findings

Table 7.2 represents our main conclusions about the factors that affected the outcome of the three case studies we have examined. These factors have been grouped into technological (running and development costs, available equipment); economic (market, geographical location, coal reserves and quality); strategic and organisational (business plan, management team, legal advice, financial backing, time); and political (trade union, local authority and party support, British Coal's attitude). These enable us to see why Tower succeeded, Monktonhall opened but passed eventually into private hands and Thurcroft foundered. Tower had technological and economic advantages, exploited by an effective strategic and organisational plan which generated universal political support. Monktonhall had good economic prospects but poor technological infrastructure, never properly acknowledged in excessively optimistic strategic and organisational plans. Local authority and trade union opinion was divided. At Thurcroft both technology and market prospects were adequate but strategic and organisational planning was pressurised and inexperienced. The local authority was supportive but the NUM at area and national level reneged. There was no nationalist or regional identification with the project. For whatever reason, British Coal effectively sabotaged it.

TABLE 7.2 THE ECONOMIC VIABILITY OF EACH COLLIERY AS A WORKER TAKE-OVER

	Thurcroft	Monktonhall	Tower
Technological			
Running costs	Relatively small colliery – low overheads and running costs	Large colliery – expensive to run especially pumping water from shafts	Relatively small colliery – low overheads and running costs
Development status	Faces and roadways developed	No development	Ready for mining; capital development required in five years
Equipment	Up-to-date and reliable equipment still underground	No underground machinery	Fully equipped with modern machinery
Economic			
Coal market	Coal suitable for non-ESI, 'niche' market, therefore potential higher revenue	Locally available markets, limited local competition	Niche market, local and national; high revenue
Location	Central coalfield pit, therefore local competition	Peripheral pit not in central coalfields and therefore was not seen as a threat to BCC	Very little competition in domestic market; BCC no longer in a position to obstruct
Coal quality/reserves	Good quality, medium-low sulphur, moderate reserves	Good quality coal, large reserves	High-quality product – anthracite; moderate reserves
Strategic/organisational			
Business plan	Mine plan unconvincing	Under-capitalisation	Realistic and well presented; required only modest initial injection of capital
Management team	No management team	Management team in place but experience questionable	Management team experienced and in place; original workforce intact
Legal advice	Solicitors experienced in buy-outs but not mining and mineral laws	Solicitors experienced in mining and mineral laws	Sound advice from experienced firm
Financial backing	No firm financial backers	Men prepared to risk £10,000	Men: £8,000, plus loan from Barclays Bank
Time	Negotiations rushed because BCC not prepared to cover costs of maintaining mine	Pressure to get coal out without adequate preparation	Part of privatisation plans of government, therefore propitious timing
Political			
Trade union	Trade union support withdrawn	Trade union hostile	No national or area support but well-organised campaign and planning by lodge
Local authority	Support of local authority	Local authority hostile	Local authority very supportive
British Coal	British Coal obstruction and refusal to cover care and maintenance	British Coal mothballed – care and maintenance paid for	Care and maintenance paid for; BCC no longer a significant actor
Political parties	Over-reliance on an expected Labour victory in April 1992	Local Labour hostility; Scottish Nationalist support	All-party support sought and received; nationality a factor

Such a portrait immediately points to a list of conditions propitious for a worker take-over of a mine with implications for any future proposals. But we have also argued that the ethos of any worker take-over has tangible effects upon its success, measured in economic or ideological terms. Table 7.3 compares the principles and practices of the three projects in terms of such ideals. Tower had a clear set of guiding principles converted into a practice which drew a fine line between ideals and commercial realities. Monktonhall had a more strictly economic agenda which soon deteriorated into practices committed to economic solvency at all costs. Thurcroft espoused similar principles to those of Tower but never had the opportunity to test them out in practice.

A Future Role for WTOs in the Coal-mining Industry?

The interaction of these groupings of factors is clearly a matter of some complexity in any individual example. Nevertheless, a set of optimum conditions emerges for a successful worker take-over in the mining industry – though, with amendments, these may also apply to worker take-overs in other industries. They are as follows:

1. goodwill and good faith on the part of the parent company;

2. sound existing technology and a healthy pit infrastructure;

3. favourable geological conditions with plentiful, easily developed reserves;

4. niche markets involving a diversity of separate customers;

5. a credible and enthusiastic leadership, capable of organising the take-over bid and inspiring the confidence and support of relevant parties;

6. a pre-trained, adequately skilled and committed workforce;

7. commercial pragmatism (i.e. a willingness to adapt personnel, methods, etc. to gain the approval of financial backers);

8. a sufficiently competent management team which has the confidence of employees and looks credible to financial and political audiences;

9. advisory, financial and practical support from sympathetic institutions, such as trade unions, 'free professionals' and the co-operative movement;

10. similar support from external institutions, most notably government, financial backers and 'paid' professionals (e.g. accountants and legal advisors not necessarily aligned with the labour movement);

11. the support of the local community and wider general public; and

12. sufficient capital investment involving limited financial risk to employee-shareholders.

TABLE 7.3 MANAGEMENT PRINCIPLES AND PRACTICE AT EACH COLLIERY

	Thurcroft	Monktonhall	Tower
Principles			
Main priority	Rescuing jobs the main priority	Creation of jobs a priority	Creation of jobs a priority
Guiding philosophy	Commitment to collectivist principles	Commercial philosophy dominant	Commitment to collectivist principles wedded to business acumen
Worker control	Set up as a company limited by guarantee with intention of being 51% mineworker-owned	Began as one member, one vote at Annual General Meeting or Emergency General Meeting. Two-tier employees. In 1994, 167 owned 51% of company – other 93 had no share. Shares bought out in 1995 by investment company	Wholly owned by mineworkers; structured as an ESOP
Unionisation	Pro-union although some disagreement as to which to join	May 1993, non-union – only one member in NUM; 90% unionisation by 1996	100% unionised
Locality ties	Locally and community-based – 86.5% ex-Thurcroft miners, 13.49% ex-local closed pits and 1 non-miner (a miner's son)	Few ties with local community – no more than 15% ex-Monktonhall miners	Strong local ties; although miners travel from across South Wales coalfield, the majority worked at Tower before closure
Practice			
Management	Not applicable	Running of company given over to management team – members not kept regularly informed	Running of mine left to management but with increased consultation
Democracy	Not applicable	Some members not aware of the details or nature of their investment – just bought a job	Participation and democracy at regular meetings
Wages	Not applicable	'Sweat equity' – good wages not always paid, extra time put in unpaid	Higher than other companies; dividends also paid
Other benefits	Not applicable	Below BCC levels	Better than any other available in coal-mining in the UK
Safety	Not applicable	Questionable	Given top priority

There are wider factors, too. As Paton (1989, p.73) points out, government can play a pivotal role in this process by providing the necessary financial and practical incentives and facilitating structures, e.g. cancelling outstanding debts, placing orders, paying consultants and setting up special loan funds. Only time will tell whether the British Labour party and trade union movement wish to move beyond a conventional capitalist economy. If they do, then our case studies suggest that the model of the worker take-over should not be easily dismissed and that detailed examination of its principles and practices might pay significant dividends – and not merely to the shareholders.

In successfully taking over and running their own mine the workers at Tower staved off the collapse of the local economy. They managed to retain, rather than being forced to replace, the staple local industry. Elsewhere, where retention of the pit was not an option, other means had to be found to replace the economic foundation of community life which a mine had historically provided. How this was attempted in the UK and mainland Europe is the subject of the next section.

NOTES

1. The advanced face system of long-wall coal-mining involves the driving of roadways (usually two) in order to keep up with an advancing coal-face that runs between the two roadways. Roadway development and coal-cutting are thus part of the same mining operation. It had the advantage for Monktonhall of being the quickest way to start production.

2. Retreat mining is a system of long-wall mining using pre-driven roadways which are then worked back from the furthest point. This has the advantage of divorcing roadway development from coal-face production, thus simplifying operations. It is the most successful method used in UK coalmines but has the disadvantage for small operators of requiring significant investment in driving roadways with very little coal produced in the development period.

PART IV:
THE ECONOMIC REGENERATION
OF MINING COMMUNITIES

8   Coalfield Regeneration in the UK

INTRODUCTION

Previous chapters outlined the economic, cultural and psychological effects of pit closures. In this chapter we review attempts to regenerate communities which have lost their main industry and its way of life. Nearly all regenerative efforts in ex-coalfield areas can be seen as aiming to achieve one or more of three objectives:

1.   physical renewal, such as remedying despoliation and improving the local infrastructure;

2.   the creation of new employment opportunities via job replacement and re-skilling strategies; and

3.   the empowering of local communities, by enabling people to identify their needs and determine how to respond to them, rather than having such definitions imposed by external agencies (cf. Barr 1995; Taylor 1995).

Recent attempts to regenerate coalfield areas are not unique. Other areas of heavy industry – steel, textiles or shipbuilding – have already experienced decline and attempted regeneration. The North-East of England is an example. Some mining areas, notably South Wales, had to confront the problem much earlier than others. We begin the chapter by reviewing evaluations of regeneration programmes in these two areas. We then recount our own study of regeneration initiatives as they existed in 1995 in three coalfield areas: South Wales; South Yorkshire; and North Nottinghamshire (Parry 1996). The most authoritative policy document on coalfield regeneration has been that of the Government's Task Force (Coalfields Task Force 1998). We describe its recommendations and the Government's response. A comparative regional study commissioned by the Joseph Rowntree Foundation is the most recent contribution (Bennett et al. 2000), one which raises some issues of how regeneration and related terms are conceptualised. The findings of this study are also examined in this chapter. In the conclusion, we concentrate on two issues central to the ongoing debate on coalfield regeneration, the role of local institutions and the significance of community initiatives.

Regenerating Regions

The regeneration of industrial regions historically dependent on steel production has focused on the key areas of the North-East of England and South Wales.

The North-East of England

In Derwentside a major economic crisis followed the closure of its major steel works at Consett (Beynon et al. 1991; Hudson 1994; Hudson and Sadler 1992; 1995). Despite local opposition it closed in 1980 with the loss of 3,700 jobs. Consett became a test case for regeneration, 'the touchstone against which a variety of dogmas and policies about local economic development could be judged' (Hudson and Sadler 1992, p.317). The two main strategies turned out to be job creation and fostering small businesses. Responsibility for leading economic recovery fell to two principal agencies: British Steel Corporation's own British Steel (Industry) – BS(I) – and a newly created body, Derwentside Industrial Development Agency (DIDA). Both institutions offered packages of business and financial assistance and advice. BS(I) was eventually subsumed by DIDA.

BS(I) was formed a year before closure, aspiring to replace all the jobs lost within five years. By its own figures only 2,000 new jobs were created between 1979 and 1985, indicating 'a substantial gap between expectations and outcome' (Beynon et al. 1991). Launched in a 'blaze of publicity' DIDA 'sought to promote an enterprise culture via creating a (temporarily) supportive and highly state-subsidised environment for potential entrepreneurs' (Hudson 1994, p.200). It attracted £50 million of public and £70 million of private investment between 1980 and 1988. DIDA claimed to have created 4,500 new jobs, largely in the manufacturing sector, but this claim was not supported by government figures suggesting a lower total of 1,270 jobs. Either way, it was limited compensation for the 8,000 manufacturing jobs lost locally between 1978 and 1981.

Small businesses fared even worse. Hudson and Sadler (1992) report the high fatality rates of 36 per cent for existing firms supported and 44 per cent for new start-ups. Most surviving enterprises were established by 'entrepreneurial immigrants', attracted by 'grants, loans and the mass of unemployed people desperate for waged work' (Hudson 1994, p.201). The dominant employment sector in Derwentside at the end of the 1980s was concerned with the management of unemployment. Twenty-seven per cent of the local workforce was employed in local government, 2,800 people were on temporary government job-schemes and 3,500 registered unemployed (Hudson and Sadler 1992). Hudson (1994, p.201) concludes that regeneration measures in Derwentside largely had 'a cosmetic and superficial effect', endorsing the value of entrepreneurship with few tangible results.

As Hudson (1994) explains, the above two strategies and three other variations were applied, with a similar lack of success, throughout the North-East as a whole. A third strategy employed within the region was to attract the outposts, or 'branch plants', of multinational corporations. This type of strategy requires ad hoc institutions to promote the area to potential inward investors by outlining the availability of grants or loans, emphasising the favourability of the local built and natural environment, and extolling the adaptability, flexibility and passivity of local workers. Such institutions are typically 'pseudo-corporatist' in form, frequently involving selected trade unionist representatives with ambitions to reel in a single-union deal. For example, the Northern Development Company played a key role in attracting Japanese companies like Fujitsu and Nissan. The transformation from the old industrial basis to a more mixed local economy produces a younger, lower-skilled, more feminised, non-unionised and poorer-paid workforce (Hudson 1994; Hudson et al. 1992). Nevertheless, Hudson (1994) concedes that transnational companies may stimulate local economic development where they regionalise their operations and cluster together specialist functions in research and development, production and distribution.

The fourth strategy Hudson calls the 'consumptionist solution', involving the development of tourism and heritage centres, such as the conversion of South Tyneside into 'Catherine Cookson country'. Such 'sanitised' and 'romanticised' restorations of the past represent a 'politics of despair', a tacit recognition 'of economic marginalisation in areas that were once focal points in an accumulation process that now increasingly by-passes them' (Hudson 1994, p.206)

A final regenerative strategy was the conversion of former working-class production spaces into sites of middle-class residence and consumption. These are often identified with urban development corporations, non-elected but generously funded corporatist institutions, given the responsibility of transforming old industrial areas 'via a speculative, private-property-led redevelopment strategy' (ibid., p.207). Examples from the Teesside Development Corporation included the creation of a £10 million technology park on the site of a disused shipyard and the development of a £40 million marina on the former Hartlepool coal-docks. The jobs created tend to be menial, poorly paid, part-time or casual, and non-unionised, throwing into sharp relief the contrasts with the affluent in-comers.

Hudson (1994) concludes by highlighting how 'localised thick institutional structures' – trade unions and local civic institutions – stifled opposition to orthodox regeneration strategies. During the 1980s, for example, the Labour-dominated district and county councils ensured that alternative grass-roots proposals for remedying the problems confronting Derwentside were marginalised in favour of more conventional solutions: 'Under these circumstances, it would seem that localised institutional thinness may have held greater emancipatory and radical transformatory potential' (ibid., p.212).

South Wales

In the early 1980s Wales lost 100,000 jobs in coal, steel and metal manufacturing. Regenerative efforts have been led by the Welsh Development Agency (WDA), operating under the Welsh Office. It 'has played an almost continental European role as animateur or orchestrator of some remarkably innovative initiatives to regenerate key elements of the Welsh economy' (Cooke 1995, p.44).

Founded in 1976, when devolution was a salient political issue (Morgan 1997), the WDA set out to attract substantial inward investment from western Europe, Japan and the USA. Its achievements were spectacular. Cooke (1995, p.45) dismisses as 'marketing hyperbole' WDA claims to have been attracting 20 per cent of total UK foreign investment in the early 1990s, estimating 13 per cent to be more realistic. He nevertheless concedes this to have been 'a remarkable achievement for a part of the UK with only a 5 per cent share of GDP'.

Cooke attributes the WDA's success to both 'the relatively straightforward and traditional methods of hard-sell, regional assistance and property rental packages', and labour costs in Wales being 10 per cent lower than in the UK and 50 per cent lower than in Germany. Crucial to this success was the commitment of the WDA and Welsh Office to creating partnerships which integrated components of the regional economy. For example, 'Source Wales' was a development programme bringing suppliers into contact with potential customers, creating local business clusters. The programme also set out to raise the competence of such suppliers, improving their long-term attractiveness to newfound clients. A complementary service was provided by 'Eurolink', which forged commercial links outwards with companies in France, Germany and Spain.

As Morgan (1995, p.204) explains, 'Because of its deeply entrenched Labourist traditions, South Wales never embraced the free-market credo of Thatcherism.' He argues that the five-year Programme for the Valleys, launched in June 1988 by Secretary of State for Wales Peter Walker, was pivotal. It established the principle of partnership between the private and public sectors as 'a key mechanism for the regeneration of urban areas' (ibid., p.208). With government expenditure of £751 million the programme claimed to have achieved: £700 million of private-sector investment, creating or safeguarding 24,000 jobs; 2,000 acres of land clearance; over 2.5 million acres of new industrial floorspace; and the improvement or refurbishment of 7,000 homes (Morgan 1995). However, it only marginally decreased unemployment in the valleys.

Inward investment strategies have been derided by Morris (1995) as 'McJobbing', with severe decreases in the wages and skill levels of new jobs. Morgan (1997) disputes this, arguing that occupational upgrading has progressively occurred in the new electronics and automotive components plants. What is less disputed is that unemployment rates in the valleys are double the UK average (in some cases, 30 per cent or more), that rates of pay are substantially lower than in the remainder of South Wales and that the chief beneficiaries of economic regeneration have been the sub-regions away from the valleys.

Morris (1995) offers a political critique of the 'democratic vacuum' caused by local authority strategy and decision-making being steered rigidly from London by the Welsh Office. Cooke (1995) cites as an example the

WDA-instigated Urban Joint Venture programme for environmental upgrading. The WDA decided what upgrading was relevant and which local authorities should receive funding. Consequently it required conformity to its own vision, which not all local authorities shared. Rhonnda Valley councillors declined to accept a regional role as a tourist centre so were marginalised in the WDA's plans. By contrast, the Welsh TUC was co-opted into a strategy of attracting inward investment at any cost. Opposition in such an instance is practically impossible. 'Either they accept the agenda or are left out of the process totally' (Morris 1995, p.57).

These two case studies, of North-East England and South Wales, demonstrate the difficulty of constructing any universally applicable model for the economic regeneration of ex-industrial areas. While the causes of decline are global the resolutions have to be local. In both cases a regional development agency was the driving force. Though wanting and needing the co-operation of other public and private institutions this was frequently on the agency's own terms. Claims about new jobs or businesses remained contentious. Even where accepted, they often disguised unevenness within the region.

Of the range of regeneration measures some appear easier to achieve than others. Given adequate resources the reclamation of land is achievable. While its environmental and psychological benefits are discernible its economic effects are not. Attracting branch plants is quite simply the most effective way to replace employment but there are hidden costs in incentives provided, the quality of jobs and the ever-present threat of plant relocation. Re-skilling the workforce faces the paradox that training for available jobs in an ailing local economy inevitably means low levels of skills and rewards. Training for high technology jobs is a hopeful investment in the future which both agencies and the unemployed may be reluctant to make. Of all the regenerative strategies that of creating small businesses seems to owe more to ideology than economic reality. The idea that those made redundant from manufacturing or extractive industries have the skills, confidence and attitudes to set up their own businesses is rarely supported by any reliable evidence. The final strategy, heritage and tourism, seems more likely to benefit the image of a region than to make any substantial contribution to its economic recovery. Such were the potential problems posed by the decline of the steel and coal industries. In the next section we examine the solutions proposed for coal at the national level.

Coalfield Regeneration: Structures and Strategies

The main agent of regeneration policy in the coalfields throughout the 1980s and 1990s remained central government. State intervention was indirect through quasi-non-governmental organisations (quangos) – such as the Urban Development Corporations (UDCs) and the Training and Enterprise Councils (TECs) (Parkinson and Evans 1990). The role for local authorities was reduced, even though many had their own economic development units. In practice, local government, the TECs, UDCs, Enterprise Agencies, English Partnerships and a plethora of other agencies and consultancies all competed for the limited resources available from successive government initiatives.

Between the start of the miners' strike in March 1984 and the election of the Labour Government in May 1997 a few initiatives were aimed specifically at coalfield regeneration. These were:

- a sum of £185 million awarded to British Coal Enterprise in 1984 to cover a ten-year period;

- the emergency aid package of £200 million over two years, unveiled in the wake of the Heseltine announcement;

- two allocations of European (RECHAR) funding in the periods 1990–3 and 1994–7 (subsequently extended to 1999); and

- a £350 million investment (spread over ten years) in English Partnership's coalfield programme.

We now describe and analyse these and related initiatives pre-dating the election of New Labour.

British Coal Enterprise

British Coal Enterprise (BCE) was established in 1985. Its two main roles were to create new job opportunities and provide training for redundant miners. Financial assistance (amounting to £500 per job or 25 per cent of start-up costs) was advanced to new businesses, workspace was provided (sometimes custom-built) and help offered in the placement and retraining of redundant miners.

Early attempts to stimulate entrepreneurship amongst middle-aged miners met with little success. Self-employment was consistently low, for example only 2–3 per cent at the South Yorkshire pits surveyed by Turner and Gregory (1995). Rees and Thomas (1989) found initial enthusiasts in South Wales to be deterred by financial uncertainties. Consequently, most small businesses created or encouraged by BCE were neither new nor run by former miners (Rees and Thomas 1989; Trotman and Lewis 1990; Turner 1992). BCE-sponsored small enterprises may even have displaced others, since 'new firms subsidised by cheap loans, accommodation or government grants undercut or put their competitors out of business' (Edwards 1991, p.59).

As the prospect of creating an 'enterprise culture' receded BCE's emphasis shifted to employment counselling and training. Employee evaluations of these services varied. In South Yorkshire Turner and Gregory (1995) found ex-miners from Markham Main to have a higher opinion of BCE than those from Brodsworth. Most saw the practical help as limited and some suspected it was all a ploy to get redundant miners off the unemployment register to avoid political embarrassment. Nevertheless, the Coalfield Communities Campaign survey of miners made redundant at five pits in the 1992 round of closures indicated that 75 per cent of those using BCE rated it as useful or very useful (Guy 1994).

The training scheme for miners was called the Job and Career Change Scheme (JACCS). Available within six months of redundancy it paid ex-miners £50 a week with a small allowance for adult dependants. Semi-skilled jobs such as driving, welding and security were the target. The Coalfield Communities Campaign national survey (ibid.) revealed a consistently low take-up, fewer than 10 per cent undergoing long-term training. Our own Thurcoft survey (Critcher, Parry and Waddington 1995) indicated a higher take-up of the JACCS scheme than earlier. Re-employment for those taking courses was higher (65 per cent) but the skills acquired were low-level, mainly driving and some welding. Often, the need and request for training emerged after the time qualification had expired.

BCE's claim to have created over 100,000 new job opportunities in its first ten years was challenged, especially by Fothergill and Guy (1994). They estimated the real figure to be nearer 16,000 though conceded that replacing one in fourteen jobs lost was still a considerable achievement. While the work of BCE was valued by other regeneration agencies it made little inroad into the high levels of unemployment in coalfield areas following pit closure. The suspicion lingered that 'the objective of British Coal Enterprise in relation to former miners would seem to be the transfer of men into any type of economic activity as soon as possible in order to demonstrate the limited impact of colliery closure upon mining areas' (Witt 1990, p.47).

The Role of the Training and Enterprise Councils

One hundred and four TECs were set up in England and Wales in 1990–1, 'to plan and deliver training and to promote and support the development of small businesses and self-employment within their area' (Department of Employment 1988, cited in Bennett et al. 1994). TECs were defined as business-led and community-based agencies with executive responsibility for determining and responding to local training needs. 'As well as managing on behalf of government a wide range of training and enterprise programmes, each TEC has the wider responsibility to act in a catalytic and co-ordinating role to ensure that training and enterprise activities are relevant to individual needs and local services' (Employment Service 1992, p.2). Organised as limited companies with business people the majority on their boards (70 per cent nationally), they shared an annual budget in the mid-1990s of £2.3 million, 74 per cent of which was devoted to training the unemployed.

Though locally based, TECs worked under national guidelines. There were some variations in practice, dependent on the quality of relationships with other regenerative agencies (Peck 1994), but otherwise the essence of the TECs' work was similar everywhere. TECs have been criticised by those in the field as well as by academics. Priority was given to government schemes and filling immediate, often low-skill, vacancies. Strategic policies aimed at higher-order skills were not implemented. In order to justify their budgets TECs concentrated on programmes that would produce apparently impressive performance indicators. The emphasis was on matching skills to whatever employment was locally available. Critics argued that the consequence was an oversupply of low-grade, easy-to-learn trades such as painting and decorating, with some schemes apparently designed to keep young unemployed people occupied. They produced 'short-term, low-cost training, for high turnover, low-skill sections of the labour market' which sidelined 'training for mid- and higher-level skills' (Boddy 1992, p.178).

The Heseltine Package

In the immediate wake of the Heseltine announcement of October 1992 the Government announced a package of aid to assist regeneration in the affected communities. In addition to redundancy payments the Government promised £200 million of further aid. Seventy-five million pounds were earmarked for TECs and the Employment Service for retraining, with a similar amount allocated to English Estates (later, English Partnerships) for the provision of factory and office space. BCE and the Rural Development Commission were authorised to establish schemes for the retraining of redundant miners, involving loans at low rates of interest of £5,000 per job for a five-year period. The Government promised new funding for the creation of Enterprise Zones in the neediest localities. Finally, despite being 'in many ways the bodies most experienced in local economic development activity' (Guy 1994, p.43), local authorities were to be supported by a much smaller Coalfield Areas Fund of £5 million for promoting skills or attracting new investment. Overall, the government package was judged inadequate. 'It is quite incredible that such a scheme could be considered acceptable as any sort of compensation for the loss of what was said to be 30,000 jobs but turned out to be a loss of nearly 40,000' (Coates and Barratt-Brown 1997, p.73).

Enterprise Zones are a case in point. Turner (1997) doubts their ability to deliver substantial economic benefits. He cites the zone created in the early 1980s at the Langthwaite Grange industrial estate in the former mining area of South Kirkby in West Yorkshire. Between 1990 and 1991 the number of full-time jobs showed only a 'modest' increase of 905, from 1,215 to 2,120. Most 'new' jobs resulted from the relocation of nearby firms:

> *The biggest employer in the enterprise zone in 1990, arriving in October of the same year, was a men's outfitter, providing 370 jobs. On moving into the zone, however, the company closed one factory in South Kirkby itself and one three miles away. This local relocation involved neither an increase nor a decrease in the number of jobs available. There was, therefore, no stimulus to the local economy. Other relocations included a chemical company, a glass recycling company, a security company, and a Christmas hamper packing company, all from close by. (Turner 1997, p.36)*

English Partnerships' Coalfield Programme

A coalition of smaller agencies concerned with housing and urban development, English Partnerships (EP), was formed in 1994. It aims to encourage area regeneration via the reclamation, development or redevelopment of land and buildings. Late in 1996 it acquired 56 disused coalfield sites from British Coal. English Partnerships' own £69 million was to be supplemented by specially targeted European funding and £750 million of private-sector funds. Physical renewal was intended to improve morale: 'The agency's aim is not just to improve and regenerate the sites themselves, but also to create and revive prosperity and generate a new sense of optimism within the coalfield communities' (Howe 1998, p.362). Six regional offices were briefed to target particular local needs and aspirations. Two early examples of EP's development work were projects developing former colliery sites at Glasshoughton in Castleford, West Yorkshire, and Dawdon colliery in Seaham, County Durham. At Glasshoughton, £8 million-worth of investment was devoted to reclaiming and developing the 330-acre (133.7 ha) site into a multipurpose industrial, residential and leisure complex. At Dawdon, a land reclamation and sewer improvement project, costing £4 million, was the first phase in the planned creation of an industrial park. Overall, development of the fifty-six sites aimed to produce 20,000 new jobs and 2,500 new homes. An EP representative claimed that, 'Coalmining may never come back to these areas, but new industry, and with it jobs, will start to bring new optimism to the coalfield communities' (Inman 1997, p.19).

European Funding

Throughout the 1990s British coalfield communities were entitled to apply for financial assistance from a variety of European Structural Funds. Foremost among these sources are the European Regional Development Fund (ERDF), which is used to promote economic development, and the European Social Fund (ESF), aiming to enhance employment primarily through training. After protracted negotiation and lobbying the allocation of structural funds up to 2006 was finally agreed in 2000. Qualification for this, the biggest funding source, requires an area to have fallen below 75 per cent of the EU average Gross Domestic Product (GDP). There are also a small number of Specialised Community Initiatives that distribute funds to areas traditionally dependent on one industry, such as shipbuilding, textiles, steel and, latterly, coal (RECHAR [Reconversion Charbonnage] programme).

To qualify for ERDF or ESF funding applications must be consistent with one or more specially designated European Community objectives. Objective 1 aims to narrow the gap between more prosperous and less favoured regions. Until 1999 UK coalfields were excluded because per capita GDP exceeded the 75 per cent threshold. Objective 2 seeks to rejuvenate regions experiencing serious economic decline, while Objective 3 is concerned with the reduction of unemployment, especially among young people. Objective 4 prioritises the adaptation of workers to industrial or product change. Objective 2 grants alone have typically been worth around £200 million per annum to the UK regions.

The RECHAR scheme 'represents a "silver lining" to the "cloud" of the mid-1990s coal closures' (Ball 1998, p.355). RECHAR owes its existence to political lobbying in the late 1980s by European Action for Coal Communities (EURACOM), an alliance of the CCC and its equivalent European organisations. The programme was formally approved in December 1989. Its specific aim is 'to assist economic renewal in EC coalfields that have lost large numbers of jobs in recent years and which suffer from important handicaps to regeneration' (Fothergill 1995, p.192). RECHAR obtains 80 per cent of its money from the ERDF. There have been two major phases of RECHAR funding. RECHAR 1, covering the period 1990–3, was worth 300 million ecus. RECHAR 2, initially running from 1994–7, subsequently extended to 1999, provided 400 million ecus. The regeneration measures eligible for RECHAR assistance are: environmental improvements, the development of factories or workspaces, the promotion of small or medium-sized businesses, tourism, the development of economic conversion agencies, vocational training, the retraining of ex-mineworkers, and the renovation of the economic and social infrastructure of an area (ibid.).

Two examples are cited by Coates and Barratt-Brown (1997). The East Durham Community Development Initiative assigned sixteen development workers to instigating a variety of training schemes, environmental improvement projects and pre-school childcare initiatives. South Yorkshire Coalfield's Learning Project used RECHAR money to provide ex-mining communities with 'access to a broad range of educational opportunities', enhancing employability and the value of 'lifelong learning' (ibid., p.63). An assessment of the impact of RECHAR funding on whole localities is provided by Ball (1998) for three coalfields within the West Midlands region (North Warwickshire, and North and South Staffordshire). There have been successes in land reclamation, workspace development, the refurbishment of community centres, training initiatives, and the encouraging or creating of small businesses. Less success was evident in heritage, tourism development and regional marketing.

RECHAR has not proved a panacea. A continuing problem stems from eligibility criteria. Applicants must come from an area which has lost a thousand coal-mining jobs since 1 January 1984. However, many of the areas most in need of regeneration lost their mines earlier. A related criterion – the unemployment rate within the Travel to Work Areas of mine closures – has disqualified some mining communities enveloped by relatively prosperous larger areas (Fothergill 1995). Most controversial of all in the British context has been the issue of 'additionality', which decrees that any amount of EU aid should be matched by national or local government spending. Strict financial controls on spending by UK local authorities meant that, in the late 1980s and early 1990s, 'non-additionality' was the norm. It is estimated that between 1989 and 1993 £1 billion-worth of European funding earmarked for UK mining areas was frozen (ibid.). Finally, its patience exhausted, the European Commission threatened to withhold future RECHAR and ERDF entitlement from the UK: 'Politically isolated, the subject of unfavourable publicity, and with a general election looming, the UK government conceded in February 1992' (ibid., p.203).

Ball (1998) has identified specific problems with RECHAR funding. Experience in the West Midlands suggests that the patchwork nature of RECHAR funding within particular regions can produce a lack of strategic coherence and direction:

> *Whilst it has been a catalyst for innovative thinking via the lure of the European funding, with tight performance criteria and financial monitoring, the attractions set against the workloads for local applicants sometimes wear thin. There is also a potential danger of additionality, and a phasing problem in the availability of matched funding between project partners. In addition, enthusiasm for local capacity building is initially not always matched by local expertise in creating and developing it, but potential funding has had the effect of nudging partners into action that is sometimes quite innovative in design and delivery. (ibid., p.360)*

In his overall assessment Fothergill compliments RECHAR for having kindled enthusiasm for co-operation and being responsive to problems beyond solution by local actors and resources. However, he expresses the reservation that, 'It is not clear that the Commission has yet learned that regional aid must be substantial and sustained if it is to be genuinely effective' (Fothergill 1995, p.204).

The European Union's allocation of structural funds up until 2006 could represent the last opportunity for UK coalfield areas. An enlarged Europe with many ailing economies in the east is unlikely to be so generous again. Of the coalfield areas South Yorkshire and the South Wales valleys have qualified for Objective 1 funding. EU grants are available up to 75 per cent towards the cost of projects in these areas. More contentious has been the allocation of Objective 2 funding (earmarked for lagging industrial regions) where grants of up to 50 per cent of the cost of projects are allocated. Some coal districts have missed out on this source of funding and direct funding from the UK Government under Regional Selective Assistance (the so-called Assisted Areas), worth around £400 million in total per year. EU structural funds, worth over £1 billion per year, will continue to be available, however, to most coalfield areas over the next few years.

Challenge Funding and Area Regeneration

Equally important as European structural and Assisted Area funds are the competitive spatial economic policies that have been introduced over the last decade by the Department of Trade and Industry, notably City and Rural Challenges and the Single Regeneration Budget (SRB). City Challenge was the prototype. Launched in 1991, it required partnerships of local government and voluntary and private-sector agencies to compete for standard funding packages of £37.5 million over five years. Supplanted by the SRB in 1993, its basic principle of competitive funding has remained (Hall and Mawson 1999; Mawson and Hall 2000). Applicants must incorporate a strong partnership principle, demonstrate pump-priming potential, have clear targets for up to seven years, and show how regeneration and development will continue when funding ceases (Fordham et al. 1999).

In practice, regeneration initiatives depend on multiple sources of funding, from the UK and Europe. An exception to the fragmented and piecemeal approach is the Dearne Valley Partnership (DVP), a coalition of three South Yorkshire local authorities, business interests and community organisations. Described as 'probably the most polluted and despoiled area within the UK' (Salt 1995, p.70), the Dearne Valley covers 20 square miles (51.8 km) with a population of 80,000. The DVP originates from the early 1990s when fifteen local authorities were invited by the DTI to compete under the City Challenge scheme. Although, as Turner (1997, p.384) points out, the Dearne Valley 'bore no resemblance whatsoever to a "city"', it was selected as one of eleven successful bidders. The DVP adopted a supply-side strategy of land reclamation, economic development and improved infrastructure, especially for road traffic. Arguably more ambitious still was the creation of a university college to cater for local education and retraining needs.

Another example is the Midland Coalfield Area of the National Forest, described by Beaverstock (1998a; 1998b). To stimulate enterprise and create jobs in a context of 'environmental and economic sustainability' the National Forest has stimulated partnership bids for central government and European Funds. By August 1996 a series of specific projects, such as the conversion of former colliery buildings into craft and training centres, developing business units and energising the local SME (small and medium-sized enterprises) sector had been funded out of the RECHAR II scheme. A host of land reclamation, tourism enhancement, renewable energy and recreational and educational projects had also been funded by the Rural and SRB Challenges.

So far we have looked at the regeneration strategies and agencies, providing examples of detailed assessments of their impact. The general tendencies have been to centralise policy whilst devolving its execution to quangos, to multiply the number of agencies involved whilst exhorting co-operation and co-ordination, and to provide short-term funding on a highly competitive basis. The RECHAR programme has been a partial exception but even there problems of eligibility criteria and the lack of long-term investment have proved to have limitations. How all these national and European strategies have impacted specific areas or particular kinds of projects has been examined in several important studies. The first is a study conducted by one of the authors.

Parry's Interregional Comparison

Between 1993 and 1995 David Parry carried out a comparative analysis of regeneration attempts in the key coal-mining regions of South Wales, Nottinghamshire and South Yorkshire. Using in-depth interviews and secondary sources the study evaluated regenerative policies in each region up until 1995. A full account of this research is given in Parry (1996). This summary provides a snapshot in the mid-1990s of the progress of regeneration in three coalfields most affected by pit closure. In each, three aspects were examined: physical renewal, job creation or training, and the empowerment of local communities.

South Wales

Environmental regeneration in South Wales aimed to rid the region of its spoil-heap image, release development land for inward investment and house incoming managerial and technical staff. The first initiative was the 'greening of the valleys' spearheaded by the WDA, which had built nearly 6,000 new homes. By 1996 it involved forty projects aimed at the restoration of 3,000 acres (1,214.1 ha) of former industrial land. A second major initiative, the Cardiff Bay Development, aimed to transform 2,700 acres (1,092.7 ha) of former docklands into offices and high-tech modern business sites (see also Raco 2000). Though centred beyond the valley areas it was claimed as beneficial to the entire region, particularly as skills audits suggested that 49 per cent of employees travelled outside the valleys daily. It still attracted criticism that it diverted resources from other parts of the region. A third example was the infrastructural improvement programme, including the development of the M4 motorway and the building of twenty-three new railway stations in Mid- and South Glamorgan between 1984 and 1992. The M4 development stimulated growth along its corridor and in the east of the region but had limited impact on the valleys, though links to the main motorway were being improved.

Job creation in South Wales rested on the region's ability to attract more inward investment, at a far higher and more consistent rate than any other UK region. However, doubts remained about even this apparent success. The process of foreign investment had been notably uneven, with the valleys receiving only one-third of inward investment by 1992. This had been insufficient to stem the ongoing decline in jobs in manufacturing: between 1988 and 1992 12,000 jobs were created in 73 new and 203 expanded plants but this could not prevent the net loss of 18,400 jobs. Real unemployment figures for the valleys were estimated to be as high as 33 per cent. The quality of new jobs, their pay and conditions, was also the subject of concern.

Community empowerment had been encouraged through the Community Business arm of the WDA, stimulating community enterprises that were locally controlled but business-oriented. Examples included projects in the Amman Valley, Betws and Cynon Valley, which provided services – cafés, bars, community halls and transport – rather than goods manufacturing. Though culturally important, their economic impact was limited. The Valleys Initiative for Adult Education (VIAE) and its offshoot, the Community University of the Valleys, saw regeneration as dependent on individual and collective empowerment through education. The VIAE was finding it difficult to promote education in coalfield communities. Ingrained attitudes and widespread apathy were proving intractable.

Nottinghamshire

In Nottinghamshire, there was no single project of the built environment designed to arrest decline and stimulate economic growth. Mining villages are scattered across a largely rural landscape so that pockets of deprivation are small compared with South Wales or South Yorkshire. In Nottinghamshire County Council's 'New Deal' for the area 'transport and infrastructure improvements' and 'improving the environment' were two of its six priorities. The transport project with the highest profile was the Robin Hood Line, rebuilding a railway line which had been closed in the 1960s to restore a transport link through the heart of the county.

Nottinghamshire's employment base was considerably diluted during the 1980s by large-scale job losses in engineering and pharmaceuticals as well as in coal-mining and textiles. The region responded by promising incentives and factory space to promote internal growth and inward investment. This policy paid some dividends, such as the Toyota plant near Derby or Toray Textiles and the automotive furnishings manufacturer, Johnson's Controls, in Mansfield. However, unemployment in the assisted area of Mansfield increased from 14 per cent in 1989 to 16 per cent in 1994. The construction of different measures for unemployment – or 'non-employment' (Balls and Gregg 1993) – suggested that real unemployment in the Nottinghamshire coalfields was 19 per cent rather than the 11 per cent officially registered.

Community Business developments were limited in Nottinghamshire. Community projects included the Rural Development Commission's (RDC) plans for four part-time community resource centres at Blidworth, Bilsthorpe, Langold and Newstead. The RDC also part-sponsored the Warsop Regeneration Project, whose aim was the environmental, economic and social renewal of the area.

South Yorkshire

Property developments in the South Yorkshire coalfield were few, though leisure complexes had been established at The Dome at Doncaster and The Metrodome at Barnsley. One of the Dearne Valley Partnership's plans for the revival of the area was The Earth Centre, a proposed educational and business enterprise which attracted £50 million from the Millennium Fund in October 1995. The centre was projected to attract some 2 million visitors a year. A proposed new university development was stymied by the Government's capping of student numbers.

The transformation of former colliery sites, coke works and chemical plants into country parks or factory units was proving a slow and difficult process. The DVP's target for land reclamation over the five-year City Challenge period was 1,944.2 acres (786.8 ha); after two years, they had achieved 673.1 acres (272.4 ha) (35 per cent of the target in 40 per cent of the time). The construction of the £30 million Dearne Towns Link Road was designed to upgrade the infrastructure. However, as better road links were built, rail passenger and freight lines were being closed.

In South Yorkshire, approaches to employment creation usually fell into two categories: inward investment and indigenous growth. There had been some foreign investment. Koyo relocated on a former colliery site in Barnsley and Kostel in the Dearne Valley but these were rare examples. The shortage of greenfield sites was thought to be partly responsible. Business growth had been held back by the lack of a local enterprise culture. The rate of coalfield unemployment remained high, Beatty and Fothergill (1994) estimating the real level of unemployment in pit villages to be 28 per cent, rather than the 15 per cent officially registered.

A few projects targeted community empowerment, such as Community Development Trusts in the Dinnington and Kiveton areas of Rotherham. The most comprehensive was the Dearne Enterprise Centre, opened in 1986. It provided career and business advice and training, a base for a writers' workshop, welfare rights project and urban farm, as well as being the focal point of political lobbying. Inspired by the VIAE in South Wales, the Coalfield Education Project was trying to promote education as a basis for confidence-building towards possible future employment.

Implications

Parry's study argued that, ultimately, regenerative strategies in all three regions involved a commitment to a post-industrial solution, recognising that the tertiary sector has expanded while extractive and manufacturing industries are in decline (Allen and Massey 1988a; 1998b). The solution advocated had been to adjust the local economy to national and international trends. The most effective strategy seemed to have been the stimulation of inward investment, attracted by a plentiful supply of labour to be selectively recruited and grants available in Enterprise Zones, Assisted Areas and City Challenge locations. Nevertheless, even though some parts of the regions under study had been able to adjust, there was little evidence that former coal communities themselves had been, or were likely to be, the beneficiaries of any significant economic growth. A second strategy had been to encourage in the local economy the flexible specialisation taken to be characteristic of post-Fordist economies. The emphasis on small businesses and networking was an attempt to stimulate growth patterns similar to the more successful regional economies, encouraging flexible specialisation firms at the high end of the skill, knowledge and value-added chain. However, there was little evidence of the predominance of such firms in any of the three regions, much less in the coalfield areas.

In practice, coalfield areas had been economically marginalised. Communities with closed collieries had a wide range of disadvantages including poor infrastructure, environmental dereliction and substandard housing. Their labour markets exhibited problems in skill acquisition and educational attainment. The local culture was perceived as inimical to entrepreneurial activity (Rees and Thomas 1989; Turner 1992; 1993). In a shifting economy such localities could not easily move from the periphery to the centre.

The policy of 'market shock' (Amin and Thrift 1995, p.44) and deregulation had inevitably led to a concentration of resources, including physical infrastructure, skills and power, in areas where the highest and quickest return on investment is possible. Regional disparities had increased rather than decreased (Amin and Thrift 1994). The relocation of capital to low wage de-regulated areas (Jonas 1995) demanded cheaper labour and flexibility – task, temporal and contractual (Hudson 1988). Industrial networking (Cooke and Morgan 1993), high-tech, high value-added, high quality, high skills had all been much less evident.

Rectifying imbalances within global, national and regional economies had proved beyond the scope of policies in these regions. South Wales's comparative success in regeneration appeared unlikely to be replicated in the other two regions, at least in the medium term. The explanations were specific: the longer-term efforts to address the region's economic problems; the unique nature of regional agencies; and even such contingencies as motorway connections to the affluent South-East and West of England. Even here, the coalfields had been the last to benefit from spin-offs from the region's economic improvement. Parts of the South Wales valleys had remained stubbornly resistant to renewal. In South Yorkshire and Nottinghamshire, coalfields lacked the context of long-term intervention, strong regional institutions or links to prosperous neighbouring regions. The very factors which had aided regeneration in Wales were conspicuously absent from the other two regions where 'socio-spatial segregation' and 'social containment' (Hudson 1994, pp.208-9) seemed the more likely outcome.

The Coalfields Task Force and Government Response

The election of a Labour government in May 1997 raised expectations in coalfield areas that more resources for regeneration would be released. In October 1997 Deputy Prime Minister John Prescott commissioned a special Coalfields Task Force to investigate the particular needs of mining communities and make recommendations for their regeneration. Its brief was to:

set the framework which will empower coalfield communities affected by pit closures and job losses to create their own new start, forging their own sustainable and prosperous future, and to engage the active support of all partners, particularly the government, in its delivery. (Coalfields Task Force 1998, p.1)

The thirteen-person Task Force, with its one woman as chair, was drawn mainly from the civil service, local authorities and the voluntary sector. It took evidence from over 200 organisations, held five regional hearings and one themed seminar, and commissioned two locality studies. Its report, delivered within seven months in June 1998, contained thirty-nine recommendations, summarised in Table 8.1 below.

TABLE 8.1 THE COALFIELDS TASK FORCE RECOMMENDATIONS

Policy type	Immediate action and impact	Immediate action/ medium-term impact	Strategic action/ long-term impact
Improving access to existing funding	4	2	2
Providing new sources of funding	3		
Regional development strategies		4	3
Improving local services	3	1	
Pension compensation	1	1	
Encouraging partnerships		2	1
Co-ordinating government departments		3	
Improving the environment		3	
Extending English Partnerships	2		
Other	1	2	1
Total	*14*	*18*	*7*

The first four policy types covered twenty-two of the thirty-nine recommendations. Improving access to existing funding aimed at Objectives 1 and 2 for the EU, the RECHAR programme, matched funding, lottery grants, the SRB budget, and Standard Spending Assessment. Providing new sources of funding aimed at public or business advice services and community projects. Regional development strategies targeted job creation, roads, action areas and inward investment. Local services needing improvement included transport, roads and housing.

This was a set of highly practical proposals in that they worked within existing and proposed structures and agencies. While the document did discuss the need for empowerment this was not taken as involving any radical disturbance in policy formulation or implementation.

The Government's response was bound to reflect New Labour's policy to integrate coalfields into its more general area regeneration strategy. Its basic principles are 'fivefold: integration; decentralisation; regeneration; partnerships; sustainability' (Hall and Mawson 1999, p.5). This stance was evident in measures undertaken before the publication of the Task Force Report. A government discussion document (DETR 1997) confirmed that New Labour would continue to prioritise competitive challenge funding for area regeneration. A December 1997 White Paper, Partnerships for Prosperity in the English Regions, outlined five key areas of activity to be undertaken by new Regional Development Agencies: economic development and regeneration (including administration of the SRB Challenge Fund); competitiveness; business support and investment; skills; employment; and sustainability.

In July 1998, as the Task Force was reporting, the Government revealed the outcome of its Comprehensive Spending Review. Central to its package of reforms was the establishment of a 'New Deal for Communities', whereby £88 million would be set aside for improving housing and enhancing employment opportunities in seriously deprived neighbourhoods. A commitment was made to reform the SRB to ensure that 80 per cent of resources would reach the most deprived areas.

Hence, in its response to the Task Force report (DETR 1998), the Government emphasised how ex-mining communities would benefit from applications of existing government programmes, with only a few new policies specifically designed for coal communities. A ten-year programme was unveiled for combating deprivation in the coalfields. While said to involve some £354 million of 'additional money', the package actually incorporated £196 million that had mostly been pledged to English Partnerships in 1996. A second undertaking, to earmark £70 million from Round 5 of the SRB for the coalfields, arguably incorporated money already destined for the coalfields anyway. Out of the genuinely 'new' money being made available the Government committed itself to investing £50 million over three years in a new Coalfields Regeneration Trust to support community initiatives, such as one-stop shops and welfare-to-work related projects. A further £15 million would be invested across the same period (via a Coalfield Enterprise Fund) to stimulate and support the development of small firms, while £28 million was allocated over three years to a Housing Investment Programme for coalfield councils. Action would be taken to ensure an improved take-up of lottery funding in coalfield areas, raising it at least to the national average. Finally, responsibility for developing and co-ordinating the economic, physical and social regeneration of the coalfields would now rest with eight Regional Development Agencies (RDAs).

The Coalfield Communities Campaign has since published two separate assessments of progress (CCC 1999; 2000). The foreword to the more recent evaluation reports that 'valuable progress' had been made in key areas, none the less adding, 'But there are still weak points as well, where good intentions and sensible ideas seem so far to have come to nothing' (CCC 2000, p.3). More positively, the CCC noted that the Coalfields Regeneration Trust, enlarged to include Scotland and Wales, had received more than 1,000 applications from community and voluntary organisations by August 2000. More than £20 million had been awarded. A further twenty-five coalfield sites had been added to English Partnership's portfolio and its ten-year budget of £350 million enhanced by £40 million for three years. Despite the estimated cost of £116 million for restoring the extra sites, English Partnerships expected to finance it from sales and grants. The Government had committed £18 million to the Housing Investment Programme. The CCC regarded this as inadequate, since £85 million was needed just to raise the housing stock in the Nottinghamshire Meden Valley to minimum standards.

The CCC criticised the slow progress of the Coalfield Enterprise Fund which 'compares unfavourably with the speed with which a broadly similar (and larger) fund was established as part of British Coal Enterprise in 1984–5' (ibid., p.9). The lack of access to lottery funds had been researched but no specific action taken. The CCC was agnostic about the potential of the RDAs. In its statutory guidance to the RDAs the Government had directed them to have 'special regard for coalfield areas' in their economic strategies. That two regions, the West Midlands and the North-West, had initially omitted any mention of the coalfields in their draft strategies did not bode well. Reservations were also expressed about SRB allocations. The amounts going to coalfields under SRB5 and SRB6 had increased but their proportional share remained static: 'the stability of the coalfields' share of SRB grants indicates that they have not been given any extra priority since the publication of the Government's response to the Task Force' (ibid. p.14).

In September 2000 a team commissioned by the DETR also produced an interim evaluation of the Task Force initiative (DETR 2000). This research took the themes of the Task Force as its starting point and looked at the conditions in the former coalfields to provide a baseline for evaluating policy. Assessment of progress pointed up the need to focus public-sector intervention. Some coal districts had recovered better than others and did not require significant further assistance. Community involvement and partnership building was much encouraged but the authors warned against reliance on previously established patterns of community behaviour. They doubted the ability of coal communities to help themselves, stressing the need to rebuild community capacity. Institutional inertia, significantly targeted as a major barrier to regeneration, was evident in the lack of co-ordination between central government departments and regional or local organisations.

The 2000 Spending Review provided another injection of cash for the Regional Development Agencies and a new Neighbourhood Renewal Fund. This £800 million fund covers over eighty areas until 2004. Allocation is based on the new Indices of Deprivation 2000. The intention is to discriminate between coalfields showing signs of recovery and those still in dire need. Two of the latter have been examined in another recent study.

The Rowntree Report

In a project funded by the Joseph Rowntree Foundation, Bennett et al. (2000) focused on thirty community initiatives in the coalfield areas of Mansfield, North Nottinghamshire and Rhonnda Cynon Taff, South Wales. The study's premise was that 'formal sector top-down policies have been unable to provide jobs of adequate quality and quantity to replace those lost from coal mining' (ibid., p.22).

All but one of the initiatives sampled were involved in service provision rather than goods manufacture. The exception, an Arts Factory in South Wales, produced plants, pottery and woodcrafts. Other projects provided subsidised furniture, advice about loans and savings, crèches or childcare facilities, out-of-school activities, drop-in or counselling services, transport, landscaping, café or catering facilities, fine or performing arts, and educational or vocational courses and training. All depended largely on public-sector funding and tended to develop when formal agencies allied with small numbers of local residents. The attitude of most local people to initiatives foisted on them from the outside was 'sometimes, at best one of indifference, at worst one of confrontation and opposition' (ibid., p.28).

The authors argue that, whilst community initiatives provide few jobs, they none the less provide satisfying forms of work and valuable services that the labour market otherwise fails to deliver. However, participants in community initiatives are often discouraged by 'what is often seen as bureaucratic indifference, a constant battle to secure funding, and the resultant threat – or reality – of the collapse of projects' (ibid., p.31).

Funding applications are time-consuming and complicated. Financial support is typically short-term and often requires matched funding. The chances of success are often slim. There is an excessive emphasis on 'quantifiable outputs'. Less tangible outcomes – such as making people feel included or valuable, or restoring their self-esteem and confidence – seem to count for little. The requirement to form partnerships leads to 'marriages of convenience' in which community representatives are marginalised, excluded from strategy formulation and included only as 'token representation to ensure that a tick could be placed in the relevant box on an application for funding' (ibid., p.41).

Bennett et al. conclude that coalfield areas should continue to receive substantial funding from national government and European sources but that local people should be fully involved in the formulation, implementation and management of community initiatives. The current accent on short-termism should be abandoned; funds should be made available for as long as any given project is likely to require them; and there should be scope for risk-taking: 'Local initiatives that start and then "fail" may be as important as those that start and then "succeed", recognising that both success and failure are open to competing interpretations' (ibid., p.46). A flexible view should taken of how projects meet the needs and objectives of the local population.

Bennett et al. appear sceptical about whether New Labour's proposals for coalfield regeneration will meet these requirements. They note that the new money is less than the Treasury has accrued from surpluses in the miners' pension fund. The general approach of the Government, that 'the key to regeneration of deprived place lies in their integration into the formal economy through economic development policies' (ibid., p.40), implicitly assumes that the market, if stimulated, will solve the problems which the market has produced. Regional Development Agencies will not resolve problems of overlapping programmes, competition for funds or spurious partnerships. Moreover, they will reproduce one of the most long-standing problems in regeneration: the tendency to devolve responsibility for achieving regeneration objectives whilst retaining centrally the power to define eligibility criteria and allocate funds.

Bennett et al. conclude that a major problem at the heart of regeneration is the term itself and others coexisting alongside it: 'partnership', 'community' and 'empowerment'. As they explore in detail, each of these terms has significantly different meanings depending on who is using it, in what context and for what purpose. From a top-down perspective, regeneration is primarily a question of economic renewal; partnership a matter of co-ordination and efficiency; community a process of consultation; and empowerment a form of self-help. From a bottom-up perspective, regeneration is the revitalisation of a whole way of life; partnership a requirement of funding agencies; community an expression of local interests; and empowerment the devolving of power from economic and political institutions. Groups using the same language do not share common meanings. In the following conclusions we discuss how these ambiguities have been reflected in regenerative strategies at the national, local and regional levels.

Conclusions

Coalfield communities are examples of the uneven development of capitalism that have been forced in to decline by world forces (Sadler 1992). This chapter and other reviews of research suggest that much regeneration policy has become, in practice, the management of social exclusion (Hudson 1994; Brown and Crompton 1994; Kennett 1994). There have been significant improvements in land reclamation, infrastructural improvement and housing renovation. Job creation and retraining have occurred but on too small a scale to compensate for the number of lost jobs and have resulted in deterioration in pay and conditions. The process of recovery is perhaps best illustrated by the fact that South Yorkshire and the South Wales valleys now qualify for

Objective 1 funding. This could be interpreted as an indictment of previous regeneration policies. After 150 years in the engine-room of the UK economy they are now ranked amongst the most failing regions of Europe.

Overall, the limitations of the results of regeneration strategies reflect the scale of the problems based. An extractive and manufacturing base cannot be replaced overnight. The resources involved have not been commensurate with the dimensions of the problem. The emphases on competition and the creation of a plethora of agencies has meant that regeneration has been largely piecemeal and unco-ordinated. Many problems are untouched. Huge tracts of housing remain dilapidated and educational attainment is substandard. The rate of unemployment in ex-mining villages remains three times the national average. For all that, there is evidence within this chapter of possible ways forward. We want to draw attention to two such directions: the importance of institutions, especially at the regional level; and, at the other end of the scale, the value of locally run and managed projects.

The Role of Institutions

The objectives and strategies of regeneration policies depend crucially on the institutions which execute them. Though much activity has appeared local, it has in effect been nationally driven by government, with the same institutions – TECs and BCE, local authorities, English Estates and the Rural Development Commission – playing key roles in each region. There has been some variation in the precise relationship between national agencies like TECs and localised 'socially embedded' institutions (Peck 1994). Even 'Growth Coalitions' (Barnekov et al. 1989; Loftman and Nevin 1994), such as the Dearne Valley Partnership or the Urban Development Corporations of Sheffield and Cardiff, have been defined by national strategies. National programmes, such as City Challenge or the Single Regeneration Budget, have encouraged local coalitions but only on condition that they competed with each other.

Agencies and tiers of regional government have been directed by central government, with policy prescriptions uniform throughout the UK. Central government has exerted more control by 'rolling back' the local state and squeezing it financially, promoting quangos and competitive funding programmes, all distributed according to government-defined criteria. Thus, 'Without a more supportive national economic framework, it will be difficult if not impossible to achieve anything other than little victories at the regional level' (Morgan and Price 1992, p.12). As Peck (1994) points out, it has been striking how 'unlocal' many policies have been. Yet at the local level they have often duplicated each other and lacked co-ordination (Peck and Tickell 1994). Open or covert rivalry between local authorities and between agencies has hindered the efficient and effective implementation of policies: 'all concerned with attracting a slice of the cake, but uninterested in, or unable to affect its size, and downplaying other broader questions such as the quality of jobs and the general conditions of employment' (Beynon et al. 1991, p.xix).

However, there has been considerable regional variation in the sense of identity, the flexibility and durability of local institutions and the ability to co-ordinate regenerative efforts. South Wales's regional identity has been built on nationality, embodied in the special institutions of the Welsh Office and the Welsh Development Agency, from which identifiable advantages have accrued. Despite some criticism their very existence has provided an 'institutional thickness of the region' (Amin and Thrift 1994), bodies with clear responsibility for and resources to undertake systematic regeneration. Though apparently unique, the WDA's qualified success should at least stimulate a rethink about how regions are governed and how they can implement regeneration policies (Morgan 1995). Larger units of governance, or coalitions of local government, can be more effective in regeneration policies. The evidence appears incontrovertible that a regional tier of policy implementation can have significant regenerative effects on a regional economy, even if its impact upon particular coalfield localities is indirect and long-term. This appears, however, to require substantial autonomy from national government.

Community Initiatives

Local community-based initiatives are frequently found in ex-coalfield communities but their resourcing has been inadequate. The formation of the Coalfields Regeneration Trust may in time improve the position. It is recognised that community empowerment can 'reap limited but real gains' (Lawless 1996) to ameliorate the impact of 'structural disempowerment' (Amin and Thrift 1995). As examples in this chapter have shown, in isolated coalfield communities small initiatives can contribute to educational and training opportunities and physical renewal of neighbourhoods, increasing employment potential. However, despite the inclusion of such ideas in a great deal of literature, orthodox economic development still tends to dominate.

Since there is no hope of returning employment levels to those of a thriving coal industry scaled-down expectations and projects are much more likely to work, especially if they are located in and controlled by the community they are trying to help. As Chanan (1996, p.83) suggests, the issue is not just that this approach has 'economic value', but 'whether policy, both domestic and global, can be made more accountable to the ethos of community activity'. The physical renewal of community buildings and their use as educational and training facilities controlled by the local people give mining communities the chance to sustain themselves in a limited but valuable way.

Simmonds and Emmerich (1996) have argued that significant job creation is possible in the 'social economy'. Their 'regeneration through work' strategy addresses the types of problem evident in coalfield communities and combines all the four components of regeneration. It argues that the 'employment demand deficit' (ibid., p.4) is not inevitable and that, by creating intermediate labour markets employing people in socially useful jobs not covered by private or public enterprise, successful regeneration is possible. Policies to set up 'Community Enterprise Corporations' and 'Community Enterprise Zones' could provide an appropriate institutional structure to complement 'regeneration through work' (Thakes and Stauback 1993). Since it has not seriously been tried, the economic potential of such an approach remains unknown but its psychological benefits, in restoring some sense of control and morale, would almost certainly be positive.

The portents for creating an enabling and empowering national approach to coalfield regeneration are admittedly not good. As Bennett et al., amongst others, have shown, the present range of competitive funding regimes are often restrictive and demoralising. Funding is short-term and non-renewable. Criteria are complex and arbitrary. The requirement for partnerships gives rise to bogus coalitions smacking of political expediency.

New Labour and Regional Development Agencies

The Labour Government's regeneration strategy appears to recognise the importance of both regional institutions and community empowerment. However, structural reform has been circumspect and orthodox. The need for a new level of governance in the regions capable of co-ordinating and sustaining economic development was accepted but the model chosen was for more effective, bigger quangos with little devolution of political power. The associated regional assemblies presented additional problems and Government has been much more cautious about setting up another layer of political power. This has left the RDAs open to the charge of lack of accountability (Bennett et al. 2000).

Incrementally, the role of the RDAs has been enhanced. Budgets from 2000 onwards have been significantly increased and the RDAs have taken over allocation of Single Regeneration Budget funds. Potentially, these organisations will have significant power and exercise strategic control over economic development. However, as the Coalfield Communities Campaign point out (CCC 2000), the voices of coalfield areas may not be heard in regions dominated by metropolitan interests.

The crucial problem for RDAs may be whether they can be legitimately perceived as achieving the goal of 'institutional thickness'. This refers not to the size or number of regenerative institutions but how they are interlocked with other significant political and economic institutions, both nationally and locally. It is not clear whether RDAs represent a new kind of institution 'which would allow more of a smooth and incremental adaptation of local economic and social life to the broader exigencies of national state policies and global political-economic change' (Hudson 1992, p.212). It does not immediately seem that RDAs are designed to fulfil this role. They are defined as 'business-led' with a role 'to help further economic development, regeneration and promote business efficiency, investment and competitiveness in the regions' (DETR 1998, p.15). This is uncomfortably close to the ethos and structure of the much criticised Training and Enterprise Councils.

In similarly orthodox fashion, community participation and empowerment is assumed to be realised by yet more exhortation of partnership:

> *Where SRB coalfield partnerships are felt to be weak, the most common problem is lack of genuine community involvement and participation of the voluntary and private sectors. The Government wants every former coalfield community to take an active role in a Coalfields Regeneration Partnership; and will welcome SRB Round 5 bids that build upon existing schemes to strengthen partnership coverage of coalfield areas. It also wishes to see up to 10% of resources per scheme going to community capacity building activity. (DETR 1998, p.13)*

None of this seems to add up to institutional thickness. Regenerative agencies are not to be embedded within regions but superimposed upon them. The success of the Welsh Development Agency stemmed in part from its contingent autonomy from other government departments. Such autonomy and the difficult political questions it raises about regional government are clearly not on the agenda.

There were and are viable alternatives, especially evident in the experience of coalfield decline in other European countries, where there have been different shapes and dynamics to the relationships between national, regional and local policies and institutions. We consider these in the following chapter.

9 Coalfield Regeneration in Europe

INTRODUCTION

The decline of the coal-mining industry and its communities has occurred in several west European countries.[1] This shared experience enables comparative analysis of how decline has been managed and regeneration attempted by different nation and local states. In this chapter we look at three recent examples: Belgium, Germany and Spain. In concluding, we also briefly reflect on the policy implications for the restructuring coal industries of central and eastern Europe.

In Belgium, coal-mining ceased in the early 1990s. Pit closures and regeneration efforts were guided by a ten-year 'Future Contract' (1987–96). This was a state-led programme endorsed by the EU and regional and provincial levels of Belgian politics, designed to revitalise the Limburg coal region by raising employment and educational levels to the national standard and converting former industrial land into recreational, educational and commercial centres. This programme achieved only limited success, hampered initially by mismanagement of its primary regenerative agency and latterly by party-political infighting at the provincial level.

In Germany, where mining continues, the long-term decline of the industry has been managed through a gradual and negotiated series of national agreements, buttressed by indirect subsidies and guaranteed markets. There have been concerted efforts to induce local economic regeneration involving co-operation between federal, regional and municipal government and between the public and private sectors, all co-ordinated at a local level. While this has not wholly prevented burgeoning unemployment, mining localities have been spared the drastic economic and social consequences of mass closures and local economies have been given time to restructure.

In Spain, mining also continues but in different circumstances. Until the late 1990s a highly unprofitable industry has been wound down very slowly, mainly because of the political power of regional government and the organised labour movement. This political success has prevented significant measures to regenerate local economies, which remain highly dependent on coal. A protectionist policy, with high levels of direct subsidy and guaranteed markets, has not prevented pit closures and loss of employment, but merely postponed the demise of the industry and its consequences for local economies.

The European Union (formerly the Common Market) was founded on the two pillars of coal and steel under the European Coal and Steel Community

(ECSC) Treaty 1952. This is testimony to the former importance of these basic industries. It is necessary when comparing national policies to be aware of the transnational regulatory framework of the Treaty in ratifying subsidies and restructuring programmes.

To facilitate close comparison we focus on three principal coal regions in each nation: Limburg in Belgium; the Asturias region of Spain; and North-Rhine Westfalen in Germany. In addition to established studies (Baeten et al. 1999; Swyngedouw 1996), we draw on our own programme of work (Critcher, Schubert and Waddington 1995) including a specially commissioned study on Spain (Vázquez and del Rosal 1995).

We begin our analysis by tracing the decline of the European mining industry. We then outline the separate histories of coal-mining in each country and the balance of economic and political forces determining policy. In the three regional case studies we focus on implementation of restructuring polices and their implications for the local economy. The conclusion discusses the similarities and differences in the policy mix, institutional network and political culture of each nation and region. Finally, we consider the implications for future European regeneration policy of the possible inclusion of other coal-producing nations as EU members.

The Decline of the European Coal Industry

The recent fate of western Europe's major coal industries is inextricably linked to the wider transformation of the global energy market occurring over the past fifty years. In the two decades from 1950 coal's share of the international energy market fell from 65 per cent to 35 per cent (Chadwick et al. 1987). Since the early 1970s European coal production has declined as the result of: the loss of staple custom (e.g. steel); the increasing preference for alternative energy sources, notably gas; enhanced competition from generally cheaper foreign coal; and ever tighter environmental regulation. Between 1980 and 1994 coal production in the EU declined from 264 million tonnes to 131 million. As can be seen from figure 9.1, coal production in three EU states dropped by 85 million tonnes to approximately 100 million tonnes between 1992 and 2000. During this period mining ceased altogether in Belgium and Portugal. Production has tenuously survived in France where agreement has been reached under the 'National Coal Pact' between employers and unions to terminate coal-mining by 2005.

The resulting high levels of unemployment, even in those regions where some measure of coal-production was maintained, provoked special measures to protect the future viability of coal-mining, offset the impact of job losses and regenerate mining communities. McAvan (1993, p.172) makes the general point that what most distinguishes the pit closure programmes of Britain's European partners from the types of policy implemented by the UK government is that 'they involve long-term planning in terms of both energy and regional policy, as well as extensive consultations with local actors, including trade unions, employers and local authorities, prior to decisions being taken'.

McAvan explains, for example, how miners at Portugal's last surviving mine were retrained during working hours for the eighteen months before the pit eventually closed. In France, in the 1980s, the state-owned Charbonnages de France committed itself to securing new jobs for all miners aged under 45 and to providing additional assistance with retraining and relocation. Similar measures have been implemented at one stage or another by the Belgian, German and Spanish authorities but the historical, economic and political context has been significantly different in each case.

FIGURE 9.1 COAL PRODUCTION IN SELECTED EU COUNTRIES 1992–9

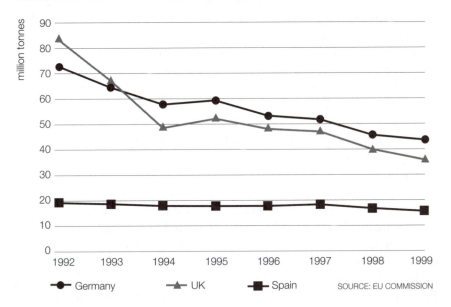

The Three Coal Industries Compared

Historically, Belgian deep coal-mining was concentrated in Wallonia (south Belgium) and in the Flemish Province of Limburg. At its productive peak of 1952 the Limburg coalfield employed 40,000 miners producing half the national output. At this stage, coal-mining accounted for some two-thirds of Limburg's total industrial employment. From the mid-1950s the industry entered a long period of slow contraction. With the closure of the last of the Walloon mines in 1981 coal-production existed only in the handful of remaining Limburg collieries. Even so, by 1986 its workforce still numbered 17,000 miners. However, in that year the Belgian Government signalled its intention to phase out all coal-mining within a decade, an objective achieved with time to spare in 1992.

The German coal industry played a major role in national post-war reconstruction. Ruhrkohle AG (RAG), a private corporation founded in 1968, owns most of the deep coal-mines. A high degree of mechanisation cannot resolve the geological problems of coal extraction. Government subsidies and rationalisation have cushioned a slow decline. In the 1980s the industry lost 19 per cent of its production and 22 per cent of its workforce. Germany produced more coal than the UK from 1993 onwards (see figure 9.1) but at a higher cost and price, the latter being three times the international market price (figure 9.2). Economically, German coal is not a very viable industry. Arguments in favour of its retention have to use other criteria.

Coal's contribution to Spain's economic development peaked in the 1950s and 1960s as a consequence of governmental isolationism and commitment to energy self-sufficiency. By the 1980s the effects of liberalisation, economic competition and especially entry into the EC rendered the uncompetitive industry ever more vulnerable, heavily dependent on contracts with the energy supply industry brokered by government. These guaranteed markets enabled expansion when the rest of the European industry was in steep decline. In the 1980s it actually increased production and employment by 1–2 per cent. The state-owned Hulleras del Norte Sociedad Anónimia (HUNOSA) dominates the industry, accounting nationally for 35 per cent of coal employment and 42 per cent of production. Hard coal is of poor quality, high in ash and sulphur content. It lies in geologically problematic strata. The mines are small and production methods crude. It has a lower rate of productivity and higher costs than the other two countries; the price of its coal is nearly three times that of the UK, four and a half times that of the international market price, prompting the comment that 'HUNOSA is probably the most uneconomic coal mining operation in the world' (Parker 1994, p.54). The economic case for the Spanish coal industry is non-existent.

Thus, at the beginning of the 1990s, coal-mining had entirely ceased in Belgium. The most economically viable industry, that of the UK, was contracting fastest and the least economically viable in Spain contracting the slowest, with Germany intermediate on both counts. Politics rather than economics was driving the course of each national industry, especially whether, why and to what extent national governments were prepared to subsidise it: 'the size of the gap between the cost of EU-12 deep-mined coal and international prices remains the basis of the politics of coal in these countries' (Parker 1994, p.29). In Spain and Germany the rate of subsidy actually increased in the late 1980s when it was decreasing in the UK. As figure 9.2 shows, in striving to match the price of imported steam coal, only the UK comes close to achieving its objective.

A Comparison of National Political Contexts

Pivotal to Belgium's post-war economic redevelopment was a carefully managed process of 'social consultation, negotiation and pacification' between

FIGURE 9.2 COST TRENDS: EUROPEAN VERSUS IMPORTED COAL 1985–98

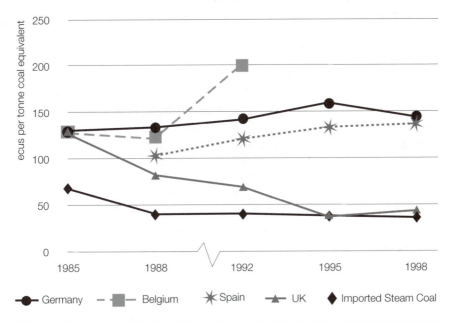

Note: Figures for Spain not available before 1988, since they had not yet joined the EU.   SOURCE: EU COMMISSION

such key 'social partners' as the trade unions, employers (including the self-employed and farmers) and the state. Consensual politics reflected and confirmed a mutual commitment to the maintenance of social peace. 'National interest organisations' provided the main means of representing and negotiating sectional objectives. State spending was geared to balancing competing claims and assuaging discontent. Most regional policy-making bodies, such as the Provincial Development Corporations, 'were nationally organised and mirrored the national power relations and national policy initiatives' (Swyngedouw 1996, p.1507).

Whilst this corporate institutional framework worked highly successfully during periods of economic prosperity it was destabilised by economic recession. In the 1980s governments experienced unprecedented budgetary crises. The reduction of state spending as an aim forced successive governments into bypassing traditional forums of negotiation:

This process implicitly challenged the choreography and the relationships of power. Altering the spatial scale of governance (the 'hollowing' out of the state) and the development of a parallel circuit of state or quasi-state institutions became part of a strategy to alter social power lines without resorting to overt struggle and outright overt dismantling of the 'Fordist' bargaining system (as in the UK, for example). The emergence of new local and supra-national forms of governance announced a creeping process of

marginalising workers' and other social organisations and to forge a new, albeit
contested and internally fractured, alliance between a slimmed-down
(entrepreneurial) state and 'global' business elites. (Swyngedouw 1996, p.1508)

The reconstruction of post-war West Germany helped develop a consensual goal of 'social peace' within the 'social market'. Towards that end, long-term planning for economic and social policy has been the guiding principle, even for the ruling Christian Democrat Party. Consensual planning as a practice has been endorsed by the constitutional framework. The federal structure of the country means that key elements of political and economic policy lie with the regional government. The Länder habitually negotiate with municipalities and other interest groups. Such institutionalisation of consensus has important consequences for the processes of both industrial restructuring and regional economic regeneration.

In Spain, the democratic constitution constructed after democratisation deferred to nationalistic claims by defining regions as 'Autonomous Communities' with considerable legal and financial powers. Regional and municipal authorities are responsible for more than a third of all public expenditure. Nominally a federal structure, there are considerable tensions between central and regional governments, especially where nationalistic aspirations are evident. The early dominance of Spain's socialist party, the Partido Socialista Obero Español (PSOE), cemented relations with regions where it was dominant but also made economic reforms politically sensitive.

Political structures and ideologies were everywhere an important determinant of policy in relation to the coal industry and coalfield communities. Whatever solutions emerged they were likely to be directed from the centre in the UK, consensually negotiated in Belgium and Germany and compromised in Spain. Such factors did not necessarily predetermine the policy outcomes but affected the mix and institutional forms of policies. The complexity of this web of interactions and institutions is evident in each regional case study.

Case study 1: Limburg

The Limburg coalfield started in 1901 when seven mines were sunk to provide coal for the thriving steel industries of Wallonia and France. For the next half-century employment in coal-mining grew rapidly, from 20,600 to 40,775 between 1930 and 1950. Such heavy reliance on a single industry resulted in 'a failure to establish a capitalist-entrepreneurial tradition in the region' (Swyngedouw 1996, p.1504).

Decline Management

From the 1950s onwards the Limburg coal industry progressively declined, along with the rest of Belgian mining. Until the mid-1960s the Government had been willing to divert funds from an otherwise sound national economy in order to sustain its ailing coal sector. However, in 1965, in order to reduce subsidies the Government decided to close six Belgian mines, five of them in Wallonia. A strike was instantly called which culminated in the police shooting two protesting miners. As a result of this shock to the system a new accord was fashioned between the state and organised labour. The 'Akkorden van Zwartberg' ('Agreements of Zwartberg') of 1966 specified that no further pit closures would occur unless alternative jobs were made available. Additionally, the Belgian Government would cover the losses of all remaining mines until 1996:

> *This agreement had a major impact on the subsequent development of the region. On the one hand, it prevented Limburg from becoming a social disaster area. On the other hand, it was no longer necessary to consider a more fundamental restructuring of the region's economy. The trauma of the events also entrenched Fordist regulation of labour-management relations – centred on negotiation, compromise and wage deals – deeper into the practice of local social regulation. The Limburg social economy consequently bubbled on in lethargy for the next decade or so. (Baeten et al. 1999, p.250)*

By the mid-1980s Limburg produced the EC's easily most expensive coal, costing $250 per tonne (per 1,000 kilos) (McAvan 1993). With public debt reaching unsustainable levels and despite local unemployment rates which 'were about to turn Limburg into a social desert' (Baeten et al. 1999, p.250), the decision was taken to phase out the province's five heavily subsidised but loss-making pits. This objective was to be accomplished via an extremely ambitious ten-year reconversion plan, the 1987 'Future Contract for Limburg', signed by representatives of all levels of the Belgian Government (provincial, Flemish and federal) and the European Union.

Two billion Belgian francs (£2.2 billion) were to be set aside by the Belgian Government, partly to finance redundancy payments but also with the intention of ensuring that, within ten years, local unemployment would be reduced to the national average and educational attainment raised to national standards. Housing improvements would be facilitated and the urban landscape extensively revitalised. The European Recreation Centre (ERC) would convert former mine sites for educational, cultural and recreational purposes.

With these commitments in place Limburg's five remaining coal mines were gradually phased out: the first three were closed down between September 1987 and March 1988; the remaining two on 1 January 1993. These closures were accompanied by confrontations between protesting miners and the police (McAvan 1993). The responsibility for administering the closure programme rested with the Kempische Steenkoolmijnen N.V. (KS), founded in 1967 by amalgamating the five Limburg mines. In 1987 KS was brought into state ownership under the leadership of Thyl Gheyselinck, who had been head-hunted by the Belgian Government from Shell's Portuguese headquarters.

Gheyselinck was one of the principal architects of the Future Contract. The KS and its new figurehead had overall responsibility for the reconversion of the Limburg coalfield, a task carried out amidst great criticism and controversy.

Regeneration

The appointment of Gheyselinck represented a radical departure from the traditional Belgian social partnership approach. In agreeing to take up his post at KS Gheyselinck insisted on total control over the 2 billion Belgian francs (£2.2 million) of public reconversion funds. The Belgian Government agreed because it enabled them to evade responsibility for closing mines and allocating restructuring funds which would otherwise have jeopardised relations with traditional 'social partners'. The Government's strategy seems to have been influenced by any future EU regeneration funding being conditional on 'the existence of an effective strategy to halt the endless streams of subsidies to the [Belgian] coal sector' (Baeten et al. 1999, p.251).

The singularly 'authoritarian and maverick style' adopted by Gheyselinck involved little partnership. Local entrepreneurs were successfully nominated on to key decision-making boards within KS and its subsidiaries, such as the Limburg Investment Company. In the absence of regional or national accountability this local elite alliance sanctioned a major ideological shift in the region's reconversion strategy. Its flagship project, the ERC, a commitment 'aimed primordially at generating jobs', was to be abandoned in favour of the more commercially oriented 'FENIX' development, complete with its centrepiece of a 150,000 sq m (179,400 sq yds) shopping centre. The lucrative land rents associated with this venture would yield large profits for private developers. This and other commercial activities associated with the KS became 'entangled in a web of real or perceived forms of poor management, shady financial operations and badly conceived reconversion plans' (Baeten et al. 1999, p.252).

Fortunately, this KS funding circuit was complemented by a parallel European circuit based on the equivalent of £550 million from European Structural Funds that had been advanced by the EC in 1988 in support of the Future Contract. This funding regime was administered by the Permanente Werkgroep Limburg (PWL) which, unlike the KS, was inclusive of the traditional 'social partners' within Belgian politics (including the newly formed Government of Flanders) and held together by key individuals, all belonging to the Christian-Democrat Party (CVP). Baeten et al. make the point that, while unemployment rates in 1991 were still higher than the national average, the PWL had none the less succeeded in creating a net employment increase of 24,000 new jobs since 1986 and providing retraining for thousands of ex-miners.

Since 1994, however, local regeneration activities in Limburg have collapsed as a result of local political developments. The 'Christian-Democratic hegemony' was displaced by an anti-CVP alliance, led by the Socialist Party. The implications of this political reconfiguration for regeneration activity have been profound. Many reconversion agencies associated with the CVP have had their activities curbed or terminated, creating a temporary inertia. In retaliation the CVP has been 'using its still very powerful local network of institutions, organisations, lobby groups, industrialists, mayors, etc. – painstakingly built-up during the long years of hegemonic control – to block the restructuring process in order to minimise the electoral benefit that the new political coalition could potentially reap from successful restructuring' (Baeten et al. 1999, p.255). Finally, embarrassed by recent controversies and political infighting, the Flemish Government and the EU have each distanced themselves from the regeneration process. Consequently, there is no higher tier of governance to mediate local differences of interest or philosophy.

Implications

Baeten et al. (1999) acknowledge that over BF 100 million of internal funds and substantial European spending over a ten-year period failed to reduce unemployment in Limburg to national levels or to socially and economically reinvigorate the area. National governments, under pressure from their own budgetary crises and EU opposition to continued subsidies, sought to absolve themselves by appointing a tough manager to run down an independent state industry and regenerate the region. Local business elites abdicated wider responsibilities in order to divert funds to profitable property development. Other measures within the public sector fell victim to a power struggle between the CVP and its political opponents. As the EU and the Flemish Government withdrew, any potential for an integrated policy was lost:

> *In spite of significant financial means, the socio-economic restructuring in Limburg is characterised by the absence of an overall strategy. The restructuring policies have imploded. As a corollary, money is now simply distributed among interest groups in accordance with the relative power positions and shifting coalitions they manage to forge. The choreography of regional political power, its articulation with other and higher scales of governance, and the making and breaking of alliances and hegemonic project formation are, indeed, decisive in shaping the trajectory of socio-economic restructuring in the region. (Baeten et al. 1999, p.256)*

Case study 2: North-Rhine Westfalen

North-Rhine Westfalen is the main hard-coal area of Germany, producing 86 per cent of its hard coal from mines on the edges of small towns. Though an older industrial area, it has many modern characteristics, such as developed transport, financial and small business infrastructures. Regional unemployment is nevertheless higher than the national norm.

Decline Management

Germany's post-war economic recovery was led between 1946 and 1957 by its coal-mining industry. At its peak in 1957 hard-coal production reached record heights of 149 million tonnes per annum and the industry employed 607,000 workers. However, in the next decade, German coal-mining started to decline with the increasing availability of oil and gas. By 1968 production had fallen to 112 million tonnes and employment to 264,000. Three-quarters of all mining jobs were concentrated in the Ruhr. At this time the Federal Government determined that further decline should not be left unmanaged. In 1968 twenty-six separate companies owning fifty-two mines were consolidated into a single company, Ruhrkohle AG. Privately owned by the steel industry and power generators, its economic targets were to be set by the Federal Government.

After the brief respite of the oil crises capacity was further reduced in the 1980s as a result of declining steel demand, despite guaranteed sales to power generators. By the 1990s, continuing competition from other energy sources and EU pressure to reduce subsidies rendered the industry economically vulnerable. Coal production halved between 1957 and 1990, from 150 to 70 million tonnes, and is due to halve again by 2005.

The national strategic plan for coal, 'Coal Concept 2005', made a commitment to preserve the industry, based in part on the guaranteed but shrinking markets to power stations and the steel industry. Germany retained its national security objective of maintaining reliable indigenous energy supplies. The main parties to negotiations – the employers, unions, representatives of the electricity industry, and the Federal and State Governments – agreed that the coal contract with the power stations (the 'Jahrhundertvertrag') would be temporarily maintained at 40.9 million tonnes annually but would be reduced to 35 million tonnes between 1997 and 2005. The protected annual sales of 21 million tonnes to the iron and steel industry would also reduce to 15 million tonnes by 2000. Ruhrkohle's annual subsidy was raised by the so-called 'kohlepfennig', an 8.5 per cent levy on energy bills. Standing at DM 8.2 billion in the early 1990s, it would be reduced to 7 billion by the year 2000. The projected net effect of these measures was that coal production would decrease from 66 million tonnes to 50 million tonnes by 2005. There would be reductions in the number of mines (from 26 to 17) and of jobs (from 120,000 to 80,000).

The management of restructuring has taken place with the agreement of the main trade union federation, the IG Bergbau-Energie (IGBE), who even agreed to a reduction in hours and wages to accommodate downsizing. Equally important in negotiated decline is the Zukunftsaktion Kohlegebiete (ZAK) (Campaign for the Future of Coal-Mining Areas), a federation of union, employer and local government representatives. ZAK is committed both to retaining a restructured industry and to local economic regeneration, expecting consultation over proposals for both (Steingraber 1995).

Restructuring programmes made extensive use of transfer between pits and early retirement, reducing the miners' average age to 32. As these possibilities were exhausted formal redundancy was rejected in favour of training schemes, resourced out of European structural funds, the Länder, Federal Government and the coal-producers themselves (Davies 1993; Beenken 1995; Bosch 1995). Volunteers to leave the industry were offered training whilst in employment, receiving two-thirds of their average wage. It is unclear how many miners took advantage of a new extended scheme after its introduction in 1995.

However, the combined pressures of the costs of German reunification, a downturn in the national economy, pressure from the EC to remove subsidies and environmental protests have cast doubt on protectionist polices for coal. Access to the large lignite mines of eastern Germany introduced other considerations. This coal was much cheaper and, although there were additional environmental hurdles, it did provide another indigenous source of fuel supply.

Government proposals in 1996 to hasten the rate of closure provoked mass demonstrations in mining areas and the plans were hastily revised. The new agreement, signed in 1997 by the coal producers, trade unions, the Federal Government, and the Länder of North-Rhine Westfalen and Saarland, involves reductions in subsidy by the year 2005 from DM 9.4 to DM 5.5 billion. Over the period 1997–2005 this requires a reduction in production from 50 to 25 million tonnes, in employment from 50,000 to around 30,000 and in mines from 18 to perhaps 10. Even this may not satisfy the EU. The balance of forces sustaining the management of decline is therefore very fragile.

Regeneration

Regeneration plans in North-Rhine Westfalen were first drafted during the 1958 crisis. By the late 1960s the Land announced the first of a series of regional regeneration plans to improve the infrastructure of housing, traffic, education and recreation, with subsidiary emphases on land reclamation and increases in training, private investment and regional promotion. Technology transfer was added in the late 1970s. By the early 1980s the crisis in the steel industry and attendant political protest prompted three new plans, one for the region as a whole, one for coal and steel areas and one for land reclamation. However, their implementation was not to be the direct responsibility of the Land; instead the region was divided into fifteen sub-regions, each of which was to have a regional board or conference. Comprising local authorities, chambers of commerce, trade unions and local community organisations, they would instigate regenerative projects.

Typical of the German approach was the founding of the East Ruhr Development Agency. In 1992 the Land Government proposed that land reclamation should be handed over to an independent agency and offered DM 10 million of start-up finance. Within eight months a limited company had been set up involving four major city or district councils, their chambers of commerce and trade associations, as well as five of the biggest non-mining firms in the region. Its brief was to initiate, co-ordinate and monitor projects, each involving a separate company. The target was to reclaim and develop 200 ha (494.2 acres) of land (Esterman and Roxlau-Hennemann 1995).

Evidence of the effects of such initiatives is widespread. In the first six months of 1991 almost 12,000 new companies were registered in North-Rhine Westfalen, a quarter of the national total. In 1965 there was no university; by 1995 there were six (in addition to six polytechnics and eleven technology centres). Major private-sector companies, forming the Inititativeskreis Ruhrgebeit, invested DM 5 billion and committed DM 4.5 billion of investment in the region in the first two years (Hudson 1992). New employment opportunities were encouraged by setting up industrial parks and technology centres and fostering entrepreneurship (Esterman and Roxlau-Hennemann 1995; Huggins and Thomalla 1995; Noll 1995; Buhr 1995).

A key element in restructuring has been the diversification and adaptation of the mining industry itself. In 1993 RAG (Ruhrkohle AG) employed 75,000 workers directly in mining and another 25,000 in other activities such as land reclamation, waste and product recycling. The latter generated 50 per cent of turnover in 1995 (Hessling 1995). This extension of RAG's activities away from the company's basic origins represents a form of lateral diversification (Cooke 1995). Similar processes of both lateral and vertical diversification (the latter involving the broadening of companies' activities within its host industry) have also occurred within the Ruhr's steel sector (ibid.). Equally important for the region as a whole has been the development of a 'production cluster' of firms and institutions involved in the environmental protection industry (Rehfeld 1995).

Land renewal and reclamation have been the most obvious policy successes (Wagner 1995). Progress is exemplified by activities associated with the redevelopment of 300 sq km (115.83 sq miles) of land around Essen. Between 1994 and 1999 118 projects (two-thirds of them state-funded), ranging from the conversion of mines into parks and health farms to the creation of small businesses like the wine distillery at Bergkamen, were instrumental in transforming the area. Symbolic of this conversion from old to new is the old gasometer at Oberhausen, now functioning as a high-rise exhibition centre and adventure park. The town's former mine site has been relandscaped as a 'people's golf course'. Undoubtedly the most impressive development is Oberhausen's 'CentrO', opened in 1996, which professes to be Europe's largest shopping centre (*The Independent* 13 November 1999).

Implications

The German coal industry has been maintained by a series of subsidies under increasing economic and political pressure (Schubert and Brautigam 1995). North-Rhine Westfalen remains significant within the coal industry but Ruhrkohle is becoming progressively less centred on coal.

Unemployment has risen, especially amongst the young. In 1994 the national rate was 8.1 per cent, in the Ruhr 13.3 per cent. The precise effects of retraining are hard to quantify. Some observers admit that miners have been reluctant to leave the industry, preferring the established industrial structure and mining culture. There have been considerable strides in land reclamation and development, in the transport infrastructure and in educational provision. Small business start-ups are impressive.

The cumulative impact seems to have been to insulate North-Rhine Westfalen from the worst excesses of de-industrialisation. Partly explicable by the region's relatively favourable positioning in the national economy, it is also the outcome of specifically political attitudes, structures and decisions. Regional elections make all political parties sensitive to mining votes. The federal structure has enabled North-Rhine Westfalen to influence national policy decisions.

Both restructuring and regeneration have involved a co-ordination of all affected parties. Local institutions are as much the products as the instigators of such dialogue which has necessitated 'a new understanding of the role of the state and its players in economic policy based on non-hierarchical relationships i.e. on co-operation with those affected in the economy and society' (Schubert and Brautigam 1995, p.45). The search continues for 'new forms of dialogue and co-operation between the state, institutions and companies' (Noll 1995, p.118).

The German case, as evident in North-Rhine Westfalen, contrasts sharply with the UK. The effects of the emergence of a global market in energy have been moderated in view of the potential social costs of the economic collapse of the coal industry, which has itself been diversified. Policy objectives have been on both the supply- and demand-side. Partnership and decentralisation is institutionalised at the local level. The political culture is committed to dialogue as an inherent process across the board.

The recent groundswell of opinion amongst the finance community against the managed economy and some envy of the 'British solution' to economic restructuring pose a considerable threat to the model of change management in North-Rhine Westfalen. The social and economic exclusion evident in the UK could yet be the fate of mining communities in Germany.

Case study 3: Asturias in Spain

The once powerful Asturias region has slipped from fifth to twelfth in the Spanish league table of prosperity. Production and income per capita are significantly below the national average. From 1955–85, Asturias lost 15.7 per cent of its jobs, 51 per cent in manufacturing. Comparable national figures showed a gain of 1.8 per cent in jobs, a manufacturing loss of 18 per cent. With redundancy disguised as retirement, the unemployed were mainly young people. The regional unemployment rate of 20 per cent in the mid-1990s was just below the national average. Mining locality unemployment was 25 per cent, of whom 40 per cent were under 25 years old.

Central Asturias has 40 per cent of hard coal production, and 40 per cent of the workforce. HUNOSA accounts for 82 per cent of employment and 66.1 per cent of production. Production costs are over twice the national average. Despite increases in national production, Asturias' share of coal-production fell from 67 per cent to 53 per cent between 1970 and 1992. Mining jobs decreased by a third from 32,000 to 21,000. The number of pits halved in the 1980s with just 14 left (Vázquez and del Rosal 1995, p.19).

The Asturian coalfield is the least efficient and most vulnerable in the national coal industry. Enduring traditions of organised trade union solidarity and opposition to rationalisation have managed to protect jobs. True to their militant traditions, Asturian miners have engaged in a number of protests against pit closures, invariably with public backing (*The Independent* 17 January 1998). On economic criteria alone there is no viable argument for keeping the mines in production:

> *They produce a poor coal that nobody really wants, extracted at high cost for a company that has never made a profit and never expects to do so. Here the inefficiencies of a subsidised state industry reach an extreme. But it is also here that the industrial support system is likely to persist long after it has been dismantled elsewhere. In these grim mining communities and the shipbuilding ports of the north and south of Spain, the brave new world of the free market and private enterprise meets its frontiers. (*Financial Times 8 June 1998)*

Decline Management

The response to the long-term crisis in the Spanish coal industry was the nationalisation of eighteen mining companies in 1967 into HUNOSA. Its operations were protected by import tariffs, guaranteed prices, contracts with thermal power stations and direct subsidies to production costs.

Spain's entry into the EC jeopardised these protectionist policies. Existing subsidies and agreements were initially modified to make them apparently compatible with EC regulations but by the late 1980s the government was under increasing pressure to produce a programme for the rationalisation of the industry. Commitments were made to a progressive reduction of direct subsidy and a programme of contraction for the industry as a whole, yet in the 1980s six restructuring programmes failed either to reduce the massive state subsidy or to improve productivity.

The negotiation of such plans has always been complex and highly conflictual, with many different interests represented by the company, unions, regional and local government, political parties and even the Church. Such plans were designed to protect rather than reform the industry and its jobs. None of these plans had the desired impact: production and employment decreased; productivity remained static; and costs increased. The net result was an increased level of subsidy from central Government. By the 1990s this burden had become intolerable and, in the EC's view, anti-competitive.

Two further restructuring plans were produced for 1991–3 and 1994–7. The 1991-3 plan, produced after much argument, reduced the 18,000 jobs by a third by progressively reducing the retirement age to 55. HUNOSA bore the cost of high levels of pension and social security entitlements. The 1994–7 plan aimed to maintain existing levels of production whilst reducing the workforce by another 2,000, lowering the retirement age to 47 and improving technology. HUNOSA would diversify into waste recycling and environmental regeneration.

The attempted phasing of contraction, and the use of early retirement and social security to soften its impact, only postponed the time when wholesale closure would have to be considered. The Minister for Industry did just that in late 1996 when a leaked document indicated that the deals with the electricity industry would not be renewed. Following widespread political protest a new agreement was reached in May 1997. HUNOSA would by 2000 reduce its production from 2.5 million tonnes to 2.1 million tonnes and its workforce from 10,000 to 7,000. The EU, wanting a reduction of production to 1.5 million tonnes, refused to sanction the agreement. This provoked a national strike in January 1998, during which strikers set pit props ablaze and overturned coal wagons along the main Asturias motorway, and the Civil Guard riot squad fired rubber bullets and tear-gas at pickets (*The Independent* 17 January 1998). Two months later, on 31 March 1998, the Spanish Government outlined its plans for the rationalisation and restructuring of the coal industry from 1998–2002. This involved an annual decrease in production to no more than 12.7 million tonnes in 2002 (compared with the 1998 figure of 16,380 million). The future of the industry seemed more uncertain than ever.

Regeneration

The two restructuring plans of the early 1990s included very little by way of local economic regeneration. The Government produced but failed to resource a Plan for Asturias, nor did it fund the Regional Government's own plan. Regeneration thus became the responsibility of several agencies set up mainly by Regional Government with different briefs and organisational structures. The two most important have been the Institute for Regional Development (IFR) and the Business Assessment and Promotional Service (SAYE).

Founded in the mid-1980s, initially to attract inward investment, the IFR subsequently diversified its activities into land reclamation and development; applications for EC aid; support for exports; and the financing of R&D. The SAYE targets small businesses. Both have offices in the main municipalities. Other agencies include the Foundation for the Promotion of Applied Scientific Research and Technology, a joint initiative between the Regional Government and the University of Oviedo, concerned with technology transfer; and EXPORTATSUR, a grouping of private company exporters. Additionally, there are development agencies in nine municipalities, business centres, chambers of commerce and local branches of the state-owned national innovation company Empresario Nacional di Innovación (ENISA) offering small-scale grants for business innovation.

Vázquez and del Rosal argue that this apparently 'wide institutional base for economic promotion ... presents significant deficiencies in terms of organisational structures and demonstrable results' (1995, p.69). One index of the success rate is the four-year (1989–93) achievement of the business assessment and promotional service El Servicio de Asesoramiento y Promoción Empresarial (SAYPE). It claims to have supported 2,000 projects producing 6,000 jobs. On average, each project cost 26 million pesetas (£100,000 at 1997 prices) and produced three jobs, a cost per job of 9.2 million pesetas (£35,000). Vázsquez and del Rosal conclude that 'The performance of these organisations has involved considerable effort and huge financial resources, often disproportionate to the results obtained' (ibid., p.70).

More local is the Society for the Development of Comarcas Mineras (SODECO). A joint venture of HUNOSA and a wing of the IFR, this is designed to generate venture capital for new and existing businesses. From 1989 to 1993 it invested 5,800 million pesetas (£23 million at 1997 prices) in 20 companies, producing 677 new jobs (£35,000 per job). This operates alongside HUNOSA's diversification programme and various forms of EC aid.

Assessing the overall results in the Comarcas Mineras, Vázquez and del Rosal note considerable improvements in land reclamation, environment and transport but only marginal gains in job creation or small businesses. This they attribute to four types of deficiency in regenerative agencies. First, they are fragmented, lacking in co-ordination, often overlapping in jurisdiction and unable to establish a 'critical mass' of activity. Second, they are wholly public sector with insufficient involvement of local business and so are not integrated into the local economy. Third, they are excessively bureaucratic organisations, lacking in flexibility or clear targets. Fourth, they lack long-term objectives and their short-term goals are frequently subject to political interference. Consequently, economic regenerative strategies and agencies are inadequate to the task of halting the decline of the local economy.

Implications

In Spain, the objective of protecting jobs has until recently overridden those of making the industry viable or regenerating the local economy. The pressures towards distributive measures proved stronger than those towards economic efficiency. The consequence for Asturias is a steep decline in the overall level of economic activity. Young men and women have been hardest hit, with little prospect of any but the lowest grade of jobs.

We find in Spain a set of responses quite different from those in the UK, Belgium and Germany: outright protectionism, with extremely high levels of direct and indirect subsidy. Whilst the need to restructure the industry has been recognised the actual process has been tortuous and modernisation proved impossible. Central governments, fearful of political ramifications, have been unwilling to enforce a closure programme. All restructuring programmes have been fiercely contested by an alliance of regional political interests, holding tacitly the expectation that the State should provide them with jobs, however uneconomic, and with a dominant strategic objective to wring concessions out of the State. Restructuring programmes were fatally compromised by this balance of political forces. Regenerative agencies rely heavily on regional government, lack co-ordination or clear goals and exclude the private sector. Dialogue here has been largely the adversarial process of bargaining.

In Asturias there persists a basically unviable industry, on which the region remains highly dependent. The decline of the industry and attempts at economic regeneration have been haltingly managed. Its demise, and the further decline of the region, seem imminent.

Conclusions

Assessing the precise regional effects of the regulation of industrial decline and economic regeneration is complex, since other potential outcomes remain unknown. Comparative study of the kind undertaken here must acknowledge variations in national politics, energy economics and the 'positioning' of the region which comprise 'the proliferation of special factors that inhibit direct comparison between cases' (Ferner et al. 1997, p.59).

One simple criterion that can be used in all cases is how far the overall outcome avoids the standard fate of older industrial regions: structural unemployment; skill imbalances; physical neglect; depopulation; and social disintegration (Albrechts et al. 1989). This is potentially the position in Limburg and the burgeoning reality in the Asturias. Only North-Rhine Westfalen has avoided this scenario.

In considering the exact reasons for the success of Germany, as compared with the relative failure in Belgium and the absolute failure in Spain, we shall outline the policy mix, the role of institutions and the importance of social dialogue, before assessing the relative importance of the global, the national and the local in structuring responses to economic decline.

The Policy Mix

Decisions about the de-industrialisation and economic regeneration of regional and local economies are ultimately determined by political factors at the level of the nation state. As Parker (1994) argues, the differences between national restructuring policies are politically rooted. In Belgium, the controversial and ultimately disastrous role of the KS was sanctioned by a federal government intent on bypassing the traditional social partners as part of a strategy to obtain European regenerative funding. UK policy in the late 1980s and early 1990s was driven by the centralised nature of the State, the clarity of its energy policies and its resolve to isolate and break the radical miners' union; that of Germany by a decentralised state, a more equivocal energy policy and its willingness to negotiate with a more moderate mining union. In Spain, the rigidities of regional autonomy, the absence of an energy policy and the militancy of the union and the region all helped to delay effective action of any kind. It is therefore crucial 'how the balance of opposing internal political forces determines the rate of change', so that the prime consideration 'is not about fundamental strategic direction but about politically acceptable phasing of decline' (Parker 1994, p.76).

This determination of the economic by the political also applies to local regeneration policy. Martin (1989) has reviewed the six options available: re-industrialisation; industrial de-maturation; tertiarisation; re-skilling and flexibilisation of the workforce; infrastructure renewal; and financial reorganisation. The decision about which mix of policies to adopt reflects national political views of both the ends and means of economic renewal. Germany's approach has been to maximise involvement in a comprehensive plan, the only one to incorporate all of Martin's options, including the regulation of de-maturation through the diversification of Rurhrkohle. In the UK there has been an unwarranted assumption by national government that retraining and SME support will re-stimulate the local economy. Belgium has used a similar strategy with slightly more success. Spain vacillates ineffectually between these two models. With the UK, it resorts to what Hudson (1992) calls welfare regulation, financially buttressing pensions and unemployment benefit. Such short-term measures may mitigate the worst effects of de-industrialisation but have no effect on the local economy. They have been produced by political influences: in the UK, a zealous belief in market forces; in Spain, the extreme political sensitivity of the industry and its regions. Essentially the same contrast between comprehensive planning and piecemeal short-term measures is found at the level of institutions.

'Thick' Institutions

The important factor for economic institutions is recognised to be their degree of 'thickness', not their size or number but how they are interlocked with other significant political and economic institutions locally and with the State nationally. Hudson (1992) notes that local institutions may either resist or welcome change, a persistent difference between such institutions in Spain and Germany. Resistance in older areas is more likely because existing institutions favour political and cultural continuity rather than economic change. Hence, the problem for such areas is to develop new kinds of institution which facilitate effective local economic adaptation to State policy or more global political and economic developments. Hudson remains sceptical about the viability of the necessary institutional reform.

Our case studies suggest that institutions at both regional and local level do matter, though their effects may be uneven. In the UK, central government power and centrally directed quangos enabled fast closure but prevented the development of local institutional thickness. The only exceptions have been in regions like South Wales where new institutional networks have been custom woven. In Belgium, attempts to create such institutions circumvented extant partnerships and were sabotaged by economic greed and political opportunism. In Spain, the coalition of interests rooted in local institutions has perennially resisted industrial change and ignored regenerative change. In Germany, the creation of new institutions through the 'conference' structure has reinforced their dense networking.

Drewe (2000, p.282) argues that 'it is important to realise that not only does economic decline cause social exclusion, so does economic growth if certain population groups are unable to share in a rising level of prosperity'. Our Belgian example reveals what can happen when institutional innovation is insensitive to the needs of the worst victims of industrial decline. The same point applies to the work of the Welsh Development Agency which has achieved least success in the hard-pressed valley regions. It is also applicable to international examples, such as the modern transition of Pittsburgh, Pennsylvania, from one of America's foremost coal and steel centres to an economy based on advanced technology, health care, education and financial services (Deitrick 1999; Deitrick and Beauregard 1995; Sbragia 1990).

Institutions are structures which may generate or reflect cultures. Organisation is not enough; there must be a commitment to processes of decision-making. In north-west Europe, outside the UK, this exists in the form of 'social dialogue'.

Social Dialogue

In many European countries the resolution of policy dilemmas is thought to lie in social dialogue: constructive discussion of policy options amongst producers, workers and consumers. Ferner et al. (1997) have attempted to measure the effect on member countries of the example set by the ECSC of social dialogue. They identify three different types of effect. They suggest it would have happened anyway in those countries 'with strong legal measures in support of social dialogue', of which Germany is the prime example. Nor was there any effect on countries where 'liberal market philosophies' coexist with 'weak processes of social dialogue', the UK being the most extreme case. Where the model has had most effect is 'in countries where a legal framework for dialogue exists but is to varying degrees fairly weak or uncertain', an example being Spain. This typology is very accurate for economic regulation in coal-mining areas in the UK and Germany. The case of Spain is more complex, since the typology begs the question of why, if the legal framework exists, the processes are so weak. The explanation is political. Whatever the constitution may say, the key factors are the balance of power between central and regional government and, crucially, prevalent working assumptions about the balance between dependence and autonomy for the regions. That is why the EU cannot induce dialogue where the conditions for it do not exist: 'The vitality of dialogue in each member state ... is to a large extent determined by the national institutional, cultural and legislative frameworks within which social dialogue is being conducted' (Ferner et al. 1997, p.69). The extent to which the constitution, tiers of government and new organisational alliances can manage change effectively does seem to depend on political traditions where decision-making is regarded as inherently inclusive and consensual. Only in Germany has this ambitious goal been realised.

Vertical Integration

Effective regeneration appears to require institutions committed to social dialogue. They also need a supportive political framework. It may be true that effective regional policy 'implies the decentralisation of powers of planning and implementation to the local level' (Martin 1989, p.48) but this does not specify how the local, the regional and the national need to operate in concert and the conditions needed to bring this about. The basic necessity is that the respective powers of the national, regional and local levels should achieve a kind of balance. Trigilia may be right to stress that regeneration poses 'a regulative problem of a regional nature' (cited in Peck 1994, p.165) but this is not simply a question of an institutional tier, though that may be a prerequisite. It has to be effectively interlocked with the central State, as it is in Germany and more unevenly in Belgium, but has not been in Spain. Similarly, the local should mean not penetration by the region but a genuine autonomy. If a feedback loop of political communication is lacking, the structure will not operate with the required degree of flexibility.

As the German case shows, even that may be insufficient if the national is unevenly related to supra-national institutions. EU commitment to free competition acts against subsidies necessary to the management of decline. In both Germany and Spain it is the EU which objects to planned contraction. In short, regulation at the local, regional and national level, however well designed and executed, may be insufficient if at the supra-national level there is no regulative system. As Peck and Tickell emphasise, the search for appropriate instruments of economic generation – 'a new institutional fix' – is spurious while there is no attempt to meet the need for the 'construction of a new global regulatory order' (1994, p.292). The 'hollowing out of the state' gives regions regulatory responsibility without power, whilst supra-national systems have power without responsibility (1994, p.311).

Our most optimistic case, North-Rhine Westfalen, may in the long term reposition itself as a region in the German and European economy but has exerted no influence over the global energy markets which have caused the demise of its coal industry. Limited protection for the rump of the industry is under constant challenge from European regulations designed to ensure free competition. Nor can the Länder necessarily exert control over the national energy policy and attempts to revise it in the light of economic problems following reunification.

On the basis of recent events, we cannot agree that 'With appropriate action and public and private initiative, the social impact of coal sector restructuring can be minimised and a more secure future for the coalfields can be foreseen' (IEEC [International Economic and Energy Consultants] 1995, p.9). The balance of political forces which have given some support to the coal industry and its areas seem likely to tilt against them. Whilst the basic problems of the European coal industry are economic, their resolution is a matter of political will. Ultimately, as the German example shows, effective policies, institutions and cultures depend upon a willingness to disperse economic and political power. While nation states refuse this option, ex-mining communities will lack the resources to determine their own futures and cannot be confident that those with resources will utilise them in the most effective ways.

Restructuring in Central and Eastern Europe

Looking further afield to the EU candidate states of central and eastern Europe, such as Romania and Poland, the lessons from this comparative study may have additional significance. As much of the coal industry and dependent communities of western Europe complete their restructuring those nations lying further east are in the throes of traumatic change. Despite the different political and economic context of countries emerging from centralised State management problems and putative solutions are remarkably similar (Brendow 2000).

The policy agenda adopted follows much the same direction but is constrained by perhaps deeper political and economic problems. Closure of unprofitable mines, re-deployment of miners and re-conversion of mining regions have proved very difficult in relatively strong economies, as our comparison shows. In the struggling economies of former eastern bloc countries restructuring is of a different order of magnitude. Expansion of the EU will increase the pressure for effective policy responses.

The importance of the ECSC Treaty for the previous half-century has already been mentioned. Attention at the beginning of the 21st century has turned to its replacement after 2002. This not only requires a major re-negotiation of subsidy arrangements but also consideration of the prospect of extended membership. These new members will include, for example, Poland and other coal-producers. Were Poland to become a member, hard coal production within the EU would more than double and the future of 200,000 more jobs would have to be carefully considered.

Sharp energy price rises in 2000 once again reminded national governments of the vulnerability of the EU to energy shocks. The debate about Europe's future energy policy and the fate of coal has taken on a new urgency which is reflected in the publication of the European Commission Green Paper on security of supply (European Commission 2000). A future role for Europe's indigenous coal industries and the management of restructuring programmes, particularly in eastern Europe will remain important issues for some decades to come.

NOTES

1. The comparison refers to hard coal mining. Lignite mining, especially in eastern Germany, remains a significant industry and fuel source.

PART V:
COAL AND COMMUNITIES IN
THE 21ST CENTURY

10 Conclusion

The End of Coal's Reign

The subtitle of Tony Hall's *King Coal* (Hall 1981) is *Miners, Coal and Britain's Industrial Future*. Little more than a quarter of a century ago these three entities seemed inseparably intertwined. Indeed, 'from 1973 onwards, it appeared that coal was going to be the fuel of the future. Oil was too costly and in danger of running out. Nuclear power was taking a long time to develop and aroused massive anxieties. King Coal looked set to rule again' (Hall 1981, p.13). In the halcyon days of 1975 Britain's coal communities could look with less concern at the fact that the number of working mines had been reduced from 822 to 241 since 1957, that the number of miners had dropped from 704,000 to 245,000, and that yearly production had fallen from 207 to 115 million tonnes. Optimism had been rekindled by the 1974 Plan For Coal, embodying an investment programme designed to produce an extra 42 million tonnes by 1985. Three years later 'Plan 2000' upwardly revised projected demand to 170 million tonnes by the year 2000 and called for substantial investment to facilitate this extra capacity.

However, as we saw in Part I, global transformations in the world energy market, combined with processes of political machination and indifference, have since induced rapid contraction of the UK coal industry. By 2000 a mere seventeen British deep coal-mines remained open, producing an annual total of 25 million tonnes. The vulnerability to market forces or sudden political whim of these scattered outposts of coal's once-mighty kingdom was exemplified by the announcement, on 15 November 2000, that the Government was sanctioning the introduction of up to six further gas-fired power stations, with a potential displacement of 15 million tonnes of coal per year (*The Guardian* 16 November 2000). For much of the 20th century coal had reigned supreme as Britain's premier industrial fuel. In the new millennium the industry was threatened with extinction.

Coal's Suffering Kingdom

In Part II we documented the human impact of industrial contraction. First, in chapter 2, we heard from men who had lost, or thought they were about to lose, their livelihoods. Male unemployment rates in former coalfield areas are already higher than the national average. However, the true rates of mining unemployment – thought to be between 20 and 30 or more per cent in most coalfield localities (Beatty and Fothergill 1998) – are disguised by high rates of permanent sickness among former miners and the fact that employees leaving under the Redundant Mineworkers Payments Scheme were disqualified from registering as 'unemployed'.

The immediate psychological problems confronting the jobless in mining areas revolve around their loss of occupational identity, erosion of meaningful structure and loss of purpose. In some cases former miners lose contact with former workmates and retreat into social isolation, especially if unable to find new employment. They become disconcerted by the intense competition for local jobs and despair at the detected preferences among employers for younger men or non-miners unschooled in trade union militancy. Having to fill out application and claim forms or attend interviews are novel and unwelcome experiences. In sum, the foundations of their identity are being undermined as they lose breadwinner status within the home and sense the collapse of their authority.

Not surprisingly, former miners with recent experience of unemployment spoke with satisfaction and relief of re-employment outside mining. Apart from missing the camaraderie, such men were often glad to have escaped the oppressive working conditions exacted by British Coal. However, liberation had its price. For one thing, wages in non-mining are substantially inferior to those enjoyed by working miners. The work content of the new jobs is typically greatly simplified, and the new workplaces are rarely unionised. New jobs are often unstable, so that post-mining work careers of local men are frequently chequered and insecure.

In chapter 3, we examined the response of women in mining communities. The relatively small number of women displaced from the mining industry had to cope with their own as well as their husbands' redundancy. Where women had jobs when their partners did not there was always potential for conflict, though not always realised. Most employed women enjoyed their work, not least when it offered a refuge from tensions at home. These occurred most when they had underfoot an unemployed man, monitoring and criticising their housework, whilst contributing little himself. In almost all cases women had to cope with the emotional volatility of their husband. They also found themselves mediating in the consequent family feuds. On a daily basis wives struggled to stretch limited financial resources. The strain of worrying about their male partners, the family and its future, sometimes seemed unbearable, particularly as most women considered it necessary to put on a brave face to protect their men from further pressure.

There is evidence that the inevitable parental discord would be felt traumatically by their children, resulting in reduced confidence and emotional insecurity. Such feelings were compounded as children occasionally became the butt of adult frustration. In a context in which adults had a diminished capacity to contribute, psychologically and financially, to the well-being of their offspring, children became deprived, not just of basic material provisions (such as clothes and sweets), but of comfort, support and regular social interaction.

Not surprisingly, schooling may be affected by this process. Parents are liable to feel less inclined to offer encouragement and support for homework and other school-related activities. Tied up with their own problems they might be less sensitive to children's problems at school, such as bullying. The build-up of stress in their own lives could cause over-reaction to scholastic failure or criticism by teachers. Children's own relationship to school is jeopardised by the lack of employment prospects, whatever qualifications are gained.

It would be disingenuous of us to suggest that industrial contraction has wreaked universal havoc throughout the lives of local residents. For a minority at least, redundancy has brought with it a new lease of life, providing the miner and his family with an opportunity to forget the constant strain of job insecurity. However, a more general picture remains of beleaguered individuals, struggling with varying degrees of success, to adapt as best they can with economic adversity. For unemployed ex-miners this has often involved a process of resignation to a life of decreased satisfaction. Others may stave off the potential for lowered self-esteem by constructively adapting their lifestyles so as to remain usefully active and self-respecting, by developing a leisure interest or working in the informal economy. Some working miners may become more fatalistic or instrumental in their outlook. Working or unemployed, male adults in these communities may find relief from stress by drinking or occasionally using drugs.

We saw in chapters 4 and 5 how the consequences of industrial contraction are most apparent at the level of community itself. The impact on the physical fabric of community is evident in the progressive run-down of the environment and dilapidation of local housing – especially where former British Coal properties have fallen into the hands of neglectful absentee landlords. Local facilities, such as shops, welfare and recreational areas, either disappear or fall into chronic disrepair. The social fabric is similarly undermined as village cohesion is lost, social rivalries develop and people become detached and isolated from erstwhile colleagues and friends. The migration of former miners in search of alternative employment is discouraged by family and cultural ties, lack of transferable skills, or inability to sell houses. Many younger residents have taken the option of outmigration. Among those remaining, political disaffection and disempowerment translate into drug misuse or acquisitive and expressive crime, ranging from burglary to joyriding. There is a general disrespect for those formal and informal authoritative institutions, such as school, the police force and trade unions, who are no longer relevant to their lives. The threatening presence of disaffected youths on community street corners has become the focus of inter-generational conflict. Intra-community conflicts also occur between long-term residents and 'outsiders', or between those in work and those dependent on welfare benefits.

In general terms, entire communities, enveloped by profound anxiety for the future, see no respite from economic adversity. In the main, strong vestiges of 'community spirit' continue to survive in the face of economic difficulty. Nevertheless, the potential for local residents to fight back is tempered by collective feelings of powerlessness and the general sense that little is being done to rescue them from their plight. The observations we have made in this volume are generally endorsed by other commentators:

> A clear conclusion is that economic and social disadvantage are inextricably linked. The coalfields suffer from very high levels of unemployment - much of it is unrecorded - and from low levels of employment. These lead to low average wage levels in the jobs that do exist. The poverty created by low pay and unemployment is closely associated with the poor health of people and the high crime rates that they experience. Without the creation of substantial numbers of well-paid jobs and efforts to equip local residents to take up these opportunities, the poverty, ill-health and crime that presently affect mining communities looks set to persist. (CCC 1997, p.38)

Empire and Commonwealth

The two chapters of Part III reviewed industrial relations in the privatised industry after 1995 and failed or successful attempts at worker take-overs. As we heard in chapter 2, men remaining in the pre-privatised mining industry had complained about more arduous working conditions, the oppressive treatment by management and the generally confrontational atmosphere pervading the entire industry. Above all, they were gripped by insecurity about further mine closures. Miners transferring to other mines became commuters, encountering new workmates and conditions. Particularly in the newer, more impersonal mines of the Selby complex, men bemoaned the loss of camaraderie and 'atmosphere'. In some cases they were introduced to novel tasks for which they lacked the requisite skills and were inadequately retrained. Throughout the industry miners ruefully recognised their loss of industrial muscle.

The privatisation of the industry in 1995, considered in chapter 6, brought unexpected dividends in the form of more palatable working conditions and more personable styles of management, at least within the majority of pits owned by RJB Mining. Nevertheless, the process of trade union marginalisation cultivated by British Coal was perpetuated by all the private coal owners. A notable exception to this norm was the WTO at Tower in South Wales, analysed in chapter 7. There we found a remarkable success story, a pit run on co-operative principles with a real sense of the realities of management which had found a viable niche in the new coal market. Elsewhere, similar experiments had failed, the pits and their communities eventually joining the list of casualties.

Coal's New Face

Part IV evaluated regeneration initiatives in the UK (in chapter 8) and elsewhere in Europe (chapter 9). Throughout the accelerated pit-closure programme of the mid-1980s and beyond regeneration efforts in the United Kingdom have been the principal responsibility of agencies like British Coal Enterprise, the TECs, Local Enterprise Agencies, and increasingly cash-starved local authorities. Policies typically involving job retraining, the provision of requisite infrastructure (e.g. industrial space and business premises), small business advice and financial assistance and/or incentives – sometimes extending to the establishment of Enterprise Zones – were applied with the intention of attracting inward investment and employment. Especially in the 1990s, a variety of competitive funding regimes available in Britain (e.g. City Challenge and the Single Regeneration Budget) and the European Union (notably RECHAR) enabled the resourcing of a variety of social, economic and environmental renewal schemes.

Projects of this nature have brought benefits in terms of replacement jobs, environmental rejuvenation, land reclamation and new or renovated housing but the overall impact on UK mining communities has been piecemeal, marginal and lacking coherence or direction. The quality of the gains made by regenerative strategies rarely withstands close scrutiny. For example, many of the jobs created by the setting up of Enterprise Zones have resulted from a 'displacement effect' as firms have merely relocated from other, less economically attractive areas. Moreover, employment in former mining areas is increasingly low-paid, part-time or casual, and non-unionised, reflecting the progressive 'feminisation' of the workforce. Many local training schemes designed for youths or former mineworkers are perceived as cynical devices to massage job relocation statistics. Scant attention is applied to building the capacity of local communities or encouraging their involvement in the design and implementation of regeneration strategy.

The limitations and inadequacy of top-down strategies is reflected in the growth of community initiatives, which provide jobs and services that would otherwise be lacking in the locality. They also help to sustain self-worth and pride in the absence of 'conventional' employment. Unfortunately, competitive funding regimes invariably require partnerships with formal institutions with different agendas. Often, such alliances are forged on the basis of expediency rather than commercial logic. Eligibility criteria are inflexible and funding short-term. Clearly what is required is a framework for urban regeneration which combines a top-down emphasis on co-ordination and facilitation with a commitment to 'bottom-up' initiatives which prioritise democratic participation, inclusion and social dialogue.

Some of this has been evident in other major European coal-producing nations. Spain has concentrated on a purely defensive strategy, postponing closure by subsidising its massively unprofitable mines. By contrast, in Germany there has been a co-ordinated attempt to regenerate former mining areas, involving all levels of government, the employers and trade unions. Considerable environmental and industrial renewal has taken place, involving substantial industrial innovation and the creation of clusters. In Belgium, where coal-mining has now ceased, a successful job-creation programme was implemented in the early 1990s which exemplified the benefits of including all tiers of government as well as local representatives in the regeneration process. However, a second component of Belgium's regeneration strategy, involving attempts by a controlling business elite to create a flagship retail park, demonstrated how a local 'democratic deficit' permitted self-interest to displace common objectives. In different ways, each nation illustrated alternatives to the policies pursued in the UK. In particular, more federal structures of government and varying attitudes towards political consensus and 'social peace' in Germany produced partnership as an automatic solution rather than an enforced alliance. Thus, there were guiding principles for policy, largely absent in the British context.

Working Principles

Haughton (1998) advocates the adoption of five key 'ethical principles' as a basis for regeneration policy. The first of these, 'inter-generational equity', rejects employment investment programmes which achieve short-term results. Instead, there should be an emphasis on the nurturing of local capacity and the creation of durable forms of employment that will be of value to future generations. Similarly, in applying the second principle of 'social justice' policy-makers should ensure that employees occupy rewarding jobs or training schemes are paid living wages, and are concerned with the provision of 'socially valued products and services'.

The third principle of 'participation' implies that local actors should be democratically involved in all stages of regeneration, and that such inclusion should be distinguishable from 'tokenistic' partnerships sought by larger institutions. According to Haughton, 'The essence of this principle is that productive community engagement can foster a sense of local ownership and bring about important insights into how initiatives can build from an area's existing strengths' (ibid., p.874).

The two remaining principles are concerned with widening the focus of regenerative activities to enhance their sustainability and effectiveness. The fourth principle of 'geographical equity' maintains that one locality should not benefit at the expense of another in 'zero sum inter-locality competition'. The final principle, 'holistic development', recognises that policies for economic renewal, social regeneration and environmental improvement need integrating into a coherent strategy, since 'where one of these dominates the others, problems inevitably ensue' (ibid.).

Consistent with these principles Haughton calls for a novel social audit for regeneration policies. Evaluation should be based on such criteria as the quality and permanence of jobs created, as well as the proportion occupied by local people, the unemployed or socially excluded. Time-scales for initial funding and monitoring should be extended to take into account the longer incubation required for community initiatives.

Haughton concludes by explaining that:

> Community economic development should be seen as three-fold in nature: providing alternatives to mainstream market activities (products, services and jobs); helping marginalized communities link better into mainstream market activities; and making mainstream regeneration initiatives more effective by better integrating them with local communities, bringing the benefits of improved access to local resources, knowledge and legitimacy. Community economic development from this perspective does not replace conventional regeneration activities, but it does become a vital and integral aspect of local regeneration strategies. (ibid., p.876)

Such a prescription is not meant to imply the wholesale transfer of responsibility to community leaders. A new paradigm for regeneration is envisaged whereby 'diverse combinations of salaried professionals working with business and community leaders, according to jointly agreed priorities' strive to link up and co-ordinate activities occurring at the local and regional levels (ibid.).

Labour Movement

Clearly, the principles enunciated by Haughton were largely overridden by coalfield regeneration initiatives implemented prior to the election of the Labour Government in May 1997. It is important to examine the likelihood of such principles being applied in the first decade of the new millennium. Since arriving in government in May 1997 New Labour has reversed the emphasis on 'directive funding' inherent in the urban regeneration strategies of successive Conservative governments between 1979 and 1997 (Foley and Martin 2000). In recognising that 'top-down' initiatives have largely been tried and failed and that successful regeneration depends on the devolution of power and responsibility to local communities, the Government has installed a new framework for ensuring a 'joined up' area regeneration strategy (Mawson and Hall 2000) to facilitate and co-ordinate 'bottom-up' approaches to social, economic and environmental renewal.

A pivotal role in this process is now being occupied by the nine recently formed RDAs, who have been given the responsibility of managing SRB funding in such a way as to ensure the integrated physical, social and economic regional development of their regions. Within this framework a key leadership role has also been devolved to local authorities to identify local needs, organising and supporting local partnerships (ibid.). Adding to the complexity of this structure is the additional requirement for the SRB funding to link into other government programmes dealing with education, health and social exclusion.

It remains an open question to what extent this framework is capable of delivering the type of community involvement and resources necessary to guarantee the sustained revitalisation of British coalfields. Some academics have commented on the need for extensive training among RDA and local authority personnel, and seem sceptical whether the Government possesses either the patience or financial resources to follow the programme through (Foley and Martin 2000). Others have pointed to the 'democratic deficit' built into the fact that the SRB is administered by unelected RDAs:

> RDAs will be constituted as non-departmental public bodies and, thus, will be accountable to ministers rather than the local electorate. The RDA boards will, typically, comprise between 12–15 members of whom all but a small handful will be nominees of the business community or local government. The organizations cannot, therefore, reflect the political, social and ethnic diversity of the regions in their proposed form. (Hall and Nevin 1999, p.480)

Interim appraisals by the Coalfield Communities Campaign have included some heavily qualified endorsement of New Labour's attempts to regenerate the coalfields. Such appraisals also recognise that relevant policies may take as long as a full decade to eventually reach fruition. Undoubtedly, New Labour is genuine in seeking a more holistic and community-led approach to the regeneration of the coalfields. Efforts have been made to adjust institutions and local organisations to facilitate more effective policy delivery. The evidence suggests that, while this approach may be having the laudable effect of alleviating the problems caused by social dislocation, it is failing to deliver the scale of redevelopment likely to result in a lasting revival of Britain's coalfield regions.

It is a sobering reality that, despite a discernible shift in political direction since 1997, less money is currently being spent on regional assistance by the present Labour Government than by the previous Labour administration. Between 1976 and 1979 £2.2. billion was devoted to regional assistance (at 1995 prices), whilst between 1994 and 1999 this had fallen to £400 million. Statistics of this nature are bound to be taken as a further indication that New Labour is primarily concerned with managing the decline of what remains of the British coal industry, as opposed to the lasting regeneration of its communities.

Short-term political expedience apart, there are two alternative scenarios. First of all, the Government could decide that there is a future for the UK deep-mined coal industry and take steps to ensure its survival at something like its current level of output. To do that would be to encourage investment in new areas of coal as well as new cleaner-coal power stations in order to fulfil environmental obligations. It would also require a willingness to extend subsidies under revised EU rules after 2002. Second, the Government could refrain from any significant intervention, let the industry slowly die and at the same time minimise the possibility of any political or economic fallout. It is clear that the Government is not yet convinced by the first approach; therefore, it must be assumed they adhere to the second.

If this is the case, then some radical rethinking is necessary. There is, in our view, no evidence that miners and their families are being successfully retrained for alternative employment, setting up their own businesses or moving in search of work. Nor can we find much evidence that attempts to regenerate the local economy can succeed in providing the quantity or quality of jobs sufficient to replace those lost with the closure of the mine. Those who assert the efficacy of such measures may delude themselves and seek to delude others. Those who live, work or conduct research in mining communities do not share such illusions. They are in no doubt about the debilitating effects of long-term unemployment or very low paid work, on ex-miners, their wives and families and the communities they have created.

The cruel logic of market economics with its arid terminology seems indifferent to the social consequences of the policies it advocates. Those directly affected are not merely units of labour any more than a pit is a site of production. They are ordinary men and women who seek neither charity nor condescension, only the right to work and live in communities with some hope for the future. That is, surely, not too much to ask.

Appendix: Methodology in the Doncaster Study

The Selection of Communities

Selecting our mining communities proved difficult. Our initial research design was predicated on the notion that we would identify and focus on three contrasting collieries defined as 'closed', 'threatened' or 'safe'. However, in the constantly changing environment of the coal industry in 1992 and beyond, assigning any one pit to these categories proved extremely hazardous. None of the pits originally selected for study was eventually confirmed. The pit initially deemed about to shut gained a reprieve; the one thought safe suddenly became vulnerable and the one thought insecure was suddenly closed down.

We eventually minimised uncertainty by choosing one pit which had been shut for some time: Brodsworth near Doncaster which closed in September 1990. We studied reaction to the announcement, in December 1991, of the closure of another Doncaster pit at Askern, which became our short-term closure. An apparently secure pit was Rossington, generally regarded as profitable. Since these three pits were all in the Doncaster area, we selected a fourth, insecure pit from that area, at Hatfield. Thus, when our survey began in May 1992, we had a sample of four Doncaster pits: one closed for eighteen months (Brodsworth) and another for six months (Askern), one insecure (Hatfield) and one safe (Rossington). These remained their status for most of our fieldwork period; but by the end of the project, Hatfield had shut entirely and Rossington had been mothballed. Ironically, both pits were subsequently reopened and remain so today.

The Survey

Sample

Despite variations in the size of workforce at each pit we adopted a uniform sample. A total of 400 seemed logistically viable and enabled 10 per cent of the workforce to be included. Since half of these were to be miners' wives we wished to select 40 men and 40 women from each pit. Samples were to be random since there was no reliable basis to control for such variables as age or skill level. We always intended to have a control group of people living in mining communities but not employed in the industry. This should ideally have been spread across the four communities but this proved logistically impossible. We therefore took a quota sample of 40 men and 40 women, controlled for age and occupation, from the community least likely to anticipate any secondary effects of pit closure on allied industries, which was Rossington.

Since British Coal was unable to release any details about employees at past or current pits, we used apparently comprehensive membership lists from the National Union of Mineworkers. Preliminary results of the survey showed the union lists from Hatfield and Askern to include men who had accepted voluntary redundancy prior to pit closure. Whilst this meant additional interviewing, since they had to be replaced, we now had an additional useful sample: 40 ex-miners who had chosen to leave the industry and an equivalent number of their wives. Our overall sample was thus:

ex-miners long-term pit closure	40	
wives of ex-miners long-term pit closure	40	
ex-miners short-term pit closure	40	
wives of ex-miners short-term pit closure	40	
miners at threatened pit	40	
wives of miners at threatened pit	40	
miners at safe pit	40	
wives of miners at safe pit	40	
main sample		*320*
voluntarily redundant ex-miners	40	
wives of voluntarily redundant ex-miners	40	
voluntarily redundant sample		*80*
local residents not employed in mining male	40	
local residents not employed in mining female	40	
non-mining sample		*80*
TOTAL SAMPLE		*480*

The initial survey, commissioned from Sheffield Hallam University's in-house survey unit, was eventually completed by June 1992 and the readjusted samples by December.

Questionnaire

The questionnaire, containing 40 main questions requiring 145 responses, was divided into 5 sections:

1.   biographical background: e.g. gender, age, length of residence, marital status, household composition;

2.   family relations: e.g. network of relatives, frequency of contact;

3.   community perceptions: e.g. local facilities, perception of community, sense of change, effects of pit closure;

4.   work: e.g. occupation, site, hours, career changes, changes in mining industry;

5.   stress and coping: e.g. definition of stressful experiences, past/current sources of stress and coping, measures of health and well-being, informal and formal sources of help.

The questionnaire was piloted in February 1992 using a sample of thirty interviewees drawn from two pits not included in the final selection. We encountered the most difficulties in arriving at a satisfactory measure of stress. Given the lack of academic consensus about how to define stress, we adopted Pearlin's (1989) definition of stress as a response to a 'threatening or noxious condition' and his subdivision of key elements as those of stressors (e.g. life events or chronic strains), mediators (notably coping and social support mechanisms) and outcomes (such as psychological distress or behavioural manifestations, such as drinking alcohol). We saw no inherent tension between this version and the literature relating stress to unemployment and job insecurity (Elder and Caspi 1988; Hartley et al. 1991), especially as affecting 'vulnerable communities' (Brenner and Starrin 1988).

Our original research design anticipated use of the twelve-item version of the General Health Questionnaire (GHQ) (Goldberg 1978) to measure respondents' levels of stress. However, we soon concluded that this measure was inappropriate. The GHQ focuses exclusively on the subjective psychological states of individuals and comprises some quite extreme statements of what has been specified as psychiatric disorder (cf. Warr et al. 1988). Here, we drew on our existing knowledge of the culture of mining communities and the outcome of our pilot study, which led us to believe that statements about lack of self-worth would not be recognised or admitted, especially by men, and that mental health would be closely related to physical health (Warr 1985). In general, we chose to emphasise behaviour rather than state of mind.

We therefore looked for a measure which incorporated a range of symptoms of stress. We adapted Fimian's (1984) Teacher Stress Inventory, which measures psychological, physical and behavioural symptoms. Some items specific to teaching were reformulated and others revised in the light of pilot work. This produced a twenty-one-item scale divided into three sections. We also asked a series of questions about respondents' perceptions of their own stress-related behaviour and of differences in behaviour imputed to gender.

In-depth Interviews

Miners and their Wives

The original research design specified the selection of a sub-set of 60 questionnaire interviewees for follow-up in-depth interviews. Rather than draw a simple random sample, we decided to weight the 60 according to 4 key variables:

1.   Male employment status: subdivided into miner (including redeployed as transferees and private contracting); ex-miner re-employed; and ex-miner unemployed (including short- and long-term unemployed).

2.   Female employment status: subdivided into full-time paid employment; part-time paid employment; and no paid employment.

3.   Age of potential respondent: subdivided into young (under 35); middle (36–45); and old (46 and over). The stage in the lifecycle was potentially an important mediator of perceptions of actual or potential unemployment.

4.   Total stress score from the survey: subdivided into high (a score of 16 or more); medium (6–15); or low (0–5).

This could not be an orthodox stratified random sample but provided a reasonable cross-section of case studies, incorporating a range of circumstances in which miners and their wives had to, or might be forced to, contemplate redundancy from the mining industry.

Semi-structured interviews were carried out from June to September 1992. Thirty men were interviewed by one of the male principal researchers and 30 women by the project's female research assistant. Since there were fewer sub-categories of 'male employment status' in Rossington (miner and contract worker only) and Hatfield (miner and voluntarily redundant), we decided to do fewer interviews there than at the short-term (Askern) and long-term (Brodsworth) pits. Each husband and wife out of 6 married couples were interviewed separately but simultaneously so that their viewpoints could be directly compared. Out of the 6 couples, 3 were voluntarily redundant men and their wives from Hatfield, while the other 3 were contract workers and their wives from Rossington.

Interviews elaborated issues central to the survey, such as perceptions of community, work and unemployment, family life, the impact of actual or potential pit closure, the politics of industrial contraction, and stress and coping strategies. Conducted at the interviewees' homes, interviews lasted seventy minutes on average.

Key Informants

Sixty interviews across the four communities were held with key informants from professions and community organisations. These included: the local social work team; one health centre, including a GP, a practice nurse and a member of a health-visiting team; local school headteachers from the first, middle and secondary schools; a local vicar (C of E); two community constables and one officer of higher rank; at least one Education Welfare officer; one youth worker, one Citizen's Advice Bureau worker; one careers officer; and three local councillors.

Interviews were conducted at the workplace in private and lasted about an hour. We requested that key informants give a brief description of their work, before asking them to tell us about their contacts with and perceptions of the mining community. More specific questions were tailored to their particular areas of professional responsibility, especially where they were of relevance to the impact of industrial contraction. As with our community interviews (miners and their partners), all the interview material was transcribed and coded using the 'Ethnograph' package.

References

Albrechts, L, Moulart, F, Roberts, P and Swyngedouw, E (1989) 'New Perspectives for Regional Policy and Development in the 1990s', in L Albrechts, F Moulart, P Roberts and E Swyngedouw (eds), *Regional Policy at the Crossroads*, London: Jessica Kingsley.

Allen, J and Massey, D (1988a) *The Economy in Question*, London: Sage.

Allen, J and Massey, D (eds) (1988b) *Uneven Redevelopment: Cities and Regions in Transition*, London: Sage.

Allen, S (1989) 'Gender and Work in Mining Communities', Paper Presented to British Sociological Association Annual Conference, Leeds.

Allen, S and Measham, S (1994) 'In Defence of Home and Hearth? Families, Friendships and Feminism in Mining Communities', in Communications, Media and Communities Research Centre (eds), *Coal, Culture and Community: Proceedings of a Conference*, Sheffield: PAVIC Publications.

Allen, VL (1981) *The Militancy of British Miners*, Shipley: The Moor Press.

Amin, A (ed.) (1994) *Post-Fordism: A Reader*, Oxford: Blackwell.

Amin, A and Thrift, N (eds) (1994) *Globalisation, Institutions and Regional Development in Europe*, Oxford: Oxford University Press.

Amin, A and Thrift, N (1995) 'Institutional issues for the European regions: from markets and plans to socioeconomics and powers of association', *Economy and Society* 24 (1), pp.41–66.

Baeten, G, Swyngedouw, E and Albrechts, L (1999) 'Politics, institutions and regional restructuring processes: from managed growth to planned fragmentation in the reconversion of Belgium's last coal mining region', *Regional Studies* 33 (3), pp.247–58.

Ball, R (1998) 'RECHAR II in the West Midlands: the anatomy of a community initiative', *Local Economy* 12 (4), pp.355–61.

Balls, E and Gregg, P (1993) *Work and Welfare: Tackling the Jobs Deficit*, London: Institute for Public Policy Research.

Barnekov, T, Boyle, R and Rich, D (1989) *Privatism and Urban Policy in Britain and the USA*, Oxford: Oxford University Press.

Barr, A (1995) 'Empowering communities – beyond fashionable rhetoric? Some reflections on Scottish experience', *Community Development Journal* 30 (2), pp.121–33.

Baruch, GK, Biener, L and Barnett, RC (1987) 'Women and gender in research on work and family stress', *American Psychologist* 42, pp.130–6.

Bate, P and Carter, N (1986) 'The future for producers' co-operatives', *Industrial Relations Journal* 17, pp.57–70.

Baxter, S (1992) 'Valleys in the shadow of coal', *New Statesman and Society* 11 September, pp.12–13.

Beatty, C and Fothergill, S (1994) 'Registered and Hidden Unemployment in Areas of Chronic Industrial Decline: The Case of the UK Coalfields', paper presented to the Regional Studies Association conference 'Tackling Unemployment and Social Exclusion', London.

Beatty, C and Fothergill, S (1998) 'Registered and Hidden Unemployment in the UK Coalfields', in P Lawless, R Martin and S Hardy (eds), *Unemployment and Social Exclusion*, London: Jessica Kingsley.

Beaverstock, JV (1998a) 'Economic regeneration in the Midland coalfield area of the National Forest', *East Midland Geographer* 21 (1), pp.92–7.

Beaverstock, JV (1998b) 'Local economic development and the English National Forest', *Local Economy* 12 (4), pp.364–72.

Beenken, H (1995) 'Training as a Means of Promoting the Restructuring of the Coal Regions', in C Critcher, K Schubert and D Waddington (eds), *Regeneration of the Coalfield Areas: Anglo-German Perspectives*, London: Pinter.

Bennett, K, Beynon, H and Hudson, R (2000) Coal Regeneration: *Dealing with the Consequences of Industrial Decline*, Bristol: The Policy Press/Joseph Rowntree Foundation.

Bennett, R, Wicks, P and McCoshan, A (1994) *Local Empowerment and Business Services: Britain's Experiment with Training and Enterprise Councils*, London: UCL Press.

Beynon, H, Hudson, R and Sadler, D (1991) *A Tale of Two Industries: Contraction of Coal and Steel in the North East of England*, Milton Keynes: Open University Press.

Binns, D and Mars, G (1984) 'Family, community and unemployment: a study in change', *Sociological Review* 32 (1), pp.662–95.

Bjorkland, A and Eriksson, T (1999) 'Unemployment and mental health: evidence from research in the Nordic countries', *Scandinavian Journal of Social Welfare* 7, pp.219–35.

Blyton, P and Turnbull, P (1994) *The Dynamics of Employee Relations*, London: Macmillan.

Boddy, M (1992) 'Training and Enterprise Councils and the Restructuring of Training Provision', in M Campbell and K Duffy (eds), *Local Labour Markets: Problems and Policies*, Harlow: Longman.

Bosch, G (1995) 'Industrial Restructuring and Further Training in North-Rhine Westfalen', in P Cooke (ed.), *The Rise of the Rustbelt*, London: UCL Press.

Bostyn, AM and Wight, D (1987) 'Inside a Community: Values Associated with Money and Time', in S Fineman (ed.), *Unemployment: Personal and Social Consequences*, London: Tavistock.

Brendow, K (2000) *Restructuring and Privatising the Coal Industries in Central and Eastern Europe and the CIS*, London/Geneva: World Energy Council.

Brenner, SO and Starrin, B (1988) 'Unemployment and health in Sweden: public issuers and private troubles', *Journal of Social Issues* 44 (4), pp.125–40.

Brown, GW and Harris, T (1978) *Social Origins of Depression*, London: Tavistock.

Brown, P (1990) 'Schooling and Employment in the UK', in D Ashton and G Lowe (eds), *Making their Way: Education, Training and the Labour Market*, Milton Keynes: Open University Press.

Brown, P and Crompton, R (1994) *A New Europe: Economic Restructuring and Social Exclusion*, London: UCL Press.

Buhr, R (1995) 'Product Development as the New Function of Business Promotion', in C Critcher, K Schubert and D Waddington (eds), *Regeneration of the Coalfield Areas: Anglo-German Perspectives*, London: Pinter.

Bulmer, S (1975) 'Sociological models of the mining community', *Sociological Review* 23, pp.61–92.

Burchell, B (1992) 'Towards a social psychology of the labour market. Or why we need to understand the labour market before we can understand unemployment', *Journal of Occupational and Organizational Psychology* 65, pp.345–54.

Burchell, B (1994) 'The Effects of Labour Market Position, Job Insecurity and Unemployment on Psychological Health', in D Gallie, C Marsh and C Vogler (eds), *Social Change and the Experience of Unemployment*, Oxford: Oxford University Press.

Burchell, B, Day, D, Hudson, M, Ladipo, D, Mankelow, R, Nolan, JP, Reed, H, Wichert, IC and Wilkinson, F (1999) *Job Insecurity and Work Intensification: Flexibility and the Changing Boundaries of Work*, York: York Publishing Services.

Campbell, B (1993) *Goliath: Britain's Dangerous Places*, London: Methuen.

Cartwright, S and Cooper, CL (1997) *Managing Workplace Stress*, London: Sage.

CCC (Coalfield Communities Campaign) (1993) *Memorandum on the State of the Coal Industry, Yorkshire 1993*, Barnsley: CCC.

CCC (1997) *A Fair Deal for Coal – A Fair Deal for Britain: A Strategy for Coal for a New Labour Government*, Barnsley: CCC.

CCC (1998) *A Market for Coal: How to Avoid Pit Closures and Secure Britain's Energy Supplies*, Barnsley: CCC.

CCC (1999) *How Much Difference? Progress in Implementing the Government's Response to the Coalfields Task Force*, Barnsley: CCC.

CCC (2000) *How Much More Difference? Further Progress in Implementing the Government's Response to the Coalfields Task Force*, Barnsley: CCC.

Chadwick, MJ, Highton, NH and Lindman, N (1987) *Environmental Impacts of Coal Mining and Utilisation*, Oxford: Pergamon.

Chanan, G (1996) 'Regeneration: plugging gaps or pushing frontiers?', *Local Economy* 11 (2), pp.98–103.

Cherry, N (1984) 'Nervous strain, anxiety and symptoms amongst 32-year-old men at work in Britain', *Journal of Occupational Psychology* 57, pp.95–105.

Coalfields Task Force (1998) *Making the Difference: A New Start for England's Coalfield Communities*, London: DETR.

Coates, K and Barratt-Brown, M (1997) *Community Under Attack: The Struggle for Survival in the Coalfield Communities of Britain*, Nottingham: Spokesman.

Coffield, F, Borrill, C and Marshall, S (1986) *Growing Up at the Margins: Young Adults in the North East*, Milton Keynes: Open University Press.

Colling, T (1991) 'Privatisation and the management of IR in electricity distribution', *Industrial Relations Journal* 22 (2), pp.117–29.

Community Support Unit (1997) *Community Safety Survey*, Nottingham: Notts CC Social Services Department.

Cooke, P (1995) 'New Wave Regional and Urban Revitalization Strategies in Wales', in P Cooke (ed.), *The Rise of the Rustbelt*, London: UCL Press.

Cooke, P and Morgan, D (1993) 'The network paradigm: new departures in corporate and regional development', *Society and Space* 11, pp.543–64.

Cooper, CL and Roden, J (1985) 'Mental health and satisfaction among tax officers', *Social Science and Medicine* 21 (7), pp.747–51.

Cornforth, C (1983) 'Some factors affecting the success or failure of worker co-operatives: a review of empirical research in the UK', *Economic and Industrial Democracy* 4 (2), pp.163–90.

Cornforth, C, Thomas, A, Lewis, J and Spear, R (1988) *Developing Successful Worker Co-operatives*, London: Sage.

Coulter, J, Miller, S and Walker, M (1984) *State of Siege: Politics and Policing in the Coalfields*, London: Canary Press.

County Homelessness and Housing Team (1996) *Stopping the Rot: The Warsop Vale House Condition Survey*, Nottingham: Notts CC Social Services Department.

Coyle, A (1984) *Redundant Women*, London: The Women's Press Ltd.

Cragg, A and Dawson, T (1984) *Unemployed Women: A Study of Attitudes and Experiences*, Research Paper 47, London: Department of Employment.

Crick, M (1985) *Scargill and the Miners*, Harmondsworth: Penguin.

Critcher, C, Dicks, B and Waddington, D (1992) 'Portrait of despair', *New Statesman and Society* 23 October, pp.16–17.

Critcher, C, Parry, D and Waddington, D (1995) *Redundancy and After: A Study of Ex-miners from Thurcroft in the Aftermath of Pit Closure*, Sheffield: PAVIC Publications.

Critcher, C, Parry, D and Waddington, D (1999) 'Regulation, Restructuring and Regeneration in Coalfields: Three European Cases', in P Edwards and T Elger (eds), *The Global Economy, National States and the Regulation of Labour*, London: Mansell.

Critcher, C, Schubert, K and Waddington, D (eds) (1995) *Regeneration of the Coalfield Areas: Anglo-German Perspectives*, London: Pinter.

Crouch, C (1990) 'Afterword', in G Baglioni and C Crouch (eds), *European Industrial Relations: The Challenge of Flexibility*, London: Sage.

Crow, G and Allan, G (1994) *Community Life: An Introduction to Local Social Relations*, London: Harvester-Wheatsheaf.

CTRU (Civic Trust Regeneration Unit) (1992) *The Warsop Area: Working Together*, Nottingham: Notts CC.

Dabinett, G (2000) 'Regenerating communities in the UK: getting into the information society?' *Community Development Journal* 35 (2), pp.157–66.

Daniel, WW (1978) *Applied Nonparametric Statistics*, Boston: Houghton Mifflin.

Davies, S (1993) *Training and Retraining Policies and Practices. Revitalising the Older Industrial Regions: North-Rhine Westfalen and Wales Contrasted*, Cardiff: University of Wales.

Deitrick, S (1999) 'The post industrial revitalization of Pittsburgh: myths and evidence', *Community Development Journal* 34 (1), pp.4–12.

Deitrick, S and Beauregard, RA (1995) 'From Front-runner to Also-ran – The Transformation of a Once-dominant Industrial Region: Pennsylvania, USA', in P Cooke (ed.), *The Rise of the Rustbelt*, London: UCL Press.

Dennis, N, Henriques, F and Slaughter, C (1956) *Coal is Our Life: An Analysis of a Yorkshire Mining Community*, London: Eyre and Spottiswoode.

Dennis, N, Henriques, F and Slaughter, C (1969) *Coal is Our Life: An Analysis of a Yorkshire Mining Community*, London: Tavistock (second edn).

DETR (Department of the Environment, Transport and the Regions) (1997) *The Way Forward for Regeneration*, News Release 445, London: DETR.

DETR (1998) *Making the Difference: A New Start for England's Coalfield Communities: The Government's Response to the Coalfields Task Force Report*, London: DETR.

DETR (2000) *Regeneration of Former Coalfield Areas: Interim Evaluation*, London: The Stationery Office.

Dew, MA, Bromet, EJ and Schulberg, HC (1987) 'A comparative analysis of two community stressors' long-term health effects', *American Journal of Community Psychology* 15, pp.167–84.

Dicks, B, Waddington, D and Critcher, C (1993) 'The quiet disintegration of closure communities', *Town and Country Planning* 62 (7), pp.174–6.

Dooley, D, Rook, R and Catalano, R (1987) 'Job and non-job stressors and their moderators', *Journal of Occupational Psychology* 60, pp.115–32.

Drewe, P (2000) 'European Experiences', in P Roberts and H Sykes (eds), *Urban Regeneration: A Handbook*, London: Sage.

DTI (Department of Trade and Industry) (1993) *The Prospects for Coal: Conclusions of the Government's Coal Review*, Cm 2235, London: HMSO.

DTI (1998) *Conclusions of the Review of Energy Sources for Power Regeneration and Government Response to Fourth and Fifth Reports of the Trade and Industry Committee*, London: The Stationery Office.

DTI (2000) *Market Reforms and Innovation* ('The Energy Report'), London: The Stationery Office.

Edwards, CY (1991) *Restructuring the European Community Coal Industry: A Study of the Social Consequences for the UK Mining Areas*, Kingston Business School Occasional Paper Series, Kingston: Kingston University.

Edwards, C and Heery, E (1989) *Management Control and Union Power: A Study of Labour Relations in Coal-Mining*, Oxford: Clarendon Press.

Elder, GH Jr and Caspi, A (1988) 'Economic stress in lives: developmental perspectives', *Journal of Social Issues*, 44 (4), pp.25–45.

Employment Service (1992) *Local Action for Employment*, London: HMSO.

Epstein, D, Elwood, J, Hey, V and Maw, J (eds) (1998) *Failing Boys? Issues in Gender and Achievement*, Buckingham: Open University Press.

Esterman, H and Roxlau-Hennemann, F (1995) 'The Eastern Ruhr Development Agency: A Public Private Sector Initiative for Structural Change', in C Critcher, K Schubert and D Waddington (eds), *Regeneration of the Coalfield Areas: Anglo-German Perspectives*, London: Pinter.

European Commission (2000) *Towards a European Strategy for the Security of Energy Supply*, Brussels: EU Energy and Transport Commission.

Ezzy, D (1993) 'Unemployment and mental health: a critical review', *Social Science and Medicine* 37 (1), pp.41–52.

Fairbrother, P (1994) 'Privatisation and local trade unionism', *Work, Employment and Society* 8 (3), pp.339–56.

Farmer, V (1986) 'Broken heartland', *Psychology Today* 20 (4), pp.54–62.

Ferner, A and Colling, T (1991) 'Privatization, regulation and industrial relations', *British Journal of Industrial Relations* 29 (3), pp.391–409.

Ferner, A, Keep, E and Waddington, J (1997) 'Industrial restructuring and EU-wide social measures: broader lessons of the ECSC experience', *Journal of European Public Policy* 4 (1), pp.56–72.

Fieldhouse, E and Hollywood, E (1999) 'Life after mining: hidden unemployment and changing patterns of economic activity in England and Wales 1981–1991', *Work, Employment and Society* 13 (3), pp.483–502.

Fimian, MJ (1984) 'The development of an instrument to measure occupational stress in teachers: the Teacher Stress Inventory', *Journal of Occupational Psychology* 57, pp.277–93.

Fine, B and Millar, R (eds) (1985) *Policing the Miners' Strike*, London: Lawrence and Wishart.

Fineman, S (1987) 'Back to Employment: Wounds and Wisdoms', in D Fryer and P Ullah (eds), *Unemployed People: Social and Psychological Perspectives*, Milton Keynes: Open University Press.

Foley, P and Martin, S (2000) 'Perceptions of community led regeneration: community and central government viewpoints', *Regional Studies* 34 (8), pp.783–87.

Fordham, G, Hutchinson, J and Foley, P (1999) 'Strategic approaches to local regeneration: The Single Regeneration Budget Challenge Fund', *Regional Studies* 33 (2), pp.131–41.

Fothergill, S (1993) 'The coal industry after the White Paper', *Town and Country Planning* 62 (7), pp.169–70.

Fothergill, S (1995) 'The European Community's RECHAR Programme: An Adequate Response to the Problems of Coal Areas?', in S Hardy, M Hart, L Albrechts and A Katos (eds), *An Enlarged Europe: Regions in Competition?*, London: Jessica Kingsley/Regional Studies Association.

Fothergill, S and Guy, N (1993) *The End of Coal? The Impact of the 'Dash for Gas' in UK Electricity Generation*, Barnsley: CCC.

Fothergill, S and Guy, N (1994) *An Evaluation of British Coal Enterprise*, Barnsley: CCC.

Fothergill, S and Witt, S (1990) *The Privatisation of British Coal*, Barnsley: CCC.

Fothergill, S and Witt, S (1992) *The Case Against Gas: Why Gas is the Wrong Fuel for Britain's Power Stations*, Barnsley: CCC.

Francis, H and Smith, D (1981) *The Fed: A History of the South Wales Miners in the Twentieth Century*, London: Lawrence and Wishart.

Gallie, D and Marsh, C (1994) 'The Experience of Unemployment', in D Gallie, C Marsh and C Vogler (eds), *Social Change and the Experience of Unemployment*, Oxford: Oxford University Press.

Gallie, D, Marsh, C and Vogler, C (eds) (1994) *Social Change and the Experience of Unemployment*, Oxford: Oxford University Press.

Gibbon, P (1988) 'Analysing the British miners' strike of 1984–5', *Economy and Society* 17 (2), pp.139–94.

Gibbon, P and Bromley, S (1990) '"From an institution to a business"? Changes in the British coal industry 1985–9', *Economy and Society* 19 (1), pp.151–60.

Goldberg, D (1978) *Manual of the General Health Questionnaire*, Windsor: National Foundation for Educational Research.

Gregson, N and Lowe, W (1994) 'Waged domestic labour and the renegotiation of the domestic division of labour within dual career households', *Sociology* 28 (1), pp.55–78.

Gunderson, M, Sack, J, McCartney, J, Wakely, D and Eaton, J (1995) 'Employee buyouts in Canada', *British Journal of Industrial Relations* 33 (3), pp.417–43.

Guy, N (1994) *Redundant Miners Survey: Vane Tempest*, Barnsley: CCC.

Hall, S and Mawson, J (1999) *Challenge Funding, Contracts and Area Regeneration: A Decade of Innovation in Policy Management and Coordination*, Bristol: The Policy Press.

Hall, S and Nevin, B (1999) 'Continuity and change: a review of English regeneration policy in the 1990s', *Regional Studies* 33 (5), pp.477–91.

Hall, T (1981) *King Coal: Miners, Coal and Britain's Industrial Future*, Harmondsworth: Penguin.

Hammer, T (1992) 'Unemployment and use of drugs and alcohol among young people: a longitudinal study in a general population', *British Journal of Addiction* 87, pp.1571–81.

Harding, L and Sewel, J (1992) 'Psychological health and employment status in an island community', *Journal of Occupational and Organizational Psychology* 65, pp.269–75.

Hartley, J, Jacobson, D, Klandermans, B and van Vuuren, T (eds) (1991) *Job Insecurity – Coping with Jobs at Risk*, London: Sage.

Hart, T and Johnston, I (2000) 'Employment, Education and Training', in P Roberts and H Sykes (eds), *Urban Regeneration: A Handbook*, London: Sage.

Haughton, G (1998) 'Principles and practice of community economic development', *Regional Studies* 32 (9), pp.872–7.

HM Government (1993a) *British Energy Policy and the Market for Coal*, House of Commons Select Committee on Trade and Industry, London: HMSO.

HM Government (1993b) *Employment Consequences of British Coal's Proposed Pit Closures*, House of Commons Select Committee on Employment, London: HMSO.

Heseltine, M (2000) *Life in the Jungle: My Autobiography*, London: Hodder and Stoughton.

Hessling, M (1995) 'The Role of Ruhrkohle AG in Germany's Energy and Coal Policy', in C Critcher, K Schubert and D Waddington (eds), *Regeneration of the Coalfield Areas: Anglo-German Perspectives*, London: Pinter.

House, JW and Knight, EM (1967) *Pit Closure and the Community: Report to the Ministry of Labour*, Papers on Migration and Mobility in Northern England, Number 5, Newcastle: Department of Geography, University of Newcastle upon Tyne.

Howe, G (1998) 'English Partnerships' Coalfield Regeneration Programme', *Local Economy* 12 (4), pp.362–4.

Hudson, R (1988) 'Labour Market Changes and New Forms of Work in "Old" Industrial Regions', in J Allen and D Massey (eds), *Uneven Re-development: Cities and Regions in Transition*, London: Sage.

Hudson, R (1992) *Industrial Restructuring and Spatial Change: Myths and Realities in the Changing Geography of Production in the 1980s*, Occasional Paper No. 27, Durham: Department of Geography, University of Durham.

Hudson, R (1994) 'Institutional Change, Cultural Transformation and Economic Regeneration: Myths and Realities from Europe's Old Industrial Areas', in A Amin and M Thrift (eds), *Globalization, Institutions and Regional Development in Europe*, Oxford: Oxford University Press.

Hudson, R and Sadler, D (1987) 'National policies and local economic intitiatives', *Local Economy* 12 (2), pp.7–14.

Hudson, R and Sadler, D (1990) 'State policies and the changing geography of the coal industry in the United Kingdom in the 1980s and 1990s', *Transactions of the Institute of British Geographers* 15 (4), pp.435–55.

Hudson, R and Sadler, D (1992) 'New jobs for old? Reindustrialisation policies in Derwentside in the 1980s', *Regional Studies* 6 (4), pp.316–25.

Hudson, R and Sadler, D (1995) 'Manufacturing Success: Industrialisation Policies in Derwentside in the 1980s', in C Critcher, K Schubert and D Waddington (eds), *Regeneration of the Coalfield Areas: Anglo-German Perspectives*, London: Pinter.

Hudson, R, Sadler, D and Townsend, A (1992) 'Employment change in UK steel closure areas during the 1980s: policy implications and lessons for Scotland', *Regional Studies* 26 (7), pp.633–46.

Huggins, R and Thomalla, R (1995) 'Promoting Innovation Through Technology Networks in North-Rhine Westfalen', in P Cooke (ed.), *The Rise of the Rustbelt*, London: UCL Press.

IEEC (International Economic and Energy Consultants) (1995) *Reconversion Experiences in the EU's Coalfields: A Balance Sheet*. Occasional Paper, London: IEEC.

Inman, C (1997) 'Facing up to a mine-boggling challenge', *Planning* 29 August, pp.18–19.

Iversen, L and Klausen, H (1986) 'Alcohol consumption among laid-off workers before and after closure of a Danish ship-yard: a 2-year follow-up study', *Social Science and Medicine* 22 (1), pp.107–9.

Iversen, L and Sabroe, S (1988) 'Psychological well-being among unemployed and employed people after a company closedown: a longitudinal study', *Journal of Social Issues* 44 (4), pp.141–52.

Jackson, D (1998) 'Breaking Out of the Binary Trap', in D Epstein, J Elwood, V Hey and J Maw (eds), *Failing Boys? Issues in Gender and Achievement*, Buckingham: Open University Press.

Jackson, PR and Walsh, S (1987) 'Unemployment and the Family', in D Fryer and P Ullah (eds), *Unemployed People: Social and Psychological Perspectives*, Milton Keynes: Open University Press.

Joelson, L and Wahlquist, L (1987) 'The psychological meaning of job insecurity and job loss: results of a longitudinal study', *Social Science and Medicine* 15 (12), pp.179–82.

Jonas, AEG (1995) 'Local labour control regimes: uneven development and the social regulation of production', *Regional Studies* 30 (4), pp.323–8.

Jones, G (1988) 'The Future of Coalfield Communities', *Coalfield Communities Campaign Working Papers*, 5, pp.33–47, Barnsley: CCC.

Jones, D, Petley, J, Power, M and Wood, L (1985) *Media Hits the Pits*, London: Campaign for Press and Broadcasting Freedom.

Kennett, P (1994) 'Exclusion, post-Fordism and the "New Europe"', in P Brown and R Crompton (eds), *A New Europe: Economic Restructuring and Social Exclusion*, London: UCL Press.

Kessler, RC, Turner, JB and House, JS (1989) 'Unemployment, reemployment and emotional functioning in a community sample', *American Sociological Review* 54, pp.648–57.

Kristensen, TS (1991) 'Sickness absence and work strain among Danish slaughterhouse workers: an analysis of absence from work regarded as coping behaviour', *Social Science and Medicine* 32 (1), pp.15–27.

Laite, J and Halfpenny, F (1987) 'Employment, Unemployment and the Domestic Division of Labour', in D Fryer and P Ullah (eds), *Unemployed People*, Milton Keynes: Open University Press.

Lawless, P (1996) 'The inner cities: towards a new agenda', *Town Planning Review* 67 (1), pp.21–43.

Leigh, JP (1991) 'Employee and job attributes as predictors of absenteeism in a national sample of workers: the importance of health and dangerous working conditions', *Social Science and Medicine* 33 (2), pp.127–37.

Leman, S and Winterton, J (1991) 'New technology and the restructuring of pit-level industrial relations in the British coal industry', *New Technology, Work and Employment* 6 (1), pp.54–64.

Lempers, JD and Clark-Lempers, D (1990) 'Family economic stress, maternal and paternal support and adolescent distress', *Journal of Adolescence* 13, pp.217–29.

Lennon, M C and Rosenfield, S (1992) 'Women and mental health: the interaction of job and family conditions', *Journal of Health and Social Behaviour* 33, pp.316–27.

Liem, R and Liem, JH (1988) 'Psychological effects of unemployment on workers and their families', *Journal of Social Issues* 44 (4), pp.87–105.

Liem, R and Liem, JH (1990) 'Understanding the Individual and Family Effects of Unemployment', in J Eckenrode and S Gore (eds), *Stress Between Work and Family*, New York: Plenum Press.

Little, M and Reynolds, S (1991) Guidance, Training and Education: *Provision for Redundant Miners from Mardy Colliery*, Ammanford, West Glamorgan: Valleys Initiative for Adult Education.

Loftman, P and Nevin, B (1994) 'Prestige project developments: economic developments or economic myth? A case study of Birmingham', *Local Economy* 8 (4), pp.307–25.

McAvan, L (1993) 'There is an alternative', *Town and Country Planning* 62 (7), pp.171–4.

McKee, L and Bell, C (1985) 'Marital and Family Relations in Times of Male Unemployment', in B Roberts, R Finnegan and D Gallie (eds), *New Approaches to Economic Life*, Manchester: Manchester University Press.

McKinlay, A and Taylor, P (1994) 'Privatisation and industrial relations in British shipbuilding', *Industrial Relations Journal* 25 (4), pp.293–304.

Martin, R (1989) 'The New Economics and Politics of Regional Restructuring: The British Experience', in L Albrechts, F Moulaert, P Roberts and E Swyngedouw (eds), *Regional Policy at the Crossroads: European Perspectives*, London: Jessica Kingsley.

Mawson, J and Hall, S (2000) 'Joining it up locally? Area regeneration and holistic government in England', *Regional Studies* 34 (1), pp.67–74.

Mellor, M, Hannah, J and Stirling, J (1988) *Worker Co-operatives in Theory and Practice*, Milton Keynes: Open University Press.

Miller, PMC and Plant, M (1996) 'Drinking, smoking and illicit drug use amongst 15 and 16-year-olds in the United Kingdom', *British Medical Journal* 313 (7054), pp.394–98.

Miller, S (1985) 'Grimethorpe now', *London Review of Books* 7 (10), 6 June, pp.16–17.

Milne, K (1993) 'Keeping the coal fires burning', *New Statesman and Society* 22 January, pp.12–14.

Morgan, K (1993) 'Revival in the valleys?', *Town and Country Planning* 62 (7), pp.177–9.

Morgan, K (1995) 'Reviving the Valleys? Urban Renewal and Governance Structures in Wales', in R Hambleton and H Thomas (eds), *Urban Policy Evaluation: Challenge and Change*, London: Paul Chapman.

Morgan, K (1997) 'The regional animateur: taking stock of the Welsh Development Agency', *Regional and Federal Studies* 7 (2), pp.70–94.

Morgan, K and Price, A (1992) *Rebuilding Our Communities: A New Agenda for the Valleys*, London: Friedrich Ebert Foundation.

Morris, J (1995) 'McJobbing a Region: Industrial Restructuring and the Widening Socio-economic Divide in Wales', in R Turner (ed.), *The British Economy in Transition*, London: Routledge.

Morris, J and Wilkinson, B (1993) *Poverty and Prosperity in Wales: An Analysis of Socio-Economic Divisions*, Cardiff: Cardiff Business School, University of Wales.

Morris, L (1985) 'Renegotiation of the Domestic Division of Labour in the Context of Male Redundancy', in B Roberts, R Finnegan and D Gallie (eds), *New Approaches to Economic Life*, Manchester: Manchester University Press.

Morris, L (1988) 'Employment, the Household and Social Networks', in D Gallie (ed.), *Employment in Britain*, Oxford: Basil Blackwell.

Morris, L (1992) 'Domestic labour and employment status among married couples: a case study in Hartlepool', *Capital and Class* 49, pp.37–52.

Nathanson, CA (1975) 'Illness and the feminine role: a theoretical review', *Social Science and Medicine* 9, pp.57–62.

National Union of Mineworkers (1992a) *Minutes of Annual Conference, Morning Session*, 1 July 1992, Sheffield: NUM.

National Union of Mineworkers (1992b) *Minutes of Presidential Address to Annual Conference*, 29 June 1992, Sheffield: NUM.

Nolan, JP, Wichert, IC and Burchell, BJ (2000) 'Job Insecurity, Psychological Well-being and Family Life', in E Heery and J Salmon (eds), *The Insecure Workforce*, London: Routledge.

Noll, W (1995) 'The Promotion of Business Activities in the Context of Structural Policy in North-Rhine Westfalen', in C Critcher, K Schubert and D Waddington (eds), *Regeneration of the Coalfield Areas: Anglo-German Perspectives*, London: Pinter.

Nordenmark, M and Strandh, M (1999) 'Towards a sociological understanding of mental well-being among the unemployed: the role of economic and psychosocial factors', *Sociology* 33 (3), pp.577–97.

Ogden, S (1994) 'The reconstruction of industrial relations in the privatised water industry', *British Journal of Industrial Relations* 32 (1), pp.67–84.

Parker, H, Measham, F and Aldridge, J (1995) *Drugs Futures: Changing Patterns of Drug Use amongst English Youth*, London: Institute for the Study of Drug Dependence.

Parker, M (1994) *The Politics of Coal's Decline: The Industry in Western Europe*, London: Royal Institute of Economic Affairs.

Parker, M (1999) 'Confusing signals', *The Utilities Journal* May, p.33.

Parker, M and Surrey, J (1992) *Unequal Treatment: British Policies for Coal and Nuclear Power 1979–92*, Brighton: Science Policy Research Unit, University of Sussex.

Parkinson, M and Evans, R (1990) 'Urban Development Corporations', in M Campbell (ed.), *Local Economic Policy*, London: Cassell.

Parkinson, N (1992) *Right at the Centre*, London: Weidenfeld and Nicolson.

Parry, D (1996) 'Regenerating Local Economies: A Comparative Analysis of Three UK Coal Areas'. Unpublished MPhil thesis, Sheffield: Sheffield Hallam University.

Parry, D, Waddington, D and Critcher, C (1997) 'Industrial relations in the privatised mining industry', *British Journal of Industrial Relations* 35 (2), pp.173–96.

Parry, G (1986) 'Paid employment, life events, social support and mental health in working-class mothers', *Journal of Health and Social Behaviour* 27, pp.193–208.

Paton, R (1989) *Reluctant Entrepreneurs*, Milton Keynes: Open University Press.

Pearlin LI (1989) 'The sociological study of stress', *Journal of Health and Social Behaviour* 30, pp.241–56.

Pearson, G (1979) 'In Defence of Hooliganism, Social Theory and Violence', in N Tutt (ed.), *Violence*, London: HMSO.

Pearson, G (1987a) *The New Heroin Users*, Oxford: Basil Blackwell.

Pearson, G (1987b) 'Social Deprivation, Unemployment and Patterns of Heroin Use', in N Dorn and N South (eds), *A Land Fit for Heroin*, London: Macmillan.

Peck, J (1994) 'Regulating Labour: The Social Regulation and Reproduction of Local Labour Markets', in A Amin, and N Thrift (eds), *Globalisation, Institutions, and Regional Development in Europe*, Oxford: Oxford University Press.

Peck, J and Tickell, A (1994) 'Searching for a New Institutional Fix: The After-Fordist Crisis and the Global-Local Disorder', in A Amin (ed.), *Post-Fordism: A Reader*, Oxford: Blackwell.

Pendleton, A, Robinson, A and Wilson, N (1995) 'Does employee ownership weaken trade unions? Recent evidence from the UK bus industry', *Economic and Industrial Democracy* 16 (4), pp.577–605.

Pendleton, A and Winterton, J (eds) (1993) *Public Enterprise in Transition: Industrial Relations in State and Privatised Corporations*, London: Routledge.

Penkower, L, Bromet, E and Dew, MA (1988) 'Husbands' layoff and wives' mental health', *Archives of General Psychiatry* 45, pp.994–1000.

People of Thurcroft (1986) *Thurcroft: A Village and the Miners' Strike*, Nottingham: Spokesman.

Popay, J (1985) 'Women, the Family and Unemployment', in P Close and R Collins (eds), *Family and Economy in Modern Society*, London: Macmillan.

Powell, D (1993) *The Power Game: The Struggle for Coal*, London: Duckworth.

Prowse, P and Turner, R (1996) 'Flexibility and coal: a research note on workplace relations', *Work, Employment and Society* 10 (1), pp.151–60.

Raco, M (2000) 'Assessing community participation in local economic development – lessons for the new urban policy', *Political Geography* 19 (5), pp.573–99.

Rees, G and Thomas, M (1989) 'From Coal Miners to Entrepreneurs: A Case Study in the Sociology of Re-industrialisation', paper presented to the British Sociological Association Annual Conference, Plymouth.

Rehfeld, D (1995) 'Disintegration and Reintegration of Production Clusters in the Ruhr Area', in P Cooke (ed.), *The Rise of the Rustbelt*, London: UCL Press.

Reicher, S and Emler, N (1986) 'Managing Reputations in Adolescence: The Pursuit of Delinquent and Non-delinquent Identities', in H Beloff (ed.), *Getting into Life*, London: Methuen.

Richardson, R and Wood, S (1989) 'Productivity change in the coal industry and the new industrial relations', *British Journal of Industrial Relations* 19 (3), pp.33–55.

RJB Mining (1998) *RJB plc Mining Annual Report and Accounts, 1998: The Natural Source of Power*, Doncaster, South Yorkshire: RJB Mining plc.

Roberts, P and Sykes, H (2000) 'Current Challenges and Future Prospects', in P Roberts and H Sykes (eds), *Urban Regeneration: A Handbook*, London: Sage.

Rook, K, Dooley, D and Catalano, R (1991) 'Stress transmission: the effect of husbands' job stressors on the emotional health of their wives', *Journal of Marriage and the Family* 53, pp.165–77.

Ross, CE and Mirowsky, J (1988) 'Child care and emotional adjustment to wives' employment', *Journal of Health and Social Behaviour* 29, pp.127–38.

Russell, H (1999) 'Friends in low places: gender, unemployment and sociability', *Work, Employment and Society* 13 (2), pp.205–24.

Rutledge, I and Wright, P (1985) 'Coal world-wide: the international context of the British miners' strike', *Cambridge Journal of Economics* 9, pp.303–26.

Sadler, D (1992) *The Global Region: Production, State Policies and Uneven Development*, Oxford: Pergamon.

Salt, H (1995) 'Regenerating the Dearne Valley in South Yorkshire', in C Critcher, K Schubert and D Waddington (eds). *Regeneration of the Coalfield Areas: Anglo-German Perspectives*, London: Pinter.

Samuel, R (1996) 'Introduction', in R Samuel, B Bloomfield and G Boanas (eds), *The Enemy Within: Pit Villages and the Miners' Strike of 1984–5*, London: Routledge and Kegan Paul.

Samuel, R, Bloomfield, B and Boanas, G (eds) (1986) *The Enemy Within: Pit Villages and the Miners' Strike of 1984–5*, London: Routledge and Kegan Paul.

Sbragia, AM (1990) 'Pittsburgh's "Third Way": The Non-profit Sector as a Key to Urban Regeneration', in D Judd and M Parkinson (eds), *Leadership and Urban Regeneration*, London: Sage.

Schubert, K and Brautigam, M (1995) 'Coal Policy in Germany: How Durable is the Model of Consensus?', in C Critcher, K Schubert and D Waddington (eds), *Regeneration of the Coalfield Areas: Anglo-German Perspectives*, London: Pinter.

Scraton, P (1985) 'From Saltley Gates to Orgreave: A History of the Policing of Recent Industrial Disputes', in B Fine and R Millar (eds), *Policing the Miners' Strike*, London: Lawrence and Wishart.

Seabrook, J and Blackwell, T (1993) 'Coal seams stitched up', *New Statesman and Society* 9 July, pp.18–19.

Seeman, M, Seeman, AZ and Budros, A (1988) 'Powerlessness, work and community: a longitudinal study of alienation and alcohol abuse', *Journal of Health and Social Behaviour* 29, pp.185–98.

Shapiro, H (1999) 'Dances with Drugs: Pop Music, Drugs and Youth Culture', in N South (ed.), *Drugs: Cultures, Controls and Everyday Life*, London: Sage.

Simmonds, D and Emmerich, M (1996) *Regeneration Through Work: Creating Jobs in the Social Economy*, Manchester: Centre for Labour and Economic Studies.

Sinfield, A (1981) *What Unemployment Means*, London: Martin Robertson.

Smith, A and Schlesinger, A (1993) 'A model for village and community renewal', *Town and Country Planning* 62 (7), pp.186–8.

Smith, P and Morton, G (1993) 'Union exclusion and the decollectivisation of industrial relations in contemporary Britain', *British Journal of Industrial Relations* 31 (1), pp.97–114.

Smith, P and Morton, G (1994) 'Union exclusion in Britain – next steps', *Industrial Relations Journal* 25 (1), pp.3–14.

Steingraber, W (1995) 'The Campaign for the Future of Coal Mining Areas', in C Critcher, K Schubert and D Waddington (eds), *Regeneration of the Coalfield Areas: Anglo-German Perspectives*, London: Pinter.

Stern, RN and Hammer, TH (1978) 'Buying your job: factors affecting the success or failure of employee acquisition attempts', *Human Relations* 31 (12), pp.1101–17.

Strandh, M (2000) 'Different exit routes from unemployment and their impact on mental well-being: the role of the economic situation and the predictability of the life course', *Work, Employment and Society* 14 (3), pp.459–79.

Strang, J and Taylor, C (1997) 'Different gender and age characteristics of the UK heroin epidemic of the 1990s compared with the 1980s', *European Addictions Research* 3, pp.43–8.

Swyngedouw, E (1996) 'Reconstructing citizenship, the rescaling of the state and the new authoritarianism: closing the Belgian mines', *Urban Studies* 33 (8), pp.1499–521.

Taylor, AJ (1984) *The Politics of the Yorkshire Miners*, London: Croom Helm.

Taylor, AJ (1988) 'Consultation, conciliation and politics in the British coal industry', *Industrial Relations Journal* 19 (3), pp.222–33.

Taylor, M (1995) 'Community Work and the State: The Changing Context of UK Practice', in G Craig and M Mayo (eds), *Community Empowerment: A Reader in Participation and Development*, London: Zed Books.

Thakes, S and Stauback, R (1993) *Investing in People: Rescuing Communities from the Margin*, York: Joseph Rowntree Foundation.

Thatcher, M (1993) *The Downing Street Years*, London: HarperCollins.

Thomas, A (1988) 'Measuring the success of worker co-operatives and co-operative support organisations', *Local Economy* 2, pp.298–311.

Trotman, C and Lewis, T (1990) *Training and Education: The Experiences and Needs of Redundant Mineworkers at Cynheidre and Betws Collieries in South Wales*, Ammanford, West Glamorgan: Valleys Initiative for Adult Education.

Tucker, MK and Clark, MC (1991) 'Promoting organisational effectiveness - managing the risk in human relationships', *The Mining Engineer* August, pp.29–34.

Turner, RL (1992) 'British Coal enterprise – bringing the "Enterprise culture" to a deindustrialised local economy', *Local Economy* 7 (1), pp.4–8.

Turner, RL (1993) *Regenerating the Coalfields*, Aldershot: Avebury.

Turner, RL (1995) 'After Coal', in R Turner (ed.), *British Economy in Transition*, London: Routledge.

Turner, RL (1997) 'The complexities of political agenda determination: the case of the British coal industry', *Governance: An International Journal of Policy and Administration* 10 (4), pp.377–95.

Turner, R, Bostyn, AM and Wight, D (1985) 'The Work Ethic in a Scottish Town with Declining Employment', in B Roberts, R Finnegan and D Gallie (eds), *New Approaches to Economic Life: Economic Restructuring, Unemployment and the Social Division of Labour*, Manchester: Manchester University Press.

Turner, R and Gladstone, B (1993) 'Thurcroft colliery and the politics of deindustrialisation', *Political Quarterly* 64 (8), pp.351–5.

Turner, R and Gregory, M (1995) 'Life after the pit: the post-redundancy experiences of mineworkers', *Local Economy* 10 (2), pp.149–62.

Van Hooke, M (1990) 'Family responses to the farm crisis: a study in coping', *Social Work* 35 (5), pp.425–31.

Vázquez, JA and del Rosal, I (1995) 'The Effects of and Responses to Pit Closure in the Asturias Region'. Unpublished report, Communications, Media and Communities Research Centre, Sheffield Hallam University.

Waddington, DP, Jones, K and Critcher, C (1989) *Flashpoints: Studies in Public Disorder*, London: Routledge.

Waddington, DP, Wykes, M and Critcher, C (1991) *Split at the Seams? Community, Continuity and Change after the 1984–5 Coal Dispute*, Milton Keynes: Open University Press.

Waddington, DP, Dicks, B and Critcher, C (1994) 'Community responses to pit closure in the post-strike era', *Community Development Journal* 29 (2), pp.141–50.

Waddington, DP and Parry, D (1995) 'Coal Policy in Britain: Economic Reality or Political Vendetta?', in C Critcher, K Schubert and D Waddington (eds), *Regeneration of the Coalfield Areas: Anglo-German Perspectives*, London: Pinter.

Waddington, DP, Dicks, B and Critcher, C (1998a) '"All Jumbled Up": Employed Women with Unemployed Husbands', in J Popay, J Hearn and J Edwards (eds), *Men, Gender and Welfare*, London: Routledge.

Waddington, DP, Parry, D and Critcher, C (1998b) 'Keeping the red flag flying? A comparative study of two worker take-overs in the British deep coalmining industry, 1992–1997', *Work, Employment and Society* 12 (2), pp.317–49.

Wagner, F (1995) 'Land Reclamation and Economic Restructuring in North-Rhine Westfalen', in C Critcher, K Schubert and D Waddington (eds), *Regeneration of the Coalfield Areas: Anglo-German Perspectives*, London: Pinter.

Walker, P (1991) *Staying Power*, London: Bloomsbury.

Wallis, E (2000) *Industrial Relations in the Privatised Coal Industry*, Aldershot: Ashgate.

Walsh, S and Jackson, PR (1995) 'Partner support and gender: contexts for coping with job loss', *Journal of Occupational and Organisational Psychology* 58, pp.253–68.

Warr, PB (1985) 'Twelve Questions About Unemployment and Health', in B Roberts, R Finnegan and D Gallie (eds), *New Approaches to Economic Life*, Manchester: Manchester University Press.

Warr, PB (1987) 'Job Characteristics and Mental Health', in PB Warr (ed.), *Psychology at Work*, Harmondsworth: Penguin.

Warr, PB and Jackson, PR (1987) 'Adapting to the unemployed role: a longitudinal investigation', *Social Science and Medicine* 25, pp.1219–24.

Warr, PB, Jackson, P and Banks, M (1988) 'Unemployment and mental health: some British issues', *Journal of Social Issues* 44 (4), pp.47–68.

Warwick, D and Littlejohn, G (1992) *Coal, Capital and Culture: A Sociological Analysis of Mining Communities in West Yorkshire*, London: Routledge.

Wass, V (1989) *Redundancy and Reemployment: Effects and Prospects Following Colliery Closures*, Barnsley: CCC.

Wass, V (1994) 'The Psychological Effects of Redundancy and Worklessness: A Case Study from the Coalfields', in Communications, Media and Communities Research Centre (eds), *Coal, Culture and Community – Proceedings of a Conference*, Sheffield: PAVIC Publications.

Watson, TJ (1997) *Sociology, Work and Industry*, London: Routledge and Kegan Paul (second edn).

White, D (1999) 'A step in the right direction', *The Utilities Journal* May, p.21.

Wieser, O, Wright, M and Robbie, K (1997) 'Management and employee buy-outs from the Asturian public sector', *Annals of Public and Cooperative Economics* 68 (4), pp.689–711.

Wilsher, P, MacIntyre, D and Jones, M (1985) *Strike: A Battle of Ideologies, Thatcher, Scargill and the Miners*, London: Coronet.

Winterton, J and Winterton, R (1989) *Coal, Crisis and Conflict: The 1984–85 Miners' Strike in Yorkshire*, Manchester: Manchester University Press.

Winterton, J and Winterton, R (1993) 'Coal', in A Pendleton and J Winterton (eds), *Public Enterprise in Transition: Industrial Relations in State and Privatized Corporations*, London: Routledge.

Witt, S (1990) *When the Pit Closes: The Employment Experiences of Redundant Miners*, Barnsley: CCC.

Woodside, J (1997) 'Sustainable regeneration in Barnsley', *Housing and Planning Review* 52 (4), pp.17–18.

Wright, SE and Rosenblatt, PC (1987) 'Isolation and farm loss: why neighbours may not be supportive', *Family Relations* 36, pp.391–5.

Yildirim, E (1999) 'Employee buyouts and industrial relations under employee ownership: a case study of Karabuk steel mill', *Economic and Industrial Democracy* 20 (4), pp.561–82.

Youle, J (1997) 'Grimethorpe, Barnsley', *Planning* 27 August, pp.18–19.

INDEX

Page numbers in italic indicate reference to a table or figure.

Index by Caroline Wilding